HOMES OF THE CAVALIERS

THE MACMILLAN COMPANY
NEW YORK · BOSTON · CHICAGO · DALLAS
ATLANTA · SAN FRANCISCO

DOORWAY AT BRENTWOOD FARM

HOMES OF THE CAVALIERS , , ,

By KATHERINE SCARBOROUGH
...

WITH ONE HUNDRED ONE
REPRODUCTIONS FROM
PHOTOGRAPHS
.

NEW YORK
THE MACMILLAN COMPANY
1930

Md.
917.52
S
Rm

TO
HAROLD *and* FRANCES SCARBOROUGH

FOREWORD

A great daily newspaper, the *Chicago Tribune*, recently conducted an extensive inquiry into the architecture of each of the forty-eight States in an effort to discover what building might be denominated as most typical of each. In Maryland the selection was made by the Baltimore Chapter of the American Institute of Architects which reached the opinion that White Hall, the Colonial home of the pre-Revolutionary royal governor, Horatio Sharpe, epitomized all that is characteristic of a land which is abundantly supplied with architectural excellences.

In Maryland the first settlers clung close to the waterways which threaded through its deep green hills and lowlands, making a filigree. On the banks of the Chesapeake Bay and the rivers which flow into it they built their houses and here they succeeded in developing and bringing to perfection, long before its neighboring colonies accepted it, the five-part construction which is embodied in White Hall. This type of building, which is familiar to every layman as a central mass to which wings are attached by connecting wings, is distinctively a Maryland contribution to one of the most difficult, as well as one of the most beautiful of all the arts.

But even though White Hall be set apart as most typical of Maryland, it is far from being alone in its claims to interest. Few States are so lavishly endowed with worthy survivals of Colonial building and it is of many of these, as it is of White Hall that the present book treats. The book itself is the result of a suggestion made by Douglas Farwell Woolley, an associate on the staff of the *Baltimore Sun*, whom circumstances prevented from participating in what had been intended as a collaboration of authorship. In its preparation the author has consulted every book it was possible to discover which dealt with the subject of Colonial Maryland, from Father White's "A Relation of Maryland," written not long after the arrival of the first settlers in the *Ark* and the *Dove*, to Swepson Earle's "The Chesapeake Bay Country," the last edition of which appeared a year or so ago.

Invaluable assistance also was generously given by James Donnell Tilghman who placed his store of architectural knowledge completely at the author's disposal and who took many of the pictures which illustrate the text. Others to whom the author is deeply indebted and who will recognize their own part in the following pages are Dr. James Bordley, Miss Ella Gertrude Brennan and Miss Carolyn Ellsworth Coudon. To the *Baltimore Sun* thanks are returned for permission to use such portions of the sketches portraying the Hammond-Harwood House and the Chase House in Annapolis, and Long Lane Farm as appeared in its columns before the book was written.

ILLUSTRATIONS

LIST OF ILLUSTRATIONS

[x]

LIST OF ILLUSTRATIONS

[xi]

LIST OF ILLUSTRATIONS

LIST OF ILLUSTRATIONS

HOMES OF THE
CAVALIERS

CHAPTER ONE

The wind sang "a soft, half-Syrian air" as it skimmed over
the headlands of the Potomac on the morning of the third of
March in the year 1634. It dipped into the forests and took a
deep, heady whiff of pine. It played tag with the stiff cedars and
pirouetted suddenly out over the meadows, darting off to rush
down to the river and whisper tantalizingly of violets and blood
root hidden where the river could not reach them.

Stung to retaliation, the river frilled the edges of its waves
with foam. It muttered dark secrets of the great bay to which it
was going, but the wind paid no attention. On the shore the
sassafras and redbud felt the sap leap in their veins and at intervals silent men, with copper colored skins, lifted their eyes to the
east and busied themselves knowingly with their canoes.

Then, suddenly, everything was different. Night came, but
there was no sleep for the men with the copper colored skins. The
light of council fires blazed through the land and fear stalked
the banks of the river. All night and all the next day the suspense
continued and then, on the morning of the fifth of March, over
the rim of the horizon came the white gleam of sails. An hour
or so later the good ship Ark, with its pinnace, the Dove,
dropped anchor in midstream. Over the sides of the boats
clambered the figures of white men, almost hysterical with
happiness with the ending of a long, terrible voyage across the
Atlantic, and the first of Lord Baltimore's colonists waded to the
land. They had reached St. Clement's Island, known now as
Blackiston's Island.

Acting upon the theory that it was inadvisable to locate so

high up the river, where it would be difficult to defend a settlement or to retreat in case of attack, Governor Leonard Calvert, following the instruction of Lord Baltimore "to make choice of a place first that is probable to be healthfull and fruitfull; next that it be easily fortified and, thirdly, that it be convenient for trade both with the English and the savages," pushed on after surveying the island. With Captain Henry Fleet, of the Virginia colony and an Indian trader whose experience with the Indians gave his opinion no little weight, Governor Calvert visited the Indian village of Yaocomico, taking with him on this mission a small body of men and leaving both ships and most of the colonists at St. Clement's where, it is certain, they celebrated as elaborately as the circumstances permitted.

Of Governor Calvert's visit to Yaocomico an accurate account has come down through the testimony of an eye-witness,—that Father White who conferred upon posterity his inestimable "Relation of Maryland." Governor Calvert, it is written, informed the king of the object of his coming and his desire to settle on the lower Potomac. To this, says the chronicler, the king "made but little answer, as is their manner to any new or sudden question, but entertained him and his company that night in his house, and gave him his own bed to lye on—which is a mat laid on boards—and the next day went to show him the country."

Governor Calvert was much impressed. In return for cloth, axes, hatchets, rakes, hoes and knives the Yaocomicoes agreed to permit the white men to occupy part of their town. The rest they reserved until the harvesting of the corn had been finished, promising to relinquish it all when that had been done. Immediately Governor Calvert returned to St. Clement's Island, laid the result of his negotiations before the garrison he had left there, and with them sailed down the river to the harbor which they called Saint Mary's. The landing was made on the twenty-seventh of March at what is known now as Chancellor's Point, and the Ark and Dove unloaded. This done, with pomp and with pageantry, the rollicking crew of cavaliers, retainers, peasants and laborers, rich men, poor men, including, undoubtedly, a beggarman and a thief or two, together with a "goodly parsoun," took possession of the land and fired off their absurd little cannon to show that they meant it.

The town of St. Mary's was laid out at once. But the first houses in which the Maryland cavaliers dwelt were those constructed by the Yaocomico Indians, houses built, according to Father White's "Relation," in "an oblong, oval shape. Light is admitted into these through the roof by a window a foot and a half long. This also serves to carry off the smoke, for they kindle the fire in the middle of the floor and sleep around it. Their Kings, however, and chief men, have private apartments of their own, and beds, made by driving four posts in the ground and arranging poles above them horizontally. . . . One of these cabins has fallen to me."

Soon St. Mary's City, the first capital of Maryland, came into existence on the edge of a bluff some forty feet above the water. A long headland which stretched out about a mile farther down the river combined with the plateau on which the little town stood to give it a capacious, crescent-shaped harbor. "A spot, indeed," in the language of that Captain Fleet who had urged Governor Calvert to occupy it, "so charming in its situation that Europe itself can scarcely show one to surpass it."

The first house erected by the colonists was, in all probability, the home of Governor Calvert. Though no account has come down of it, it was, undoubtedly, a log cabin. In a short time, however, St. Mary's which constituted a veritable little metropolis by comparison with Jamestown, in Virginia, which contained in 1716 only "a church, Court House and four other buildings," had "passed through the various stages of architectural transition" from cabin to substantial brick and frame buildings.

In 1664 the Assembly passed an act by which all houses which were erected after that date were required to be not less than twenty feet square and two and a-half stories high, with brick chimneys. America's first building code!

Of these houses not one is left, but along the banks of the Potomac, near the lone streams which wind through St. Mary's county, on the banks of the Chesapeake Bay, there survive today mellow old houses built of frame or dark red brick which came into being long before Maryland had completed the first century of its existence.

Most of St. Mary's conformed to the same general pattern. Mere wisps of houses we should deem them today, with outside "brick roof" chimneys and brick gables up to the line of the eaves, above which they were built of frame, though the timbers had slight resemblance to the planed millwork of today. Heavy timbers, awkwardly squared out with the axe, were fastened with mortise and tenon and sheathed with thick planks. Sometimes this crude framework was covered with clapboards or shingles, but, more often, there was little attempt at such refinement of detail. The roofs invariably were steeply pitched and were covered with hand-riven shingles, put together tightly and ingeniously with nails forged on an anvil under a tree. Nails were at a premium in the colony for many years. The free use of them marked a man as the possessor of great wealth and a covey of chimneys proclaimed him a money baron.

In a short time houses were built with gambrel roofs of a type peculiar to the colony and the hipped roof with deeply sunk mullion and dormer windows became indicative of the prosperity which had attended the adventure known documentarily as Maryland. The soil which, in the words of the "Relation," was "remarkably fertile, dark and not hard, to the depth of a foot and overlays a rich, red clay," furnished material not only for bricks with which to build houses for the rich men of the colony, but yielded great crops of tobacco which the colonists exchanged in England for the "parlor bed," "trundle bed," the "peir glass" and, a little later, the "chimney glass" which went into their homes. The leaves of the weed brought them, also, silk and worsted "bed curtains," Dutch linen sheets and napkins, things which they prized beyond measure and passed on by will to their children.

Stools and chairs, the latter scarce even in England in that day and almost non-existent in the colonies, stood in these early Maryland dwellings. Women in gowns of "spangled lace, brocades and velvets, dimities and silks" played on "harpsichord and spinnet" and dined from "the joined dining table." Brass and iron "and-irons" supported the blazing logs in their fireplaces and in their final testaments, some of which still exist, they handed down to posterity "silver knives," the "silver sack cup," the "sugar tankard," the "tea tankard," pewter cups and saucers of which not one, probably, is in existence today.

During the first forty years of the colony pewter formed virtually the only substance of the utensils which appeared on the tables of the Maryland cavaliers. Then the silver service made its appearance, massive and impressive, with coffee urns and sugar bowls large enough for the serving of a small company of militia and completing the transference to Maryland of the outward and visible signs of wealth and rank by which men and women of similar position were distinguished in England.

During the year 1637-8 provision had been made for the bounding of the manors, every holder of which was required to be trained as a soldier and to have fifteen freemen ready for military service whom the lord of the manor was bound to maintain in time of warfare—an act of Assembly which established in Maryland the institution of feudalism then gasping its last in Europe. The great landholders were privileged to exercise the rights of Court Baron and Court Leet, "royalties and privileges belonging to manors in England," which gave them virtually the power of life and death over their tenants, all of whom were required to take the oath of fealty to the lord of the manor.

Naturally, under such conditions, the great landowner's life in a land teeming with abundance was little short of idyllic. Soon aristocracy clothed itself with drooping plumes and plush-lined coats enriched with embroidery. Men wore white wigs of such size that they were forced to carry their cocked, gold-laced hats under their arms and their silken hose and jewelled garters were the envy of the yokelry. The "seale gold ring" was on the finger of every gentleman. Occasional references are to be found in the wills of those early Marylanders to the sedan chair, the "bladen" and the "horse chair." There is mention of silver, gold, cloth and leather belts, silver and gold knee and shoe buckles, silk and worsted "hoods," "head clothes" and "scharfs." Ladies of fashion devised to favored beneficiaries their "tufted Holland petticoats," their "silk gloves" and their "buckskin gloves" and provided sums of money for mourning rings before the year 1680 had closed at St. Mary's.

The whole of the little colony was strangely glamorous. Soon the building of houses had become a passion among men born to traditions of ease and luxury and something of the manner of those which were erected before the Seventeenth century had reached its meridian may be determined from their survivals which stand in St. Mary's county today.

CROSS MANOR

Photo by Aubrey Bodine

SOTTERLEY
Photo by Aubrey Bodine

Photo by Aubrey Bodine

SOTTERLEY: FLAGSTONE COLONNADE

Tradition and history unite, seemingly, in the belief that Cross Manor house, the present home of Mr. and Mrs. Charles Sterett Grason on the banks of St. Inigoes' Creek, is the oldest brick house in Maryland. The estate was granted in 1639 to "the Hon. Thomas Cornwaleys," who first built a water mill and then proceeded to "build a house to put my own head in." Exactly when his house was completed it is impossible to say, but the year 1643 is accepted by Mrs. Grason, whose mother's family had owned the place for six generations, as the probable date of its erection. In 1645 its owner made a claim against the British crown for silver and valuables stolen from his mansion, so this date must be approximately correct. So radical are the changes which have been made in its contours that its original architecture can only be approximated, but the lines of demarcation between the bricks of the old walls and the new are clearly marked. From all indications the original house had a gambrel roof which later was changed to one of the gabled persuasion, complete with foliated dormer windows.

The gardens, laid out on the side of the house next the water, apparently are as old as the original house with great masses of box, some of which measure forty-five feet in circumference, grown to the size of trees.

The rooms, generous in size, are filled with interesting old furniture, Hepplewhite chairs and tables, an old clock and a sideboard so dark it is difficult to tell whether it is made of ebony or mahogany. A Duncan Phyfe table and a Sheffield silver waiter find appropriate setting, too, in the old manor house. The Hon. Thomas Cornwaleys became one of the wealthiest men of early Maryland, but the history of his home after his death is wrapped up for years in the mists which envelop so much of the story of the colony after St. Mary's City vanished from the map. About a hundred and fifty years ago it became the property of Captain

Randolph Jones from whom it descended in direct line to Mrs. Grason.

* * *

At Sotterley, on the Patuxent River, where Herbert L. Satterlee, a New York banker of international repute, and his family live for part of each year, a tie which had been broken for more than three centuries has been knit together again in Maryland. Sotterley is a subdivision of Resurrection Manor, surveyed before 1641 for Cuthbert Fenwick, who has come down as "one of the youngest and most trusty of the early colonists." Frequently they arrive by yacht, but more often the Satterlees make the trip from New York to their remote country home by airplane—a circumstance which is typical of the new day which is exerting its influence on the storied Free State and reinvesting with vigorous renaissance its historic homesteads, which are passing, one by one, into the hands of new owners.

Sotterley takes its name from "Soterlega," the English seat of the "Players" in county Suffolk, and was, originally, pronounced Satterlee. It lies directly opposite Saint Leonard's Creek and when it was separated, two hundred years ago, from Resurrection Manor, it was purchased by the Hon. James Bowles. Two thousand acres were included in the deed and during the tenure of its new owner it was known as Bowles' Separation.

After the death of James Bowles his widow, when the formal period of mourning had passed, became the wife of the Hon. George Plater, the ceremony being recorded in the *Maryland Gazette* of June 16th, 1729, in this wise:

"On Thursday last the Hon. George Plater was married to Mrs. Rebecca Bowles, relict of James Bowles, Esq., a gentlewoman of considerable fortune."

One of the children of this marriage, George, who received his father's name and who was the only son, became governor of

Maryland. He was born in 1736 and was educated at William and Mary's College. When he had been graduated Governor Horatio Sharpe, who was a close friend of the family, gave him letters of introduction to people of importance in England and in 1760 he paid his first and only visit to England. He seems to have made an excellent impression on Lord Baltimore who lost no time in communicating to Governor Sharpe his desire to have the young Marylander associated "in the affairs of the Province" with which he subsequently became more prominently connected than he had dreamed of being.

By the marriage of the governor's son, George, to Ann Rousby, the only child of Col. John Rousby (who then was lord of a famous and splendidly kept estate on the Calvert county side of the Patuxent), the third George Plater acquired not only a wife said to have been possessed of "rare personal beauty and stately elegance," so that she was known as "the White Rose of Maryland," but a fortune as well. Her patrimony, combined with his large estate, enabled them to live at Sotterley on a scale of elegance which was in keeping with their distinguished position and in full accord with their desires.

The house, which is a story and a-half high, is an intensely absorbing as well as unique model of Colonial architecture. It is of frame construction, built of stout oak timbers on a substantial brick foundation in the shape of a capital "T," with the head of the letter elongated. The steep roof, which slopes sharply to the first story, is surmounted by a cupola and cut at intervals by dormer windows which look out with a somewhat quizzical expression from under triangular hoods. The gables, like the foundation, are of brick, and brick are the porches. A stone-flagged colonnade extends along the front, recalling the long porch at Mt. Vernon.

From the cellar to the foot of the hill below the house there runs a passageway of brick, its existence giving rise to all manner of interesting conjecture concerning the use to which it may have been put. The main hall, library and the original dining-room are lined with remarkably fine panelling which extends from floor to ceiling and which has grown dark and mysterious with age. The drawingroom is finished entirely in wood, ceiling and side walls, with shell carvings reminiscent of the Middle Ages surmounting the quaint alcoves. The window frames are made of solid walnut. The door of heavy mahogany is swung on strap hinges of solid brass, extending half way across it, and as it opens, the door swings upward to clear the carpet which once covered the floor. No more perfect specimen of Colonial interior finish and decoration is to be found anywhere in Maryland.

The stairway, which leads easily to the second floor, also is built of mahogany with a grooved hand rail and a newel post. Its ingeniously contrived filigree, according to an old tradition, was devised, like the woodwork in the drawingroom, by a mechanic whose name was Bowen and who was one of the king's "seven-year-convicts" transported to Maryland. According to a tradition in the Plater family this convict was purchased by the Hon. George Plater under whose regime the interior decoration of Sotterley was completed between 1730 and 1736 and who liberated the talented mechanic in recognition of the work he accomplished there.

In the early days two small, square buildings, with cone-shaped roofs, stood in the front yard. One at the garden gate was used as a wine and smoking room and the other, immediately opposite, was an office for the builder who became, some years before his marriage with the affluent Rebecca, collector of the customs and naval officer for the Patuxent district and who built the curious little structure in order that he might have abundant space in which to transact his many duties in connection with these responsible posts. Both the office and the wine room have been removed to other positions.

The collector's son, George, well educated, was one of the most publicly recognized men of his day. When he was only twenty-two he was elected to the House of Delegates. He next held the post of naval officer of the Patuxent, from 1767 to 1774, becoming, in the meantime, judge of the provincial court. In 1773 and 1774 he was a member of the Council and in 1776 he was a member of the Council of Safety of Maryland. That same year he was a member of the constitutional convention of Maryland and was president of that body in 1784. During the years from 1788 to 1791 he was a delegate to the Continental Congress, being also a member of the convention for the ratification of the constitution of the United States and president of that body in 1788. In 1792 he became governor of Maryland.

For more than half a century the name of Governor Plater appears on the records of the country's history, identified with almost every phase of the struggle for American independence and a leading spirit in the transition of his native State from the position of a colony of the British crown to a separate commonwealth of full and complete autonomy. His death occurred at Annapolis on February 10, 1792. His body, given honorable escort by officials "of the Council and State," was borne next day on a barge by way of the South river to Sotterley where it was buried in the rose garden. No marker, unfortunately, was placed above the coffin to indicate the grave of a statesman. Only the old sundial, still well preserved, stood near, with its inscription in many tongues to mark off the hours of eternity for the man who lay beneath the sod.

There is a story that in the old days those who stayed out late at night sometimes could hear the wheels of the governor's ghostly chariot and four, and the hoof-beats of his outriders' horses as he drove up from the capital. And sometimes it was the splash of the oars they heard of the governor's funeral cortege as it made its way over South river, across the ferry, to Sotterley.

Governor Plater's grandson, George, lost Sotterley throwing dice with Colonel Somerville, who owned Mulberry Fields, a lordly estate on the Potomac. Colonel Somerville soon sold it to Col. Thomas Barber and through him the mansion and part of the land descended to the Briscoes, who made many changes, including the raising of the roof of three bedrooms and the hall on the river front. Mr. Satterlee obtained possession in 1910, and after five years of study to establish the original outlines of the house, restored it to its Colonial dimensions.

Innumerable traditions concern themselves with Sotterley, but there is more than tradition to the story that "Long Arm," the pirate, made an unsuccessful raid on the estate while Governor Plater was giving a hunt breakfast one morning. Duels have been fought there, too, and even as late as the Civil War Sotterley was the scene of many historic episodes. The property now includes 1,550 acres of the original tract.

* * *

The Plains, in the early days of the colony, was known by the more picturesque title of Orphans' Gift and included then the large estate known as Chesley's Hill. It, too, is situated on the shore of the Patuxent, with an exceptionally beautiful location, and belonged to the Jowles family which was one of great distinction in Colonial times but the name is now apparently extinct in Maryland.

In the old graveyard on the place are crumbling tombstones, one of which marks the burial place of "Colonel Henry Peregrine Jowles, who departed this life the 31st day of March, 1720, in the 49th year of his age." In the "God's acre" at Chesley's

Hill is a stone succinctly cut to the benefit of posterity in this wise:

> This monument is erected to the memory of John Chesley of Saint Mary's county, who died December the 5th, 1767, in the 64th year of his age. He was magistrate of said County for upwards of 30 years, during several of which he presided as judge of the Court, and always distinguished himself for ability and uprightness.
>
> Beneath this stone the cold remains are laid,
> Of one who has the debt of nature paid,
> Truth as she passes drops the silent tear,
> Laments the Husband, Parent, Friend,
> Duty and love have thus inscribed his name,
> But virtue ranks it in the Book of Fame.

By various intermarriages The Plains passed from the Jowles family into the hands of the Sothorons who still reside in Maryland. The mansion house is built of brick, large and commodious, and is said to have been erected before the Revolution by the Hon. Henry Greenfield Sothoron. There is every reason to believe that this was the case but although it escaped the ravages of war during that conflict, its mellow old walls still bear the scars of the part it bore during the War of 1812, when the Maryland militia, stationed at The Plains, engaged the British fleet off shore in an effort to prevent the fleet from making its way farther up the river.

CHAPTER TWO

Deep Falls, the home of the Thomas family, is a quaint and profoundly peaceful place near the village of Chaptico. No family is more completely entwined with Maryland than that of the Thomases. They have been landholders, lawyers and bankers, always preserving the traditions of hospitality and pleasant living which they brought with them when first they set foot in St. Mary's.

Deep Falls came into possession of the family through a proprietary grant of March 26, 1680, and was then designated as Wales, but when "the improvement known as 'the falls'," to quote James Walter Thomas, the historian of St. Mary's county, was completed the name was changed to the one by which it is known today.

From the public road the approach to Deep Falls is through a luxuriantly wooded avenue which leads up to the house on its lone eminence. Much like an English country house it seems, with its group of chimneys which lift impressively above the roof line and the simplicity of its mass. Sixty feet long across the front and forty feet in width, it appears even larger by reason of its wide piazzas, upheld by massive pillars which run the entire length of the house, front and rear. Here the Thomases and their visitors, who always have been innumerable, have spent delicious summer days for almost two hundred years, and many are the juleps, mixed by expert hands, which have trickled seductively down parched throats in the shade of those hospitable verandas.

The house is of frame, mounted on a thick brick foundation

and brick-gabled to the upper line of the first story, where the brick work branches into the great, outside chimneys. Within, the house is characterized by the same simplicity which marks the exterior. The hall deviates from the usual passage-like space and spreads out into a large, well finished square room, distinguished by the stairway which is introduced at the rear by a beautiful arch. The sides of the stairway are panelled and carved and the newel posts are of maple, with rosewood tops, tipped with an ivory button. The stair rail itself is of rosewood and, with the balusters of bird's-eye maple, extends invitingly upward to the corridors above.

On one side of the hall is the drawingroom, furnished in old mahogany and rosewood and, on the other side, the diningroom, separated from it by a partition formed of a series of folding doors. At the rear of the hall, running at right angles to it, is a long passage, through which access is to be had to the rear piazza and, beyond that, to the garden.

Carrying along the front line of the house is a long corridor, with a wing, a story and a-half high at the end. This constitutes the culinary department where have been prepared through almost two hundred years those delightful dishes which are characteristic of Southern Maryland and many of them have been concocted by special recipes which the Thomases have cherished from one generation to another.

As delightful as the house are the gardens which are approached by a series of five terraces, each a hundred feet long and ten feet deep, to a plateau below. About two and a-half acres of the plateau have been laid out into a garden of Queen Anne design, and ornamented so that it was, at one time, the show place of the colony.

Not since the day of the builder has Deep Falls been out of the possession of the Thomas family. The house was erected about 1745 by Major William Thomas, who was the son of John Thomas of Charles county where he was born in 1714. Early in life he removed to St. Mary's and was a delegate to the Revolutionary convention of 1775, in addition to being a member of the Committee of Safety for St. Mary's county in the same year.

John Thomas, father of the builder of Deep Falls, was the son of James, who was the eldest son of Thomas Thomas, first of the name in Maryland and one of the early settlers on the Patuxent river, there being a survey known as Broad Neck made out for him in 1651. Twenty years afterward his will was recorded and left to his daughter, Grace, among other items, "2 pewter dishes, 1 pewter Bason, 3 porringers, 6 spoons, 1 Dutch pott and pott hookes and 1 dish." His other children were equally well remembered.

Upon the death of William Thomas his son, William, inherited the homestead and became one of the most prominent men of his day. He held the commission of major in the Maryland Line of the Continental army, was a member of the House of Delegates and for twelve years before his death, which occurred in 1813, he was president of the Maryland Senate. From him Deep Falls descended to his eldest son, James, who was a physician and was educated at St. John's College, Annapolis. He married his cousin, Eliza, daughter of Major William and Elizabeth Thomas Coates, and in 1883 was elected governor of Maryland. His body is that of the second governor of the Thomas family to rest in the old graveyard at Deep Falls which has restored to their native earth generation after generation. The other was "Maj.-Gen. James Thomas, Ex-Governor of Maryland, born March 11, 1785, died December 25th, 1845, aged 60 years, 9 months and 14 days." The inscription on his tombstone also hymns: "This Monument is erected as a tribute of affection by his children.

Green be the turf above thee,
    Friend of my better days;
None knew thee but to love thee,
    None named thee but to praise."

During the careless years of the latter part of the Nineteenth century the old mansion at Deep Falls bogged into a condition of utter decay and neglect. Its destiny seemed to matter little to any one until James Walter Thomas, of Cumberland, lawyer, historian and author, to whom it descended through James Thomas, son of William, son of the builder, inherited it. Then halcyon days came again to the place, for the new owner, interested in everything which pertained to the Colonial life of Maryland, restored the estate, down to the smallest detail, and the Thomas family again lived at Deep Falls, for part of the year, at least, in the same expansive way which the first William inaugurated nearly two hundred years ago. Deep Falls is one of the very few estates in St. Mary's which still is in the family of the original proprietor.

* * *

On the one-time manor of West St. Mary's, at Bacon's Wharf, is Porto Bello, now the home of Mr. and Mrs. J. Allan Coad. Porto Bello is the old Hebb homestead and stands on the shores of St. Mary's river, almost directly opposite St. Mary's City. The house, like Deep Falls, is a large frame building, with a stack of brick chimneys, brick foundations and gables, a hipped roof and semi-dormer windows.

In common with almost every house of importance in St. Mary's, it commands a magnificent water view, with glimpses of the leisurely turns and twists which the river insinuates into the land on its way to the Chesapeake Bay. The interior is simplicity itself. No attempt was made anywhere at elaboration, the builders evidently relying on excellence of material for their effects except in the drawingroom, where an enormous mirror, built into the brick wall and said to have been placed there when the house was erected, rests above the fireplace.

Porto Bello is said to have obtained its name in a manner at once intensely personal to its owner and historically interesting. William Hebb, the story goes, his friend, Lawrence Washington, and his neighbor, Edwin Coade, midshipmen in the British navy, named their estates on their return to the colonies after the war between England and Spain, in remembrance of persons and places connected with the conflict. Hebb called his Porto Bello in honor of the celebrated battle of that name in which he was a participant. Coade named his land Carthagena in memory of the Spanish town and Washington denominated his beautiful home on the Potomac Mount Vernon in compliment to Admiral Vernon under whom all three had served.

Another version of the beginnings of Porto Bello gives Edwin Coade as the builder, so there seems to be room for doubt who the builder really was. In a corner of the old burying ground is a grave marked "Col. William H. Hebb," but there are not wanting historians of excellent reputation who ascribe its origin to Coade,—later spelled without the final "e".

As it stood originally, before it was enlarged by its present owners (who did their work with excellent conformity to the original lines of the house and with complete understanding of its spirit) Porto Bello, while not imposing, was typical of the building which went on in Maryland before the Georgian influence reached the colony. Splendidly adapted to the climate, it is long and low and rambling, with rooms opening from one into the other for no apparent reason whatever. When it was built brick was scarce. Contrary to the familiar story which insists that virtually all Maryland houses of a certain age, or older, were built of brick brought from England, there is no authenticated instance of any house having been built from such material. Nor was there any reason for such a procedure, for the soil of Maryland was excellently adapted to the making of bricks and was used for this purpose. Traces of old kilns survived on many an ancient place for generations and the romantic story of the old houses loses nothing by dropping the supposedly English origin of the bricks and substituting for it the truth which makes them more completely genuine, more intensely the product of a great country.

The builders of Porto Bello, however, placed not their faith in brick, but sent into the forests indentured servants who hewed down the lordly trees and squared them by hand for its walls which were put together with wooden pins. The only bricks which were used were put into the foundations and the four splended chimneys which flank the original unit of the house, two at either end. The gambrelled roof has a line of unusual grace and charm and out from it jut dormer windows giving an excellent balance to the exterior and to the interior a quaintness which is at once elusive and captivating.

The stairway, after the manner of the first of these luxuries which were built in Maryland, was enclosed between the walls, for the day of carved balustrades and splendid newel posts was not yet. Deep-set windows with wide window seats attest the thickness of the walls and arched recesses give character to the interior. From almost every window there is a view of the river which flows on in complete disregard of the glory that departed from its banks when the State capital was moved from St. Mary's City to Annapolis.

From the hands of its original owners Porto Bello passed into possession of the Dickey family, its successive owners being the Bennetts, the Traverses, Dr. J. E. Bacon, Dr. Bacon's son-in-law,

James Coppage, who bought it of his wife who had inherited it, and who later sold it to Mrs. Hyatt, the present owner, who married Mr. Coad. At one time it was used as a boarding school and for years had fallen gradually into neglect, from which it has been rescued by Mr. and Mrs. Coad.

* * *

An interesting variation of the classic portico is to be found at Tudor Hall, home of the progenitors of Francis Scott Key, situated on the edge of Leonardtown. Tudor Hall seems to belong definitely among very ancient things and to live, as age has a way of doing, completely in the past. The familiar lines of the Georgian pillared portico are there, but they are treated in a manner which is seldom to be encountered among the old houses of Maryland. Instead of jutting out beyond the line of the outer walls, the five rounded columns which adorn the front of Tudor Hall are set flush with the walls, giving an effect suggestive of Italy.

The floor of this inset porch is paved with flagstones, uneven now, but recalling a day when they produced an impression of superiority upon all who trod them. The classic simplicity of the entrance characterizes the entire mansion, flanked at either end by chimneys of a size which recall the old world and which are mute evidence of the wealth and position of the first lord of Tudor Hall. Several chimneys were as convincing an evidence of financial security in the early days of Maryland as the appearance of an imported car is today on the streets of Vanity Fair.

For many years the brick outer walls of the mansion stood undaunted, but as time went on the elements ravaged them unmercifully and they were given a thick coat of plaster to protect the weakening brick. Within is a graceful stairway of

THE HALL AT SOTTERLEY

SOTTERLEY: THE "GREATE" ROOM

INSET PORTICO AT TUDOR HALL
The Key Homestead in St. Mary's County

LONG LANE FARM

mahogany with its handsome railing, almost black with age, which constitutes the magnificence of the center hall. The rooms which open off from it are very large and accent the air of elegance which the entire house begets.

Tudor Hall has been in the Key family for many generations. Lieut. John Ross Key, the father of Francis Scott Key, lived there and fought during the Revolution in the Maryland Rifle Battalion as an officer under Gen. Otho H. Williams. With it, he was present at Yorktown in Lafayette's company at the surrender of Cornwallis.

The grounds adjoining the mansion have run quite to seed. Lawns have developed into hills and hollows, but there is a superb view from the place. Breton Bay goes busily on its way past the once-luxuriant garden which sloped to the water's edge and now is obliterated, and turns in and around inquisitively along the shore as if to make sure that the old house is still there.

* * *

Of far different character is Susquehanna, a two-hundred-and-fifty-year-old house on the shores of the Patuxent. No evidence here is to be found of architectural beauty or sensuous complacency but a sinister atmosphere which hints of dark deeds and foul play. It might easily have been a smugglers' rendezvous in the days of the not-too-mythical "Rob of the Bowl" despite the beauty of its location on a terrace overlooking the river.

At the end of a long, straight, uncompromising driveway it stands, scowling and uninviting. The four dormer windows which break the roofline repel, rather than beckon. And with reason, for more than two hundred years ago Susquehanna was the *mise-en-scene* of one of the most tragic melodramas which have come down in the annals of a romantic country. To it was assigned the part of background for a tale of a hectic quarrel at sea, a murder, escape in the darkness and rescue by a devoted wife only to arouse the suspicions of blood-mad woodsmen, and a final refuge in a mountain cave. And today, in the center of a cornfield, a grave covered by a broken and crumbling slab of stone and almost obliterated by heavy undergrowth, conceals the body of the victim who rests, his hot lifeblood cooled forever, at Susquehanna. But to begin at the beginning.

Among the first settlers of Maryland was Christopher Rousby, who with his brother, John, came from England where they had been men of elegance and fashion. With them they brought great quantities of finery and purses of gold, absurdly unaware of the primitiveness of the land to which they were coming. When they reached this country each built himself a house of splendid proportions for a struggling colony, Christopher calling his Susquehanna and presiding there in elegant superiority as collector-general for the king, a post which invited many a bitter quarrel and culminated in the one which cost him his life.

In pursuit of his official duties Christopher Rousby had boarded the Quaker Ketch, a British man-of-war, and after a few preliminary passes had been made Christopher's remarks incurred the wrath of Col. George Talbot, a cousin of Lord Baltimore and a councillor of the province. His station in life and his position had not taught him self control, however, and anger on the part of this choleric individual meant action. Quickly he whipped out a knife and lunged at Christopher Rousby who was unable to defend himself, stabbing him to death.

The captain of the Quaker Ketch was beside himself with fury and with fear. He did not dare permit the murder of Rousby to come to the ears of authority, but kept the body concealed on his ship for several days. A trusted underling was sent ashore to lock the doors of Susquehanna in order that the keys might be taken aboard the Ketch. This order was carried out and was followed by another demanding the strictest secrecy.

But such a secret could not long be kept and even the cousin of the powerful Lord Baltimore had to make a run for his life. Straight made he for Virginia shore, tacking about in swamps, eating roots and berries, travelling by night, sleeping by day. Finally he was caught by Sir Francis Howard, Baron of Effingham, then governor of Virginia, tried and sentenced to death. Lord Baltimore rushed at once to the rescue of his kinsman to whom he was devoted. He would not submit to the jurisdiction of the Virginia court, but determined to have Colonel Talbot tried in England. Swift messengers were sent with an order for his release, but when they reached the prison Talbot's cell was empty.

Swifter than the law had been Talbot's wife. With a small baby in her arms she had sailed down the Chesapeake Bay in an open shallop, unmindful of the penetrating midwinter winds which swept the waters. With her went a maid and four friends in the disguise of Irish soldiery. Together they contrived the escape of Colonel Talbot, who accompanied them back to his estate in Cecil county named, strangely enough, like that of the man he had killed, Susquehanna. A posse of men, eager for revenge, pursued, but the little party managed to elude them, although Talbot was forced, tradition says, to hide in a cave where he was fed by trained ravens which brought him fish from the river. Finally, Lord Baltimore's efforts in his cousin's behalf, which had been redoubled after Talbot's escape, had their reward and royal clemency was vouchsafed. Talbot emerged from his cave and resumed his place in the world.

John Rousby, the younger brother who had built Rousby Hall in Calvert county, just opposite Solomon's Island, soon followed his brother to the tomb, for the two had been devoted and one was not able to live without the other. The crumbling stone in the midst of that lonely cornfield was placed above the bodies of both and inscribed:

> Here lyeth the body of Xpher Rousbie, Esquire, who was taken out of this World by a violent Death received on Board his Majesty's ship, 'The Quaker Ketch,' Captain Thomas Allen Command'r the last day of Oct'r 1684. And also Mr. John Rousbie, his Brother who departed this natural Life on board the Ship Baltimore, Being arrived in the Patuxent River the first day of February, 1685. Memento mori.

A skull and cross bones complete the inscription.

Christopher Rousby never married. After his death Susquehanna again became the property of the Maryland proprietary in which its title was vested until the year 1700 when it was granted to Richard Smith, attorney-general of the proprietary, in a patent executed by Mary Darnall, wife of Col. Henry Darnall, the agent of the proprietary, an unusual instance of the exercise of such power in that day by a woman. Afterwards it belonged to Capt. Henry Carroll who pledged his love to a baby sweetheart and wooed her with toys and toffee. Hopefully he waited for her to grow to womanhood and when she was still in her teens his devotion was rewarded. Araminta Thompson returned his love and the two celebrated a royal wedding and entertained hospitably at Susquehanna.

*　　*　　*

Among the early colonists who came to Maryland, although his arrival took place about two decades after the landing of the Ark and the Dove, was one Lieutenant-Colonel John Jarboe, whose name seems first to have been spelled Jarbo and, at other times, Garbo. Lieutenant-Colonel Jarboe was a native of Dijon, France, and came to Maryland from Virginia as a soldier in the service of Lord Baltimore with whom he seems to have been on terms of closest friendship. His house, more than two hundred and fifty years old, still is standing in St. Mary's county, about fifty yards back from the shore of the Chesapeake Bay, with a broad sweep of thick green turf between. The place is known now as Long Lane Farm and belongs to Marcel Longini, formerly of Chicago, who resides in Baltimore and has a summer home on the property which is not far from the little settlement known as Pearson.

The old house is representative in every detail of the first homes of the Maryland colonists. It belongs to the type which has come to be known in Southern Maryland as the Marine Colonial, houses built for the most part by men whose interest was in ships, houses with jerkin roofs pitched steeply from the ridge pole and extending down, front and back, to cover the porch which always faced the water, and the rear rooms on the first floor. From the roof long, attenuated dormers, with triangular caps, look out like spy glasses. It was an easy matter for the owner of a vessel, anxious for its return, to scan a considerable stretch of water from the vantage point of these dormers, or, if that scrutiny told him nothing, to clamber out and up to the top of the roof where he had a still more extended range of vision.

The walls of Lieutenant-Colonel Jarboe's home were built of brick and laid, two feet thick, in that interlocking Flemish bond which makes them as strong and impregnable as the walls of a fortress. The front and rear facades are clapboarded, for such was the fashion of the day, and two immense, free-standing chimneys, with ornamental caps, rise several feet above the ridge pole,—one at each end of the house—their curious outlines and intricate construction offering a long chapter of fascinating study to the person who finds absorption in old brickwork. In the cellar the foundations of the chimney take the form of a semi-circle, with a line of curious compartments around the rim of the opening. The use of these compartments never has been explained. Concerning them one can only conjecture.

Beside the chimney, on one end of the house, is a door leading into the old kitchen, and on the other side a low archway, covered by a shed roof. Just beyond is the most interesting characteristic of the structure, a curious little penthouse, with thick brick walls and lighted by a single, four-paned window close up under the eaves of its shed roof. The penthouse connected by a doorway with the bedroom back of the old kitchen and at ground level is hollowed out, possibly six feet or more below the ground. Into this curious little place went the entire family when the dreaded war whoop announced an Indian raid, pulling aside the heavy planks of the floor and dropping down into the little home-made fort. As soon as the last member of the family had descended to safety, the floor planks were replaced in position and certain strategic bricks were removed from the wall at ground level, making almost invisible apertures through which to shoot at the Indians.

The first floor of the house includes, in addition to the kitchen and bedroom mentioned, a large "greate" room, which opened onto a small hallway, really little more than a passage, leading to the back door, and a smaller bedroom, with a small chimney of its own. A primitive stairway, with a single landing, leads up from the "greate" room into one of the two bedrooms on the second floor. There is no hall upstairs at Long Point Farm, nor do any of the other Marine Colonial houses of Maryland show such an attribute of luxury. A vast amount of space goes to waste under the eaves of the upper rooms and the narrow, box-like recesses which culminate in the dormer windows give these little bedchambers an appearance of primitiveness which is not paralleled in Maryland outside of St. Mary's county.

Change is a thing unknown at Long Point Farm. Except for the replacement of broken window panes, and the covering of the original roof of handsplit chestnut shingles a few years ago with a new roof, this house has known no alterations whatever. It is a perfect exhibit of the day in which it was built, showing almost by its very arrangement how life was carried on under its roof. Existence was, inevitably, shorn of all unnnecessary trappings. Windows, for instance, were expensive, so the number of them was reduced to a minimum. Heat was at a premium, so the owner of the house slept in the room next the kitchen and left the door between open at night. Before he went to bed he removed the loose floor planks in the penthouse so that, should a hurried rush to safety be necessary, it could be accomplished without wasting a moment. The door of the other first floor bedroom is immediately opposite the doors leading, respectively, from the hallway into the owner's bedroom, and from the bedroom into the penthouse, affording the occupants of the far bedroom a direct route to the dugout.

In later years, when the spectre of the Indian no longer menaced and life in St. Mary's county had assumed the ease and freedom which still characterize it, revelry ran high in this house. The Platers and the Carrolls of Susquehanna, the Thomases and the Briscoes, all foregathered there, the sleeping problem being solved by all the feminine members of the gathering reclining crosswise in the big four-posters,—sometimes as many as four to a bed—in the upper rooms and the men disposing themselves as best they might in the rooms below. Only the most intimate of the family friends remained for the night unless they had been particularly bidden or were forced to stay for some other reason, most of the parties breaking up early in order to permit the revellers, lighting their way by pine torches and following the

[27]

trails indicated by notches cut in the trees, to reach home before midnight.

Lieutenant-Colonel John Jarboe was merely Lieutenant Jarboe when he came to Maryland from Virginia in 1646 to help Lord Baltimore settle some of his boundary difficulties and remained in the military service of the colony. In 1667-8 there is record of an order given to him to "press" twenty-three men out of his company and conduct them to East St. Mary's, the rendezvous for an expedition against the Nanticoke Indians on the Eastern Shore.

Everything, too, points to the then Lieutenant Jarboe's participation in the imbroglio which took place at Providence, as Annapolis then was called, between the forces of Governor Stone and the government which had been set up under the authorization of the Cromwellian parliament in England, "for the reduction of Maryland." Lieutenant Jarboe was fined one thousand pounds of tobacco for his part in that affair, the lightness of his fine said to have been the result of his ability to convince the court that he had entered into the engagement unwillingly.

Lieutenant Jarboe, having come into Maryland under the later "Conditions of Plantation" would have been ineligible, owing to his birth on French soil, to participate in the expansive generosity by which Lord Baltimore authorized his governors originally to grant land, subject to a small quit rent, to every adventurer who applied for it. Under the later "Conditions of Plantation" only persons of British or Irish parentage were eligible to land grants, but a "rider" declaring that "divers Frenchmen" and "some people who were already seated" should be capable of having grants made to them also, gave him the opportunity to become a Maryland landholder.

The first grant made to him was on Kent Island but, perhaps

because of the insecurity of these holdings from attack, or because of the more congenial atmosphere of the Catholic colony of St. Mary's, Lieutenant Jarboe took up one hundred acres of land on Breton's Bay to which he subsequently added tracts of considerable size. Old records speak of him having had a house near New-Town, in Newtown Hundred, but whether the house mentioned in this reference is the one on Long Lane Farm or not can only be conjectured as all traces of New-Town have been lost.

On July 30, 1661, Lord Baltimore, by his brother, Governor Philip Calvert, declared John Jarboe, "subject of the Crowne of France" to be a "free Dennizen" of Maryland, with the same rights as if born in the Province. Three years later he was commissioned a justice of the peace for St. Mary's county, a position of real importance for the justices of the colonial government composed the county court, a certain proportion of their number being designated a quorum every one of whom was required to be present before the court could sit, unless a member of the Council were present. This post was augmented in 1667 by the appointment of Lieutenant-Colonel Jarboe, as he had become by this time, to be high sheriff of St. Mary's. The appointment was made by Caecilius, Lord Baltimore, acting through his son, Governor Charles Calvert, later third Lord Baltimore, and was confirmed the next year. This French born Marylander also found time to sit in the Lower House and took part constantly in the councils of the province except during a short period when, in some manner or other, he seems to have given offence to the proprietary. The coldness, however, does not seem to have lasted any great length of time and preceded Lieutenant-Colonel Jarboe's various appointments to office.

In 1671 he made a will in writing. Subsequently, however, he had "another Sonne and daughter" for whom he wished to make provision but failed to do so until several years later when he fell extremely ill and was urged by his long-time friend and compatriot, John Jourdain, to put his affairs in order. Accepting this advice he urged John Jourdain to summon to his bedside the following Friday one Edward Clarke to draw him a new "will in writing" but, in the meantime, instructed Jourdain concerning his wishes and "bade him take notice that such was his will." The formal document never was drawn up and the nuncupative will was validated by the Assembly.

John Jarboe, his eldest son, received the "Seate of land" where Lieutenant-Colonel Jarboe then lived and this, presumably, is the old house on Long Lane Farm. Other tracts of land were devised to his other sons, his daughter Mary receiving no real estate because "she had some land to be made good to her by Mark Cordes and Walter Hall, gentlemen."

By various intermarriages the tract on which the old Jarboe house stands passed into the possession of the Carrolls of Susquehanna and was known for many years as Carroll's Bay Property, before it came into the possession of Mr. Longini.

Near the old dwelling is the old meat house, also built of brick, with the original, hand-forged iron meat hooks, showing the marks of the blacksmith's hammer, still ready to receive a side of beef or a slaughtered sheep. The old tobacco barn is there, too, with scarcely a nail to hold it together, the old wooden pins supporting the timbers as firmly as nails could do, and the other old granaries and out-buildings stand roundabout,—a little village in themselves.

Even with the lapse of almost three centuries, the waters in front and on both sides of Long Lane Farm teem with fish and crabs and any time a jaded appetite considers with favor a dish of terrapin, it is only necessary to go out and catch the requisite diamond-back. His tribe is legion at Long Lane Farm.

CHAPTER THREE

In Charles county, which lies at the heart of Southern Maryland and where still the patient ox toils in the tobacco fields, lived, during the Revolution, a group of men who were intimate friends of Washington and Lafayette and other leaders of the war against Great Britain. To their homes these doughty patriots came often, to dine and sup, to dance and flirt a little and play cards. And they, in turn, were frequent and welcome guests at Mount Vernon across the Potomac.

At Mulberry Grove lived John Hanson, who held one public office after another and, as president of the Continental Congress, extended to Washington the official welcome of his country when he returned to Philadelphia to make formal announcement of the surrender of Cornwallis at Yorktown.

At La Grange—its name bestowed in compliment to the Marquis de Lafayette whose home in France bore that designation—lived Dr. James Craik who was Washington's cousin by marriage and who was one of the physicians called to minister to him when the seriousness of his last illness became so manifest that Mrs. Washington sent hasty, desperate calls to Alexandria and to Maryland for the most expert of professional advice.

At Rose Hill the benign Dr. Gustavus Brown, a consultant with Dr. Craik at that same mournful bedside, dispensed pills and philtres and, with his wife, who was a famous hostess, entertained in a manner which is traditional even today in Charles county.

Just beyond Rose Hill, at Habre de Venture, lived Thomas Stone who signed the Declaration of Independence, one of the earliest copies of which, identical in size and appearance with the original, was presented by Congress to the family of the Signer and hangs upon a wall of the drawingroom today, moth-eaten and so fragile that it is touched only when necessary for fear it may fall entirely to pieces.

All of these estates cluster around the ancient and almost obliterated village of Port Tobacco which once was a thriving town and which was the county seat of Charles until the old court house was destroyed by fire more than thirty years ago. At the time of the Revolution it was a busy shipping center from which plantation owners dispatched great quantities of tobacco overseas in their own ships for their own aggrandizement,—as well as for the satisfaction of a jaded king and his prolix court.

Mulberry Grove, in the hands of its present owner, Dana Stevens, flourishes more expansively than during the tenure of the Hansons, for the old mansion has been considerably en-larged as well as restored to its Colonial condition, and the house and grounds are meticulously cared for. The house stands on a high ridge overlooking the valley which cups Port Tobacco and commands a view not only of the old Port Tobacco creek, now little more than a swamp at this point, but of a distant country-side as well. The driveway, bordered by rhododendron and laurel, makes a wide curve to the top of the hill which has been landscaped with lawns and gardens filled with old-fashioned flowers. It terminates by the side of the white clapboarded man-sion, with chimneys so enormous that they occupy almost the entire end of the house and are connected by a brick membrane through which a window has been cut.

The main wing of Mulberry Grove has a steep, pitched roof and is provided, both front and rear, with wide verandas. The smaller wing is much lower, with dormer windows, triangularly capped, breaking the roof line. Within, the distinguishing characteristic in addition to the nice proportions of the rooms is the stairway with its mahogany rail, extremely slender newel post and white spindles scarcely larger than a man's finger. The stair turns in its flight to the second floor, the twist in the railing providing an additional interest in the hall.

Inevitably, the attention of visitors to Mulberry Grove is drawn to the diningroom mantel, with its wide, eared shelf and high, bevelled panelling above. On each side of the mantelpiece fluted Ionic columns rest upon plain pedestals some eighteen inches high.

* * *

La Grange derives much of its interest from the fact that it was the home of Dr. Craik, whose descendants are said to be striving to regain possession of the place. It now is owned by Charles H. Stonestreet.

Four massive chimneys dominate the house which presents its gable end to the State road running through the estate. The odd placing of the gable windows, as well as the size of the chimneys, attest the age of the house and draw attention to the fact that the end walls are of brick, while the front and rear facades are of wide clapboarding. From the pitched roof two small dormer windows look out on each side.

Only part of the old portico, which was the distinguishing feature of the front facade, remains, the roof having been carried away a number of years ago after innumerable bouts with wind and rain. Otherwise the exterior looks exactly as it was in the days when Dr. Craik's saddle horse was brought round from the stables ready for him to mount and ride off to test his skill against the malaria which wracked the country side, or to sit up all night with a feverish child.

Three arches, separated by fluted pilasters, are formed by panelling which formerly sheathed the wall under the portico, the center arch being filled by the fanlight over the front door. The other two frame the small windows on either side. Above the portico the pilasters continue to the top of the house, supporting a roof line with modillions. In front of the house, close to the entrance, stand ancient thorn locusts said to have been brought to La Grange from Jerusalem by some religiously inclined owner of the place.

The original massive locks still fasten the front and back doors opening at each end into the hallway which runs through the house. The two doors are identical, with fanlights above and flanking pilasters. The length of the hall is broken by a fine arch, the supports of which are fluted and reeded to the top of the wainscoting, and fluted above it to the square capital upon which the arch rests. The floor boards are wide and firm, so thick that they show no wear from the innumerable feet which have trod them through more than two centuries. The stairway is built entirely of walnut, with wide, easy steps and a massive handrail which forms a spiral about the newel post on the lowest stair. A conventional spiral carving appears on the side of the stairstring.

The doors throughout the house are deeply recessed, the jambs showing bevelled panels. Little attempt at elaboration appears on the mantels, which are of massive size in the main rooms, but they have fluted friezes and smooth round columns under the high, narrow shelves.

On the second floor the hallway transverses the axis of the house, with bedrooms of good size opening upon it, each with its own fireplace.

An indication of the climate which makes it possible to spend most of the year out-of-doors in Southern Maryland is to be found in the veranda which stretches its length across the back of the house to the wing which connects with the old smoke-

Photo by Pickering

LA GRANGE

Photo by Pickering

STAIRWAY AT LA GRANGE

ROSE HILL MANOR

Photo by Pickering

HABRE DE VENTURE

house. The veranda also figures in a story connected with Colonel Manning, an Englishman who acquired the place from another Englishman, Col. Francis Newman, to whom La Grange was sold after the death of Dr. Craik. The story has it that Colonel Manning's wife died at La Grange and that the colonel carried her body back to England for burial, leaving word to the servants to wrap the large pillars on the veranda with black which was to be allowed to remain there until his return.

The draping was done as Colonel Manning had directed, but upon his arrival at New York a few weeks later he sent word immediately to his servants quickly to remove all signs of mourning, as he was bringing with him a new wife, also an English woman.

Dr. Craik, the most interesting, historically, of all the figures connected with La Grange, was born near Dumfries, Scotland, in 1730, and emigrated to America in 1750. He was a surgeon in Washington's first command and was with him in the Battle of Great Meadows in 1754. From that time forward he figured with the General in every battle Washington ever fought until the Revolution ended at Yorktown.

For gallant conduct and meritorious service at the Battle of Monongahela, in 1755, where he ministered to the dying Braddock, Dr. Craik was officially commended.

During the Revolution he was surgeon general of the Continental army. "He saw," says one of his biographers, "the gallant Hugh McMercer breathe his last on the field at Princeton, dressed Lafayette's wounds at Brandywine and was at the death-bed of John Custis—Mrs. Washington's son, at Eltham, after Yorktown."

He was, perhaps, the most intimate friend of Washington who refers to him in his will as "My old and intimate friend,

Dr. Craik." And after Washington's eyes had been closed in death he "soothed the dying moments of Martha, the wife of Washington."

Dr. Craik died at Vauclause, near Alexandria, Va., February 5, 1814. His body was buried in the lichened churchyard adjoining the Presbyterian church on South Fairfax Street, Alexandria.

The old smokehouse with which the veranda connects is the last of a group of brick outbuildings which once clustered near the mansion following the style of English manor houses of the Eighteenth century. The smokehouse is almost cubical, built of bricks laid in English bond, with brick modillions at the roof line. All of the other buildings, the spinning house, the storehouses, the mews, are traceable only by the depressions in the ground where once they stood. There was a day when the grounds of La Grange comprised about a thousand acres and included the present site of La Plata, now the county seat of Charles county, but the estate has been sold, piece by piece, down to its present extent of approximately one hundred and sixty acres.

* * *

Dr. Gustavus Richard Brown, of Rose Hill, was Dr. Craik's nearest neighbor, and was both jurist and legislator as well as a physician. He was one of the eleven children of Dr. Gustavus Brown of Rich Hill, another Charles county estate, his large family connection and his own inclinations combining with his position as a professional man to make his home the social center of the neighborhood.

Rose Hill is a ruin now. The front and back porticoes have given up the battle against the years and sag in twisted abandon on rusted nails. To enter it is necessary to negotiate a ladder built to a side door and, once inside, it is evident that the dignity and harmony for which the place was famous before the Revolu-

tion are inherent and need only the informed hand of the re-
storer to bring them to life again.

The house is of great size, the arrangement of its interior
presenting an engaging combination of formality and hetero-
geneity. The walls are of brick, laid in Flemish bond and faced,
like La Grange, with wide clapboarding, front and back. In its
heyday the driveway provided an impressive approach, wide and
well laid out, from the main road almost a mile away to the front
portico, where the doorway still shows its round engaged columns, topped with Ionic capitals, at each side and an ornamental
transom overhead. The gable ends are almost entirely taken
up by the twin chimneys which served fireplaces whose roaring
blaze could do little more than take the edge from a wintry
cold in rooms the size of those in Rose Hill. No one in Revolutionary days was revolutionary enough, however, to dream of
being comfortable in winter.

A fourteen-foot hallway runs through the center of the house,
panelled at each end to the height of the doors which are framed
in heavy, hand-hewn moulding and flanked by a small window
on each side. Heavy toe moulding and plain wainscoting, still
painted the grayish green so much in favor with early Maryland decorators, set off the arch which divides the hall across
the center. Bevelled panels appear on the soffit of the arch which
rests upon fluted pilasters, surmounted by heavy capitals. Until
recently the imported landscape paper hung in its original position on the walls.

The small stair hall opens off the main hall at the extreme
left end, its existence being announced by a small arch with a
fluted keystone at the top and a similar ornament at each end
of the curve. The narrow stairs, which turn at a landing and
reverse themselves, are not visible from the front door, or even
from the hallway. The balustrade is walnut, with a slender

newel post resting upon a semi-circular step at the bottom—the only one of its kind in Maryland.

At the left of the hall is the "greate" room, thirty feet square, with a high ceiling and light, moulded cornice. A wainscoting of wide boards, applied horizontally to the wall, extends to a height of about three feet, with a heavy baseboard moulding and matching chair rail. A six-foot mantel occupies the center of the wall opposite the doorway and has an eared architrave. On each side of the fireplace opening are small, round columns with Ionic capitals and the frieze has a plain center panel set off by moulding and a line of Greek fret above. The mantel shelf, which also has ears, rests upon miniature consoles.

Upstairs, over the "greate" room, is "Washington's bedroom," set apart for the General's use whenever he cared to visit Rose Hill. The windows look out over the garden and Port Tobacco creek and the bricks about the fireplace are laid endwise in a diagonal pattern. The mantel piece is high, with a simple, formal decoration and line of dentils cut into the edge of the narrow shelf.

From the semi-circular window at the end of the upper hall, over the front portico, there is a view over the gardens and the valley for miles, with Port Tobacco creek in the distance. The upper hall duplicates exactly the size of the lower and the house has that rarity of pre-Revolutionary building, a back hall, with a stairway which winds circularly to the second floor. Space was plentiful when Rose Hill was erected and the builders were prodigal in their use of it, but the irregularities of its planning make up in charm what they may lack in architectural economy.

All of the timbers which went into the making of Rose Hill were hewn from trees which grew on the plantation and, where they can be seen, show plainly the marks of the axe. Wooden pins fasten the rafters together, for nails were rare enough to be employed with parsimony as well as respect. No laths were used in the construction of Rose Hill, either. The plaster was applied, fully an inch and a-half thick, directly to the brick partition walls, from which it now is parting company in certain places.

Underneath the house is a dark, airless chamber into which, according to an old legend, obstreperous slaves were thrust in punishment for their misdoings. The accepted plantation custom of placing the kitchen in a building separate from the house obtains at Rose Hill, the similar small brick building, constructed for use as Dr. Brown's office on the opposite side of the house and which made for symmetry of the group, having been torn down years ago.

In front of the house stretches a broad green plateau of thick greensward, bound on its far edge by a luxuriant garden of box grown to enormous size and planted in a pattern of squares and quadrants, perfect in outline even today. Beyond the box garden the flower garden is laid out in a series of terraces and "falls." In a corner of the lowest "fall" stands the weathered marble sarcophagus which contains all that is mortal of the once-eminent Dr. Brown.

Atop the tomb is a massive slab into which is graven in letters that have withstood the summer heats and winter snows of a century and more, this tribute:

Sacred to the Memory of
Dr.
Gustavus Richard Brown

This tombstone is erected
by his Relict
Margaret Brown

In Testimony of her Respect
and Affection
And as a Monument
To his Skill as a Physician
and his Learning as a Scholar
To his Wisdom as a Philosopher
To his Patriotism as a Citizen
To his Generosity as a Friend
To his Elegance as a Gentleman
To his Hospitality as a Neighbor
To his Kindness as a Master
To his Tenderness as a Husband
and Parent and
To his Benevolence as a Man

He died 30th September, 1801,
Aged 56 years.

With its other appurtenances Rose Hill also has its ghost in
the guise of a blue dog which barks in anticipation of births and
deaths which occur in the Brown family and which has constituted itself the phantom guardian of buried treasure.

According to the legend of the blue dog, the animal belonged
to a peddler who was convivially inclined and who had imbibed
freely with some boon companions at the tavern in Port Tobacco
until the patient boniface informed the revellers that they would
have to disperse as the closing hour had arrived. The peddler
is said to have displayed a shot bag full of money during a
boastful moment and so to have aroused the greed of one of the
bystanders that he trailed the peripatetic Dives through the fields
and up the lonely lane to Rose Hill and murdered him there
for his gold.

The next morning, according to the story, the man's body
was found sprawled on the round stone which is to be seen

in the lane today and which, the more credulous people of the neighborhood insist, still is stained with the peddler's blood. No trace of the money ever was found. It has been supposed that the murderer buried it somewhere in the woods, intending to return for it, and that if one were bold enough to follow where the blue dog leads when it barks at midnight on a moonlight night, the money would be discovered.

After the death of Dr. Brown, Rose Hill passed to the possession of Dr. and Mrs. Brown Semmes, who willed it to Miss Amelia Floyd, Mrs. Mary Piet and John D. Piet. During the Civil War it was occupied for a time by General Hooker as his headquarters and tales still are told in the neighborhood of encounters between Miss Floyd, who is said to have been a tiny but redoubtable Confederate sympathizer, and the Union officers on the general's staff. Upon one occasion, it is said, General Hooker, who always was punctiliousness itself in his attitude toward Miss Floyd, announced his intention of being absent from the place for some time.

"But what will I do here, alone with these men?" inquired Miss Floyd.

"I feel certain that nothing will happen," General Hooker reassured her, "to make things unpleasant for you, but it seems to me that a woman who always carries two pistols at her belt has little to fear. If you need them, use them."

The general departed, undoubtedly much entertained by the idea he suggested, but with his going a number of his soldiers developed the idea of having chicken for mess at the expense of Miss Floyd's poultry yard. When the commotion incident to the executions reached the ears of Miss Floyd she drew her pistols, hurried to the chicken yard and informed the invaders in an ultimatum that has lived, "Leave my chickens alone, you Yankees, or I'll put ten of you in hell in five minutes!"

During the Civil War, it is said, the family at Rose Hill took no chances whatever concerning the safety of their valuables. The silver service is said to have been concealed in the tomb of Dr. Brown and other prized possessions to have been buried. After the war the property passed through a number of hands, coming finally into the possession of the late Adrian Posey, who was a large landholder in Charles county. After his death it was sold to W. Kesley Schoepf, of Cincinnati, to whose widow it now belongs.

*   *   *

Adjoining Rose Hill is Habre de Venture, of concern not merely as the home of a signer of the Declaration of Independence but full of architectural interest in its own right. No more skillfully contrived survival of Colonial days exists than this house which was constructed a decade before the Revolution and which, though it embodies some of the most striking features of Georgian designing, presents an originality of conception and execution.

The house embodies the five-part construction of a large central building with wings seen so frequently in Maryland, but instead of conforming to the accepted horizontal plan, it takes the form of a crescent at the rim of a hit-or-miss garden, fragrant with box and daffodil. The outer margin of the crescent forms the front facade of the house, almost entirely screened from the approaching driveway by enormous evergreens.

Tall and quite slender pillars outline a brick-flagged portico which extends the length of the central portion of the house and reaches to the eaves. From the portico, which is level with the ground, a short flight of steps leads to the front door, heavy and built for service, the kind of door which holds no party with the airy, fanlighted apertures of the Adam period. Over the door appears a plain rectangular transom, six panes wide, through which the light sifts into a hall and over a stairway which has been trod by some of the most famous men and women America has produced.

Within the house ostentation is, in the words of the phrase, conspicuous by its absence, yet architects whose services can be had only at fantastic figures have thought it worth their while to travel the tortuous road which leads from the State road for almost a mile to visit Habre de Venture and to spend hours in studying its proportions, making minute measurements of this moulding, and drawings of that mantelpiece. The master of the house is generous in his hospitality.

Little panelling has been used in the hall, what there is being put on in horizontal strips of varying widths and at unequal distances apart. The stairs are at the right of the entrance, facing the garden door, and present the usual Georgian manner of treatment, with slender, turned spindles and a rail of deep, wine red mahogany. Overhead in the place it has hung since the days of the Signer, swings a candle lantern with a globe of the rare etched glass of the period, now almost impossible to discover.

The drawingroom, even more than the stairway, attracts the attention of connoisseurs of Colonial interiors. This room, in 1928, yielded of its hand carved panelling and its corner cupboards to Baltimore's new Museum of Art, to be set up there in a Colonial room as the finest exhibit that Maryland, (some say the entire country) has to show of this form of early American art.

To Habre de Venture the loss is great, of course, but not as irreparable as might at first blush appear. Before the panelling was removed the present owner of the estate, Mr. Michael Stone, who is a great-great-grand-nephew of the Signer, had accurate measurements taken of every detail of the woodwork, which has been reproduced in such excellent simulacrum that the difference between the copy and the original appears only to the expert eye. Anyone disposed to be very meticulous indeed might discover that the two roses—one said to represent the red rose of Lancaster and the other the white rose of York—are missing from the new corner cupboards. All else, the dentils on the cornice, the size of the panels, the details of carving, seem exactly like the original with only the precision of the bevelling and certain other details to betray the origin of the present wall covering in a modern world.

There is, by virtue of an active chimney projecting beyond the exterior face of the walls, no chimney breast in the room. Directly over the fireplace is the great panel like those upon which the owners of the splendid Georgian houses in England were accustomed to express their ruling tastes as sportsmen or as men of literary proclivities. On the walls hang photographs of the portraits which accompanied the panelling to the art museum—pictured likenesses of Dr. Gustavus Brown of Rich Hill, and his second wife who was the mother of the Margaret Brown who became the wife of Thomas Stone, builder of Habre de Venture. The third portrait represents the Signer himself.

In the left wing of Habre de Venture, originally a low, one-story structure connecting with the kitchen (still equipped with the cavernous fireplace and its original fire irons) are to be found architectural distinctions which exist only in one or two other houses in Maryland, touches which weave their way back to the mediaeval houses of England and recall the nostalgic efforts of self-appointed exiles to reproduce their old homes in the heart of an American wilderness.

Everything about this wing combines to indicate that here is one of the very old brick structures in the State. Its special appeal, however, is to be found in the low, arched ceiling and an extraordinary chimney treatment beginning at the floor in a large, box-like structure of brick, overlaid with plaster and placed well out in the room, with the flue curling back to the wall and up to the ceiling. The entire structure has received close attention from architects—and, from an impious and ribald generation, the designation of "George Washington's nose."

This room, now used as a breakfast room, is lower by a short flight of steps than the central portion of the house and is lighted by four small and very deeply recessed windows. Five doors also are set into the room but so cunningly have the apertures been spaced that the wall surface does not seem cut up, but merely varied and well lighted.

The left wing has changed its contours a bit within the quite recent past to comply with modern demands for bathrooms. A low superstructure with a gambrel roof has been expertly added, but it does not violate in any appreciable degree the harmonies of the house. From it, as from the gambrel roof of the central portion of the house, dormer windows look out under triangular caps. Between the right wing, built of frame, and the main portion of the house a narrow passageway affords entrance from the front lawn into the garden and a long veranda across the back assigns Habre de Venture definitely to the catalogue of southern as well as Colonial architecture.

As unusual in its way as any other characteristic of the house is the brickwork of the walls. Here is none of that peculiar shade of salmon red for which lovers of old houses are accustomed to look in Maryland, but a deep, purplish red, almost a mulberry hue. A Flemish bond was used in the construction and an extraordinary effect obtained in the main building by the use of glazed headers, so dark that they are almost black, and which glint in the sunlight.

"There is no dawn here, only sunset," wrote Amy Lowell of

Charleston. Not so at Habre de Venture. Here the day begins in a sunrise of orange and gold. The fields yield bountifully of corn and tobacco and life wells from deep springs. On the one hundred and fifty-first anniversary of the signing of the Declaration of Independence by that first virile Thomas Stone another man child was born in the house, the great-great-great-grand-nephew of the Colonial patriot. And he, too, is Thomas Stone.

CHAPTER FOUR

Once the show place of all Charles county, storied with great houses, is Araby, known for almost a century as the home of the Wills family which is one of the oldest in Southern Maryland. Before that, its history can not be definitely traced but local tradition ascribes its possession first to one debonair young "Lord Ethelbert," the only name by which he is known in the Wills' traditions of the place and who, for reasons of his own, took part in the great adventure of Maryland. "Lord Ethelbert" is said to have been the builder of Araby. From him it passed to Lord Fairfax who disposed of it in turn to George Mason and from whom it was bought by Col. William Thompson, a maternal ancestor of the Misses Wills who own it now.

Dominating the entire country side, the house stands high on a series of terraces above the modern State road which leads from La Plata to Indian Head, cutting into the sky with great double chimneys and presenting its back aloofly to the road. Butter-and-eggs, narcissus and wood violets bloom in the spring along the lane which twists up the hill from the public way, brightly colored messengers come down from the once formal garden, which covered several acres of land, to greet visitors to the old house.

The thick walls of the main wing are built of brick laid in English bond. A frame wing, incongruously added at some later date, pushes out to the left and is broken midway by a flagged portico enclosed on three sides, with an elliptical opening on the garden front. Time, however, has softened the contrast between the main wing and its offshoot and Araby, though "it has known better days," presents to the world a poise which the owners of "modern Colonial" houses would give much to include in their building.

The entrance portico is wide and low to the ground, added some years after the house was built. Two Roman Doric columns stand close together at each of the outer corners and support a ridge roof sloping steeply to each side. In front, over the columns a wooden flange, painted white and unornamented except for the ogee moulding at the top, extends upward about three feet and seems materially to increase the height of the portico. Carved balustrades extend along both sides and a blind latticed door, flush with the outer walls, conceals the heavy entrance door behind it.

In "Lord Ethelbert's" regime, Araby was but a story and a half high, with hipped roof and dormer windows. A hundred years ago it was raised to its present proportions with the chimneys carried up in high stacks above the steep roof and the upstairs rooms enlarged to their present size. The gable walls are unbroken by windows until they reach the height of the second floor and on the front and rear facades the sole ornamentation of the exterior is a wide cornice with heavy modillions.

Two large rooms, a drawingroom and a diningroom, occupy the entire garden front of the house. The drawingroom is the larger of the two by the width of the front door which opens directly into it. The walls are wainscoted in broad rectangles to the height of the chair rail and panelled above it in slender lines to the massive cornice. The mantelpiece has a tambour panel in the center of the frieze and is flanked on each side by shell alcoves which are framed by fluted pilasters under an arched moulding which has an ornamented keystone. The shelves of the cupboards have curvilinear outlines and all of the woodwork is painted a deep pearl gray with a suggestion of green, the original coloring.

In the diningroom the mantelpiece forms the high light of the decorations and bears evidence of the same expert craftmanship which characterizes the one in the drawingroom. Fluted pilasters support the mantel shelf and in the center of the frieze the tambour panel repeats the motif of the drawingroom, with ovals of the same delicate fluting above the pilasters. The edge of the shelf is outlined with heavy rope carving.

The panelling in this room is confined to the wainscot, the walls being of white plaster, guiltless from the beginning of paper, with a moulded cornice at the ceiling line. This room has been the scene of some of the most splendid banquets ever given in Southern Maryland, for from the days of its first owners until recent years the masters of Araby have been men frequently immersed in public life and always hospitably inclined. Table cloths six yards long formed part of the stock of the linen closets in past generations. About the "first table" gathered the guests of honor when entire families of the countryside were entertained and when they had partaken and repaired to the drawingroom another table was laid for the children, so that often it was midnight before the feast was ended.

Araby was built long before the days when the wide hall and flanking rooms became the favored plan for Maryland houses. The stair hall opens directly back of the drawingroom and occupies the central space at the back of the house. The stairway mounts on broad, low steps, with a turn or so, to the second floor and its mahogany railing, dull now in a servantless age, was polished in the old days by slaves until it glowed with fire in the candlelight. In the old days, too, a tilt-top table stood in the stair hall, with its supply of candles snuffed and ready for the guests "to light them to bed" when the backgammon was over and they were ready to say good-night.

To the right of the stair hall is a room similar to it in size, panelled across one end where the fireplace is, and fitted with deep, closed-in cupboards in a double tier. During the Civil War, when the Union soldiers visited Araby, one of them inquired of the little girl, now Miss Charlotte Wills, mistress of the mansion, who stood, wide-eyed, at his elbow:

"Look here, missy, what does your father keep in those cupboards?"

"Powder to shoot the Yankees with," came the instant and unhesitating reply.

The room actually was used by the quick-witted little "rebel's" father as an office and study, a place where he kept his books and attended to his correspondence. Here he directed the operation of his plantation and interviewed his overseer who had charge of many slaves and here he wrote the letter accepting a diplomatic post to Central America under President Cleveland, during his first administration. When President Cleveland was returned to office for his second administration the post was immediately offered again to the master of Araby but before he could accept it he was stricken with apoplexy and died.

A room similar to the office in size but slightly more elaborate is back of the diningroom and, like the drawingroom, boasts a shell cupboard set into the panelling beside the chimney. All of the doors throughout the house are of curly maple and much of the woodwork is solid walnut.

Across the back of the house, facing the State road, a long veranda commands a view far across the valley with its green and brown fields and little clumps of woodland constantly changing color in the shifting light. The old terraces which stretch grandiloquently below it have been neglected for years and are covered with a thick shroud of honeysuckle and underbrush, but their outline is still there, firm and certain, seeming to wait the hand which shall rescue them from obloquy. The trees on the terraces have grown to forest size and their deep spreading roots undoubtedly do valiant service in holding them in place, regardless of wintry rigors and spring thaws.

In the garden once brilliant with hollyhocks and gillyflowers and mignonette are to be found exceedingly rare trees and shrubs planted there by one of the Wills who was an ardent horticulturist and imported to this home exotic plants from all parts of the world. Two of the six pecan trees he brought from the far south have grown to noble size and close to the portico trails a blue rambler rose, probably the only one in Maryland.

Spring never fails to bring with it the illusion of youth to Araby, despite the great age of the place. Fragrance of grape blossoms hangs in the air like a cloud and perennials bloom undauntedly among the tangled briers. Expectancy seems to emanate from the old house and at evening, when the shadows creep along the fencerows and darkness surges into the valley below, Araby lifts its silent walls like a banner into the cool last light and hangs in silhouette against the pale gray sky.

* * *

Across the fields and easily seen from the veranda of this courtly house, if the weather happens to be clear, is Linden, the ancestral home of the Mitchell family of which State Senator Walter J. Mitchell, who married a Miss Jenifer, a descendant of that Daniel of St. Thomas Jenifer, who signed the Declaration of Independence, is one of the most conspicuous members in this generation.

Linden also is exceedingly old, the original part having been built of logs and clapboarded later. To the collector of old houses its roof line is full of interest, being a combination of steeply pitched gable over the newer portion, and a long, graceful slope, pierced by dormer windows, over the old wing. Chimneys so enormous that they seem disposed to take the entire credit of the house to themselves provide a striking architectural effect and a veranda ninety feet long looks upon a pleasant country with the Potomac on the horizon.

Within, the house is both comfortable and homelike. A wide hall runs through the center, the product of the newer wing, with two doors opening on the left into the double parlors, which are filled with early American chairs and tables and davenports. On the right the doors open into the livingroom and diningroom. In the livingroom a carved mantel has quarter sunbursts on the center panel and ornaments of dentil and Greek fret. The old kitchen, which once occupied a house of its own, with a covered passageway connecting it with the main house, has been leveled to the ground, though marks of its foundations are still visible.

At the extreme end of the hall is a winding stair, a forerunner of those splendid Georgian affairs of spindles and mahogany. This one has a hand-hewn rail of solid walnut, black with age, which achieves its pitch by a convex upward thrust at the turn of the stair instead of the more familiar ramp with its skillful sweep.

On the lawn in front of the house five enormous clumps of boxwood excite the cupidity of landscape gardeners who find their way almost weekly to the place, and of visitors who live in steam heated apartments and have no title to a square foot of land anywhere in the world. Strangers travel to Linden from long distances, attracted by stories of the great size which the box has attained, for the shrub is of such slow growth that its increase is scarcely visible from one decade to another.

When the box was planted it girdled beds of flowers, but it has been many a year since this deep green marriage ring usurped the rights of the blooms it was planted to protect and occupied the centers as well as the circumferences of the beds.

* * *

Another very ancient place in Charles county is Causine's Manor, sometimes spelled "Causeen." This estate originally included one thousand acres granted by Lord Baltimore to Nicholas Causine "for service made in 1649-50, according to early traditions of plantation" as related by Annie Leakin Sioussat in her study of "Old Manors in the Colony of Maryland." What that service was has not been disclosed.

Nicholas Causine sat in the Assembly of 1641 as Freeman and was, probably, the original champion of woman's rights in Maryland. In that assembly he presented a vigorous defense of the justice of permitting a woman to own property after marriage and to possess in her own name property which she had owned before marriage. In addition, according to Mrs. Sioussat who, incidentally, doesn't mention his activities on behalf of her sex, he served the colony well in other "emploies."

Diligent search has failed to reveal the date of the building of his manor house with its walls of logs clapboarded on the outside and fastened together with wooden pins, its gambrel roof and dormer windows. A hall traverses it through the center, from front to back, where a veranda extends the entire length of the building and overlooks three terraces which formerly were laid out as a garden. Two upper terraces were devoted to flowers and the lowest one to vegetables. Lapping the edge of the lowest terrace are the waters of Port Tobacco creek which form a picturesque inlet at this point, almost choked with lilies.

That the house was a pretentious one for its day is indicated by the five enormous chimneys with which it is supplied, for chimneys were ensigns of wealth and social position in early

[53]

Maryland. The mantel in the "greate" room is formed of three layers of wood, each in relief, with an extremely narrow shelf. In the diningroom, across the hall, the mantel is made of iron.

The stairs are wide and boxed, sagging now from the tread of many feet. The upstairs rooms are "curious as forgotten lore" with wide, uneven floor boards and funny little dormer windows outlined by mouldings grooved in the manner of the very long ago and seldom seen today. In two of the rooms the old H-hinges remain on the doors, those in other portions of the house having been replaced by more modern devices.

Causine's Manor house is the more picturesque because of the tendency of smaller buildings to straggle off from it to one side, a tendency which can not be said to take the form of a wing and which reveals the gradual achievement of the big house from the first tiny shelters erected by the Maryland pioneers. The old house is far back from the main road, but in the days when the waterways were the arteries of travel it was easily accessible.

* * *

Shut away almost completely from the highways by vast tobacco fields and a devious, difficult road and looking inquiringly out over the confluence of Port Tobacco creek with the broad waters of the Potomac is an ancient house known as Mount Air. Originally, Mount Air belonged to the Matthews family who first took up land under the Conditions of Plantation of 1633, and who owned Mount Air until the death of Laura Frances Matthews in 1815. For the last fifteen years it has been the home of Mr. and Mrs. George Stevenson, who have rescued the place from the bats and snakes and insects which were in complete possession, and, except for the duration of an expedition to South America in the interest of scientific investigations for the government, have been wholeheartedly engaged in restoring it to its rightful vigor and character.

Once the visitor has negotiated the winding lane which leads into Mount Air (reassured by experience that another car can be passed on the way without one of the two dropping horribly over the bluff to be impaled on a treetop in the ravine below) and has achieved the uplands which surround the house, the instant impression is of a sentinel in brick and plaster, fully capable of defying the rains that may beat and the winds that may blow—and do.

Standing high on its bluff, the house seems to flaunt its own height, completely unaffected by the usual levelling influence of low wings. To the river front it presents a double veranda, roofed above the first story and open on the second. To the land it offers an entirely different aspect. Before it stretches a broad lawn leading to a boxwood maze and an old-fashioned garden beyond which traces of once extensive orchards and vineyards remain, undulating with bloom in the spring, heavy with fruit in the autumn. Close to the house itself are grandiose bushes of the thousand-leaf Microphylle rose, so much in favor with the great-grandmothers of today and renamed whimsically by Charles Countians, the Rosa Machiavelli.

A steep, covered portico leads to the doorway at the extreme right of the main wing, the deep recess of the door indicating the thickness of the walls which are bricknogged and clapboarded on the exterior. Years of neglect had contrived to impregnate the walls with dampness and after continued efforts to dry them out the present owners have covered them with a temporary black stucco which seems a bit staggering at first, though it is not unpleasant on a house exposed as this one is, with but few trees close by to give it background.

The predilection of Southern Maryland plantation owners for

brick chimneys so wide that they occupy almost the entire end of the house again is evident at Mount Air, but the roof line breaks the almost universal rule of the country and overhangs on the gable end, with a short return above the second story windows.

In the hallway the height of the walls is broken by mouldings at chair rail and lintel line. To the right of the hall is the library which occupies an entire wing. To the left two doors open into the livingroom and stair vestibule.

The doors alone at Mount Air make the place worth a journey to see, for all of them are of walnut and are fitted with massive brass locks imported from England. The window frames, like the doors, are of the same wood, with eared mouldings, and support the tradition that the builder of Mount Air had planned to create in it the handsomest house in Southern Maryland but was forced to give up the ambition for lack of funds before he had finished building.

In the drawingroom, overlooking the water front, the mantelpiece is almost completely covered with carving, done, however, with such restraint that the effect is rich without being flamboyant. Around the opening of the fireplace, which will take a cord stick with ease, the bricks are covered with plaster. On each side fluted pilasters, reeded almost half their length, are topped by rectangular panels, decorated with small rope carving and rosettes. Across the chimney breast, between the panels, stretches a wide frieze, the fillets between each line of fluting being carved alternately in rope and bead design. A band of rococo carving tops the frieze and the edge of the eared mantel shelf is finely fluted.

The mantelpiece in the one-time "stairway drawingroom" is only a shade less elaborate than the one in the great drawingroom, carrying out the same general scheme of decoration with slightly varied *motifs*. The proportions of this room, however, have been marred somewhat as the result of an intervening wall placed, according to tradition, to shut off the view of the stairway from the room. The alteration was made in conformity with the modest ideas of one Mme. Causine, a French woman living on the adjoining plantation, whose daughter had married the owner of Mount Air. When Mme. Causine visited her daughter she is said to have objected to the revelation of the ankles of the latter's feminine guests as they went up and down the stairs. Extraordinary as this story sounds it is, nevertheless, a fact that a partition has been interposed across the room, cutting directly into the woodwork of one of the windows. The story has it, too, that a mahogany rail was removed in the process in order that prudery might prevail.

"They say" that at one time the masculine occupants of Mount Air, Causine's Manor and White Hall, adjoining places, were such inveterate card players that they would bet anything and everything but their wives and that after an all-night vigil it was not an uncommon sight for a cartload of household effects or other assets to be moved from one plantation to the other the following morning.

A door from the drawingroom leads directly into the diningroom which is particularly interesting because of its rounded end. Several steps down from the diningroom is the kitchen, with floor boards a foot wide and a tremendous fireplace. The basement is unusually elaborate for a house the age of this one. In it is an elaborate labyrinth of brick partitioned rooms which show traces of their use as storage places for great quantities of hams and cured meats, as well as for canned fruits and vegetables which every Maryland housewife once thought it incumbent to have put away in great quantities for the winter. In the basement, too, it is possible to see the heavy walnut joists, hewn out by hand, which support the house and are put together with hand wrought nails.

Before the Civil War sixty slaves worked the land at Mount Air and raised tobacco which was shipped to England in great quantities and which was much in demand at court. The old quarters where the darkeys lived stood untouched until a few years ago when they were pulled down and today there is no trace of them. Every Saturday morning before the Civil War the slave women came up to the big house to polish the floors by strewing them with corn husks on which they danced with their heavy shoes.

At one time the plantation was owned by Judge Robert Digges. Later it passed into the possession of his brother-in-law, James Neale, whose two sisters, when fortunes dwindled, kept a girls' school in the house. After their death it was bought by a Miss Wills who, in turn, sold it to its present owners. In restoring the house to a habitable condition Mr. and Mrs. Stevenson have run a gamut of experience. Their first battle, which became a seven years' war, more or less, was with the local fauna which insisted upon the right of eminent domain, the spiders even going the length of travelling down threads they spun from the kitchen ceiling over the cook-stove where, apparently anaesthetized by the heat, they dropped into whatever happened to be brewing at the moment.

To make the house watertight resolved itself into an even greater problem which was attacked in various ways, none of them successful. The present sable coating, however, seems likely to be the solution to the puzzle, though Mr. and Mrs. Stevenson plan to change it to a hue more in keeping with Colonial usages when it has demonstrated completely its imperviousness to weather.

During their regime at Mount Air Mr. and Mrs. Stevenson

have met with the firm and unequivocal refusal of certain of the local negroes to work there on the plea that the place is haunted and that they prefer to run no risks. In their efforts to restore the farm lands to productivity they have imported overseers who have pursued hobbies of their own ranging from drugs to German espionage, but they are succeeding, nevertheless, in returning the land, as well as the house, to its Colonial fruition.

* * *

So lavishly was Maryland endowed by nature with richness of soil and an abundance of fresh and salt water teeming with all manner of marine life that existence in Lord Baltimore's colony presented difficulties which were insignificant by comparison with the rigors of life in the northern and New England colonies. It was necessary to do little more than scratch the soil to reap abundantly of whatever was planted in it and if the ancient "relations" of the colony speak true, fish fairly fought with each other to take the fisherman's hook.

In Charles county, which derives its name from "His Gracious Majesty, King Charles of England," even the Indians were friendly. Records of massacres are virtually non-existent. The result of such a combination of favorable conditions was to create here, as elsewhere in Southern Maryland, a life which was one long, rollicking adventure and to produce an aristocracy of the land as carefree and self-sufficient as any of which history makes record.

Estates covering a thousand acres and more were maintained by these early colonists in easy affluence, with all the luxuries life afforded theirs virtually for the taking. Of these enormous plantations one of the largest in Charles county was granted by Lord Baltimore to Thomas Hatton, who had been the bearer of the great religious Act of Toleration to Maryland and whose family had been high in official service in England since the days of Queen Elizabeth. Part of it he called West Hatton, a tract which eventually came into possession of the Stoddert family in which it has remained so long that throughout Charles county it invariably is referred to as Stoddert land.

Several houses stood on West Hatton before the present mansion was built about a hundred and forty years ago by Major William Truman Stoddert, a nephew of General Smallwood of Revolutionary memory, and a member of his staff.

In selecting the site for his home Major Stoddert chose a point of land almost completely encircled by the river and reached by a long lane which winds through well-tilled fields and then, turning sharply, runs straight for fully an eighth of a mile toward the house. On one side of the road an orchard blooms and ripens. On the other stretches the river.

A narrow strip of sandy beach interposes between the gardens about the house and the water, sloping so gradually that safe sport is available even for inexperienced swimmers. Out in the river a private oyster bar yields succulent food during the months with an "r" in their spelling and the West Hatton ducking marshes are alive with redheads and canvasbacks.

So West Hatton was in the days of Major Stoddert and so it is today with Mr. and Mrs. Foster Reeder, the present owners, who spend most of the year at West Hatton. Mrs. Reeder, before her marriage was Miss Bessie Stoddert, a descendant of the Revolutionary officer whose grave in the garden she discovered and marked with a marble slab after it had lain neglected for many years.

In all its essentials the house at West Hatton exhibits the characteristics of the ripe period of Georgian architecture in Maryland. Its walls are of brick, covered with white stucco which

DETAIL OF PANELLING AT HABRE DE VENTURE

INSET CORNER BOOKCASE IN "GREATE ROOM"
AT HABRE DE VENTURE

WEST HATTON: LAND VIEW

WEST HATTON: DOORWAY BETWEEN DRAWINGROOM AND DININGROOM

can be seen for miles from boats going up and down the river. The river front has a two-story portico with a flagged floor and tapering brick columns, placed to catch the breezes from the river. The central portion is flanked by two low wings of different size and indicative of different periods of construction. One of these, a one-story structure reached by a short flight of steps, has been remodeled by Mr. and Mrs. Reeder for use as a billiard room, though the old fireplace and mantel have been left intact and the arrangement of the windows is unchanged.

The four large chimneys of the main wing are placed inside the walls and cut through the gable roof, two at each end, stretching upward with a connecting ligature providing architectural interest as well as support to the stacks. The front portico is square, with hospitable benches against the side railings, and square columns support the simply carved cornice under the eaves. Over the door, with its characteristic brass knocker, is a fanlight of particularly fine proportions, its design outlined by a leaded tracery. The sidelights show a leaded design of segmented discs.

Enthusiasts display their interest especially in the central wing. The symmetry of its proportions have made it a model for many of the imitation Colonial houses of the newer suburbs and its mahogany stairway, which winds to the attic, looks as fragile as a spider's web, but actually is so well supported that it has not sagged the fraction of an inch in almost a century and a-half.

Between the drawingroom and the diningroom is an arched double door with a fanlight elaborately designed with beading and fine leading. The keystone of the arch is carved and a line of small scroll carving finishes the moulding around the fanlight. In both these rooms the mantels are identical in style, with eared, narrow shelves and oval medallions in the panels.

Plaster cornices in these rooms are simply moulded and on all of the window frames in the house a line of dentils appears below the sill, upstairs as well as down.

Many of the original antiques are still in the house, the massive brass locks on the doors and the strap bolts which were a protection against the winds as well as against possible intruders. In the diningroom, supporting an old mirror, are rare gilded brackets rescued, one from the kitchen where it had been requisitioned by a tenant as a support for a modern sink, and the other from a junk pile in an old outbuilding. The old sideboard, too, has been restored to its rightful place in the diningroom after having stood for years on the porch of a negro cabin, cast out at some time to make room for a modern substitute. It stands now exactly where it stood in the days of Major Stoddert, its position having been established by Mrs. Reeder after long search among the family archives.

* * *

Not far from West Hatton is Hard Bargain, also fronting on the Wicomico and long associated with the Harris and Digges families of Southern Maryland. Architecturally as well as legendarily the name seems, somehow, to fit. About the place there is lacking something of the largeness of spirit which characterizes most of the Southern Maryland homes, no matter what their size, (and Hard Bargain is not diminutive) but even the most captious person could find nothing about which to quibble in the view.

Reason for the apparent lack of graciousness about the place, it is possible, may be found in the absence of trees and shrubbery which play so large a part in making up the picture presented by many old houses south of the Mason and Dixon line. Or it may be discovered in a promise rashly made and kept unwillingly. The story goes that Gwynn Harris, then owner of Mount Tirzah, an adjoining estate, while celebrating an anniversary of his marriage to Kitty Root Harris, proposed to his brother, Tom, that if the latter would drink a glass of wine to the health of his sister-in-law, he himself would buy the adjoining farm and on it would build Tom a house. Tom Harris agreed. The health was drunk and everyone was happy until the next day when Tom Harris recalled the promise to his brother, who rued the day but kept his word. The Digges farm, accordingly, changed hands and in a short time Tom Harris found himself in possession of a handsome home where he lived to a ripe old age.

Hard Bargain is built of brick, in three sections which, seen from a distance, give the effect of giant steps. The windows are oddly placed to one side of the center in the gable end of the main wing—small apertures, with many panes. Brick modillions form the only decoration of the exterior and the main doorway is topped by a square transom. A number of years ago Hard Bargain passed from the Harris family into possession of the late Robert Crain, by whose estate it now is owned.

* * *

One of the landmarks along the Crain highway in the lower part of Charles county is Mount Republican which faces a wide curve in the road and stands at the head of an avenue of maples.

The deep salmon color of the brickwork in Mount Republican has been weathered by the suns and rains of many seasons and filmed over in places by a fine green moss which adds to the effect of antiquity. Thick English ivy hangs in festoons over the gable end and seems to cherish an ambition completely to obliterate the windows,—a precaution which might have been more necessary were Franklin Weems, its one-time owner, living there today. For Weems was one of the great *bon vivants* of Southern Maryland in his day and is said to have kept his cellar filled with fifty barrels of brandy and the best wines of which he partook freely himself and freely dispensed to his friends to whom he was host in a life-long celebration.

It is told with perfect seriousness in Charles county that Franklin Weems kept a poker game going in Mount Republican continuously for forty years. Three times a week he entertained a party of young people and many mornings he set out upon a fox hunt without having been to bed at all for more than twenty-four hours. A pack of one hundred fox hounds was maintained at Mount Republican and many of the best hunting dogs in Maryland have the blood of these hounds in their veins.

Mount Republican originally was the home of the Yates family and passed by marriage into the hands of Francis Hawkins. The house was built in 1792, apparently to last forever, for the walls are two and a-half feet thick and as sturdy today as they were when Philadelphia was the capital of the United States and there were no national banks. The whole place contributes to the impression of durability and while it has been unoccupied, save by tenants, for a number of years, comparatively little is necessary to restore it to a thoroughly habitable condition.

The chimneys at Mount Republican rise in pairs inside the end walls which they carry up above the line of the ridgepole in well-considered outlines. The wide hall is at one end of the house and contains a massive walnut stairway. Light is admitted to the hall at the landing of the stairway by the fanlight which surmounts the door leading into the garden.

All of the original mantels in the house have been removed except one in a bedroom on the second floor which shows a line of very fine tambour carving under the shelf and a center panel, fan-carved at the corners with a sunburst design in the

WEST HATTON: DRAWINGROOM MANTEL

Photo by Aubrey Bodine

MOUNT REPUBLICAN

Photo by Aubrey Bodine

HARD BARGAIN

center. On the third floor, under the eaves, are three dark, walled-off recesses with low doors and no windows where, tradition says, recalcitrant slaves were thrust to await a change of mind.

Mount Republican must have been an ideal spot in which to entertain. The guests and family occupied the main wing and in a low placed wing to one side, reached by a flight of several steps, the servants attended to the details of their comfort. The front door is wide and recessed in a generous arch with a fan-light above and sidelights—a hospitable door, indeed! The cornice at the roof line is carved with alternate triglyphs and diamonds, front and back. Otherwise the facades are without ornament. An old box garden back of the house has lost its design in the luxuriance of its growth, but once there were serenades in that garden and vows were exchanged there in the moonlight.

* * *

Of considerably more ancient date is Mount Pleasant, formerly known as Burlean Hall and probably, at least in part, one of the oldest houses in Charles county. This property has been in the Posey family since 1654, when John and Benjamin Posey settled near the head of the Wicomico river.

The house is rambling and very quaint, the center section being the oldest, built of logs sheathed with weather-boarding. Only a story and a-half high, its steep, sloping roof is pierced by a single, tiny dormer window, which has a triangular cap resting on crudely carved pilasters. To this was added a smaller wing to the right and, in later years, a frame wing of con-siderably greater pretensions at the left. Back of the house the boxwood which once outlined an old-fashioned garden has reached a height of eighteen feet.

CHAPTER FIVE

Called by the name of Mount Airey for more than two centuries, the old Calvert manor house which is said to exceed in age any building associated with the family of the Lords Proprietary and which stands a short distance from the little settlement known as Croome, in Prince George's county, is known now as the Dower House.

Nowhere in the State is it possible to touch more closely the lives led by the Lords Baltimore who brought the colony into existence and continued to influence it for generations than at the Dower House. Here, in this dim, delightful place, it is an easy matter to reconstruct in imagination the lives they lived and the dreams they dreamed. One can cross the threshold over which they passed into and out of the house, look through windows which frame the prospects they knew or stand before the great fireplace and watch the flames roar upward just as did these insouciant colonists at the close of an all-day deer hunt through the woods.

Driving from Upper Marlborough to Washington the road which leads to the Dower House turns sharply to the left a short distance beyond the "county town" and leads through a friendly farming country until a lake, covering some eight or ten acres of land, comes suddenly into view. At the far side of it is the lane which leads from the public road across the estate, past a rustic gate and into the lawn, with an unexpected glimpse of the manor house suddenly coming into view beyond a spreading circle of boxwood.

The effect is extraordinary, uncanny, even. Like a vestige of a lost world, fearful of discovery, the house seems to recede behind a magic ring drawn with the darkling boxwood to discourage intruders who would seek to deride its ways and belittle its lack of progress. A thick cloud of heavy English ivy which overhangs the walls enhances its seeming remoteness and a faintly purple wistaria vine draws an additional veil with its bloom in the spring time. In certain lights those wistaria blossoms look strangely like gray cobwebs.

From the front the house presents virtually the same aspect it bore in the days of the Calverts—the family name of the Lords Baltimore. The additions which have been made are appended at the rear so that, while additional space has been achieved at the hands of the present owner, the result has been effected without the sacrifice of the picture which greeted the great-great grandparents of the present generation when they arrived in their cumbersome, painted coaches, with outriders in attendance, to visit the hospitable Calverts.

In common with many old houses which stir the blood, the Dower House, now the home of Mrs. Tillie R. Duvall, is the composite achievement of several buildings. The oldest portion is the most captivating, a bit of English cottage architecture set down in Maryland with the modifications imposed by the limitations of new world artisans working without benefit of the books on architecture which were the mainstay of later builders. This portion of the house grows directly out of the ground, is built of brick weathered to a soft, warm tint, and covered with a gambrel roof. Extensive research has placed the date of the building of this section of the Dower House approximately at 1660, although the evidence to support this date is entirely circumstantial. At the time of its building that part of Maryland now known as Prince George's county, where the Calverts owned thousands of acres, was largely unexplored.

The forests still sheltered deer and wild turkey, foxes and other game to make the chase as exciting a sport as England afforded a hundred years before, and in the midst of this vast wilderness Charles, third Lord Baltimore, had constructed for his own use a hunting lodge which was the nucleus of the present Dower House. That first little building, however, with its huge bricks and its Liliputian windows, leaves nothing to be desired.

The whole of the lower floor was included in one enormous room, with cavernous fireplaces at each end to serve the double purpose of cooking and warmth. One of these fireplaces still is in use, with the old fire-irons fastened firmly into the brick work and its flagged hearth extending almost half way out into the room. The other has been sealed up. The old floor boards, wide and uneven but still sound, complete an early Maryland interior which has remained, through nearly three centuries, almost exactly as it was when the place resounded to the toasts and the jests of Lord Baltimore and his guests.

Just when the then Mount Airey passed from its status as a hunting lodge to its estate as a residence it is impossible to say. The first of the Calverts known to have lived there permanently was Benedict, son of the fifth Lord Baltimore and collector of the customs for the Potomac district. Benedict Calvert married, shortly after coming to Maryland, his cousin, Elizabeth Calvert. Whether it was for him or whether it was at some earlier period that an addition was built at each end of the old hunting lodge it is impossible to say, but the extension took place at a very early day and included one room which was used as an office, and a bedroom above, both of the simplest character, at one end, and a kitchen, with bedroom above, at the other. A partition also was run across the "greate" room, making two rooms of it, and a curious wing, tall and narrow, with a gable veering up above the ridgepole of the old house, was the next

MOUNT PLEASANT, FORMERLY BURLEAN HALL

Photo by Capitol Photo Service

THE DOWER HOUSE

Photo by Capitol Photo Service

THE DOWER HOUSE: ORIGINAL WING

addition. This wing, apparently, was laid out for a hall, with bedrooms above. At one end it is lighted by a small window, framed in black walnut, and at the other end a curious stairway with a primitive newel post, hewn out of a solid piece of walnut, leads to the second floor. The effect is strange, inside and out, its unusual aspect being enhanced by a fanlight over the third story window.

In such fashion Mount Airey, now the Dower House, remained until the needs of a growing family necessitated more space and the wing was built, which completed the house as it looks today from the front. A long narrow hall, with a simple stairway, was run out at a right angle to the initial hunting lodge, with a large drawingroom placed at the far end. This portion of the house was built of brick, overlaid with plaster. Two round brick columns, resting upon square bases and covered with plaster, rest on a brick-flagged porch set between the wings and support a roof above a spindle-railed gallery.

A similar porch once flanked the central portion of the house on the opposite side but this has disappeared and a modern room, reached through square headed openings from the hall, has been built in its stead. The old chapel which is reputed to have stood just back of the drawing room also has disappeared as the result of a fire which took place in 1720. It is said to have been rebuilt only to burn again and in place of it is a music room of comparatively recent origin. Placed three steps down from the drawingroom, it establishes little conflict with the old building and is supplied with a fireplace of generous depth.

In the drawingroom the only ornamentation is to be found in the simple, hand cut mouldings of the door and window frames which are excellently proportioned. In this room, in 1779, John Parke Custis, the stepson of Washington, and Eleanor Calvert, daughter of the collector, were married with much

[69]

pomp and circumstance. The wedding festivities are declared
to have lasted two weeks and during part of the time Washington
was a guest at Mount Airey, probably hoping against hope that,
with his new responsibilities as a husband, the boy of whom
his teacher at Annapolis had written, "I never did in my life
know a youth so exceedingly indolent, or so surprisingly voluptuous," would sober down and become the sensible citizen Washington wished him to be.

"Jacky" Custis had met young Eleanor Calvert during the
course of his journeys between Mount Vernon and Annapolis
where he had been sent by his stepfather to study under the
direction of the Reverend Jonathan Boucher. On these occasions he broke the journey at the home of Mr. Benedict Calvert
who was a close friend of Washington's, and fell deeply in love
with the daughter of his host whose portrait afterwards was
painted with her plump and distinguished mother-in-law. Their
wedding was the first to occur in the house, but the duration
of their married life was short. Within six years young Custis
died, at the age of twenty-eight, and was buried in the family
burying ground at Mount Airey. His widow subsequently re-
married and went to Virginia.

Benedict Calvert died in 1788. Concerning his death *The Mary-
land Journal and Advertiser* noted on January 15, of that year:
"A few days ago, in an advanced age at his Seat in Prince
George's county, in this State, Hon. Benedict Calvert, Esq., a
Gentleman whose Benevolence of Heart and many other ex-
alted Virtues justly endeared him to his Relations, and a numerous and respectable Acquaintance who have sustained an irreparable loss in his death." He was buried under the chancel of
St. Thomas' Church at Croome. His daughter, Eleanor Custis
Stuart (the erstwhile bride of "Jacky" Custis) was buried there
too, a number of years later, the burial taking place by stealth,

for the vestry had forbidden such interments. The body was carried to the church at night and, in digging the grave after taking up the floor, the gold coffin plate of Benedict Calvert was uncovered.

During the Revolution the house was occupied at one time by the British and in the War of 1812-14 served in the same capacity for the British general who mobilized in the neighborhood for the march on Washington. It was then that the Calverts are said to have buried in a lily bed in the garden a treasure of gold coin and silver plate which was carried out through a secret passage leading from the cellar to its hiding place and which never has been recovered. The treasure is said to have included about three thousand dollars worth of gold coin, small table silver and jewelry. No one has sought for generations to explore the old passage way which leads through foundation walls nearly three feet thick, but Elizabeth Biscoe Calvert, wife of Edward Henry Calvert, who inherited the estate from his father, Benedict Calvert, is said to walk the night in spirit, still seeking the long lost gold at the end of that gruesome corridor.

The wraith of Elizabeth Biscoe Calvert is not the only phantom which has brought to the house members of the London Society for Psychical Research in an effort to unravel the mysteries which are reputed to hold the place in their ghostly grasp. Years ago Mrs. Duvall and her husband, upon their return from an absence, are said to have been confronted by an eerie horseman in armor who bestrode his steed in front of the door and vanished after giving them a haughty stare. Persons unaccustomed to the house invariably are surprised to discover that the drawingroom door opens the "wrong way." An inspection of the woodwork will disclose that this was not always so. But, says Mrs. Duvall, there is a gruesome reason for this, too.

The reason, according to the story, lay in the opposition entertained by Miss Eleanor Calvert, daughter of Elizabeth Biscoe Calvert, to the use of the "parlor" as the drawingroom had come to be known in her day. She bitterly opposed having it opened for any purpose whatever and is said to have refused, when her dead brother's body lay there, to go to the funeral. Miss Calvert herself met a tragic death a few years later when an oil lamp overturned in her hands while she was descending the main hall stair, and exploded. When her body was put into its coffin it was carried into the "parlor" and the door locked, the key being taken out and placed on a table in the hall. There it remained over night. Just before the hour set for the funeral a neighbor arrived and offered assistance in any form which might be desired. His offer was accepted and he was asked to unlock the door into the "parlor" in order that the people who were arriving to attend the service might be seated, but when he went to comply the key could not be found. By this time the guests were assembling in numbers and so, instead of spending further time in looking for the key, the door was broken open. And when this had been done the key, the story runs, was discovered on a table beside the coffin. No mortal hand, the owner of the house believes, could have placed it there.

Tragedy seems to have been the portion of many of the women who have lived at the Dower House. Stories of broken hearts and frustrated devotion are made realistic by the shivery aspect of the place and the shadows which hang over it from the great trees which stand about, but when one comes upon the broad terraces laid out by L'Enfant at one side of the old hunting lodge the glooms vanish and the spirit of the Baltimores returns.

The present owner of the Dower House acquired it by purchase at public auction in 1903. About eight hundred and twenty-five acres are included in the estate which embraced ten thousand acres in the days of the third Lord Baltimore. Descendants of the Calverts who owned it for so many years still live in Maryland and in Washington. On the walls of the drawingroom in the Washington apartment occupied by Mrs. Charles Baltimore Calvert, whose husband was a descendant of Benedict Calvert, hang portraits showing the distinctive Calvert features, and Mr. George Calvert, son of Mrs. Calvert, who also lives in Washington, is the possessor of a pair of jewelled knee buckles sent from England to Benedict Calvert by his father and which the collector wore for many years.

*　*　*

Several miles distant from the Dower House is another old Calvert estate. After a series of vicissitudes as extraordinary as any which ever befell a Colonial mansion at the hands of a heedless generation, Riversdale, which is the most splendid of all the houses which belonged to this family in Maryland and which has been declared by many architects to be one of the particularly fine specimens of Georgian building in the country, now belongs to United States Senator and Mrs. Thaddeus Caraway, of Arkansas.

Set in the midst of wide lawns, responding again to the healing agency of interest and care, Riversdale conceals itself behind the screen of modest suburban homes which stand between it and the humming boulevard stretching from Baltimore to Washington. These houses make up the village of Riverdale, named for the Riversdale estate (but dropping the "s" from the spelling) and which has grown up on the land which once formed part of the extensive tract to which George Calvert, son of Benedict, held title.

The stout brick walls of the house are made of a clay not to be found anywhere in the neighborhood. This circumstance, apparently, gave rise to the story which attaches persistently to Riversdale, in spite of the thoroughgoing exposures which have been made of such fallacies, that the bricks were brought from England and hauled by an ox cart from Leonardtown,—a distance of some fifty miles,—over trails which would have been dignified by being called roads at the time Riversdale was built. Where the bricks came from is impossible to say. Old Calvert records concerning the building of the mansion which still are in existence confirm the evidence of the bricks themselves that the clay which went into their construction was not to be found in this vicinity. But whatever their source, the walls of Riversdale need no apology and are covered now with white stucco which makes the house appear even larger than it actually is. Built low to the ground, it occupies a vast amount of space even for the home of a Maryland gentleman of the blood. Its plan is that of the conventional central portion with low, flanking wings, but its program, as the architects call the restrictions under which they work, apparently found a builder who esteemed it "pastime to be bound." A small portico, wide enough for four well-spaced Doric columns which support a Grecian canopy in front, announces the entrance to the house. On each of the story and a-half wings the pediment of the portico is repeated, making it appear from the front elevation that the wings are but a single story high. The hip roof of the main structure, with wide, overhanging eaves, rests upon heavy modillions and is topped by a square observatory tower added long after the house was built. The chimneys are wide and sturdy, but subordinated as architectural features. Wide steps lead from the gravelled driveway to the portico and when the heavy entrance door swings open in response to the summons of a modern electric bell the interior is disclosed as a Colonial work of art worth travelling miles to see. The hallway runs parallel with

the long facade instead of crossing it, and is made further interesting by possessing one of the great rarities of the late
Georgian period, a Thornton staircase.

No one who has seen a Thornton staircase ever forgets it.
This brilliant West Indian, who was the first architect of the
national Capitol and whose design for that great structure won
the prize in the face of stiff competition by easily outstripping all
the others submitted, drew into his designs for his staircases a
certain splendor which makes them entirely individual in their
sweep and added a mahogany handrail so grooved on the outer
side that the fingers instinctively seek and close over it.

From the hall a doorway on a line with the front door leads
into the main salon revealing in every detail the influence of the
brothers Adam. Each of the side walls is divided into arched
panels which are decorated with bunches of grapes and conventional designs in plaster, and in the end wall a door leads
to the portico overlooking terraced gardens with a round pool
in the distance. During the regime of the Calverts this doorway
indicated the formal entrance to the house, but the present front
portal has served in that capacity for many years. A room in
which to receive the most impressive of guests and in which to
hold the most dignified of entertainments is the main salon.
The enormous drawingroom and the equally enormous diningroom open from it on either side.

In the drawingroom, as the house appears nowadays, is one of
the happiest bits of restoration,—or perhaps it would be more
correct to say substitution,—to be found in any Georgian house
in Maryland. The original mantel was removed long ago, no
one knows why or whither, but in its place the Caraways have
installed a mantel of white Italian marble, carved by hand and
brought to this country a hundred and forty years ago. The

[75]

diningroom mantel, with its shell carving and human figures, also is a substitution but one which satisfactorily fulfills its purpose.

Beyond the drawingroom is the library, with arched, built-in book shelves which have been returned to their initial condition after the hand of the despoiler had been laid heavily upon them. From this room several steps lead down to the large apartment which occupies the entire wing of the house on the side next the village and which the Caraways use as a music room. For years much of the obloquy which had come upon the house was visited upon this wing. First it was called upon to serve as a shelter for a coach of the period in which Riversdale was built and then to yield its entire side wall, which was knocked away in order that the wing might be used as a garage. As a by-product of this outrage the ancient coach which had stood in this place so long was set out on the ground, there to fall to pieces.

On the other side of the house, beyond the state diningroom, is the family diningroom, so entirely changed during the Victorian period as to be scarcely recognizable as a Georgian interior. Gargantuan mirrors placed at each end of the room and set in massive rococo frames, gaudy electric light fixtures, concealment of the fireplace and a well-placed door left only the actual dimensions of the room and the lofty windows untouched. As far as was possible the Caraways have repaired the indignities which had been committed here, as well as on the right wing.

Above stairs interest focuses on the room which, during one of the darkest periods of national history, was set apart for the use of Henry Clay who spent weeks at a time at Riversdale as the guest of the Calverts. In this room was written the first draft of the Missouri Compromise and while he was the guest of the Calverts the mediator had his portrait painted with the young son of the house, Eugene Calvert, seated upon his knee. In another room memories of Thomas Moore arise, for Moore also was a visitor to Riversdale.

It was a Belgian nobleman, a political refugee to America, who built the Riversdale house and presented it as a wedding gift, with 2,000 acres of land, to his daughter when she became the bride of the young man whose blood was as blue as her own. Baron von Stier, Lord of Aertselaer and Cleydael, had three castles and three daughters to whom he gave rich inheritances. Rosalie was the daughter who bestowed her hand on George Calvert of Mount Airey (now the Dower House) and Riversdale was her dowry. To its domain George Calvert added another two thousand acres. The house was built near the junction of the Paint Branch with the Northwest branch of the Potomac, which flow together at Bladensburg, at the time when this little hamlet was the metropolis of the country side and sea-going craft moored at its wharves to receive the hogsheads of tobacco which were rolled down from Montgomery county on what were known, because of this process, as "rolling roads."

The original entrance to the estate was from a lodge on the old Bladensburg turnpike, the driveway to the house passing under a brown stone archway and winding around to the south front. Beyond the driveway the grounds were laid out in three broad terraces, each a mile long and planted with shrubbery down to the lake. On the other side of the lake a deer park extended for miles.

The house was begun, according to family records, about 1790, and was first occupied by George Calvert and his young wife about 1800. The period of its building coincided exactly with that of the building of the Capitol in Washington and tradition maintains that the pillars on the north and south porticoes of

Riversdale were designed for the Capitol but were cut too short and were, in consequence, diverted to their present position.

Riversdale was, in every sense, the home of a gentleman. Its furnishing was in keeping with the dignity of the house and here and there in the big rooms are to be found pieces of mahogany, rescued now from their erstwhile degradation of gray paint, which stood there when the great men of the country delighted to be the guests of the Calverts. Vast quantities of silver and silver plate were kept in a steel vault, the key to which, weighing nearly a pound, now is in the possession of Mr. and Mrs. Humphrey Spence, the former dean of Maryland State College of Agriculture and the latter a descendant of George Calvert. Extensive wine cellars were stocked with imported vintages in such quantity that their contents passed from one generation to another.

When George Calvert died the estate descended to his eldest son, Charles Benedict Calvert, who was a member of the thirty-seventh Congress and introduced into the House of Representatives a bill advocating payment by the United States government to the slaveholders for their slaves, hoping by this measure to avert the war which he foresaw between the States. His humanitarian move failed, but he was more successful in his effort to elevate the state of agriculture in Maryland. At Riversdale he maintained a herd of pure-bred cattle in a tremendous octagonal barn, roomy as a cyclorama, with the name of each animal above its stall. The barn stood about a quarter of a mile distant from the house at the end of an arcade formed of osage orange.

Charles Benedict Calvert's interest in agriculture prompted him to organize the first college of agricultural research chartered in the United States. From his estate he ceded 250 acres of land to the college for its use and he was its first president.

After his death the estate was divided under the terms of his will into zones extending east and west and distributed among his heirs. The mansion became the property of the late George H. Calvert who, after a few years, conveyed it to a real estate development company of New York which laid out the present day suburb of Riverdale. Subsequently the house became by turns a summer hotel, a resort for members of Congress, the Lord Baltimore Club, and a tea house. During these changes and interchanges the landscape suffered a complete transformation. The outline of the terraces was obliterated in places, much of the boxwood was sold, the lake became a breeding place for mosquitoes and the deer park was completely overgrown. The south elevation no longer was recognized as the front of the house and the north one substituted in this capacity, a change which has been maintained.

In being called upon to fill so many roles the house suffered keenly. There was no one to care whether plaster fell or not, no one to replace worn floor boards, no one to prevent the introduction of incongruous electric fixtures or to protect the furniture from the coats of paint which were laid on with a heavy hand.

Much of the original furniture had been divided among the members of the Calvert family before the estate had been sold, but a few pieces were left, together with a great quantity of mid-Victorian furniture which changed hands with the house, and what was best of it has been restored by the Caraways.

Early in its existence Riversdale was exposed to trial by gunfire, for the house was in direct range when troops marched down the old 'pike, now become the Baltimore-Washington boulevard, to protect the Capitol at the Battle of Bladensburg in the War of 1812-14. Scars of that experience have been healed completely, however, and the little cannon which stands on the terrace before the south front of the house is a souvenir, not of this encounter, but of a much earlier day. It is one of four which are said to have been brought to this country by Lord Baltimore to protect his colony from Indians and other enemies. Another stands on the State House lawn at Annapolis, but the destiny of the other two is unknown.

CHAPTER SIX

First the home of the Snowden family and later of the Contees who were closely knit by ties of kindred to the Snowdens is Oakland which stands on the crest of a hill overlooking the tracks of the Baltimore and Ohio railroad at Contee, between Muirkirk and Laurel, in Prince George's county, and less than two miles west of the Patuxent river. Oakland is one of three great mansions built by the Snowden family in this vicinity, the others being Birmingham Manor, now fallen to ruin, which was built on the Anne Arundel side of the Patuxent, and Montpelier, considerably altered since Colonial days. Intimately related to these is Pleasant Prospect, not far from a fertile stretch of land known as The Forest, also in Prince George's county, and built by the Contees.

A distinctive relic of the ancient regime is Oakland which stands as imperturbable on its hilltop eminence as if the railroad over which the trains roar at all hours of the day and night simply did not exist. Built of brick showing blue-glazed headers laid up in Flemish bond, it holds its roof high above a collar of heavy modillions and, with the air of a fine old artistocrat, gives itself up to the contemplation of a number of things the very existence of which are unsuspected by wizards of big business who scurry past, with scarcely a glance in its direction, on their way to and fro between cloud-hung skyscrapers of New York and the halls of Congress.

In this house there was, and is, time for the cultivation of those things which have little to do with money and machines, although the builders of Oakland were wealthy folk, taking place among the largest land holders and most extensive tobacco growers of the country. Books with rare and lustrous bindings, pictures from the brushes of the masters, web-foot highboys and eggshell china found their way into Oakland, because the people who owned them had an ingrained love for such things, implanted by well-bred ancestors and cultivated by generation after generation of men and women of good taste.

Two short, thick piers of brick flank the lane which begins at the Washington-Baltimore boulevard and makes its way up the hill to the house, passing through a clump of locusts growing on both sides of the road and indicating that probably in Colonial days the entire lane was bordered by these trees which were much used in Maryland for this purpose. Near the northeast corner of the house is a grove of rugged old locust trees, broken by winds that have blown and the weight of years, and in front of the house red cedars and catalpa grow.

Virginia creeper, English ivy and trumpet vine climb the walls and off to the south is an old box garden. The doorway is a replica of many others to be found in Maryland. Its triangular canopy rests upon a plain entablature upheld by fluted pilasters, and a round transom appears above the door in its deep embrasure. No outside shutters appear to detract from the interest of the windows with their small, square panes divided by heavy muntins, and narrow, white-painted frames. Here and there a pane shows a wavy formation in the glass, token that it has been letting light into the big rooms ever since the house was built, and on a pane in one of the parlor windows appears the name of a pretty girl, Sylvia Contee, scratched there more than a generation ago. Perhaps it was the diamond of her engagement ring with which those old-fashioned letters were traced, or perhaps. . . .

All of the rooms in the house are large, some of them as

spacious as an entire city apartment, and the fireplaces are wide and deep, with mantels showing decorations of the Adam period above them, their carvings brought to life by the lights and shadows cast by the fire glow. The handrail of the stairway which leads from the lower hallway to the second floor shows the influence of the same great Eighteenth century craftsman and built into the wall of the diningroom is a china cupboard filled with china and cut glass which have been in use for a century and which is the admiration of innumerable artists and architects who constantly are knocking at the door of Oakland and asking permission to sketch its doors and windows and stairway.

Everything about the house reflects the predilection of the Snowdens and Contees for the out-of-doors. Men and women alike, they thought nothing of a day-long chase in pursuit of a fox or a ten mile tramp with a favorite setter across frost-locked fields, coming home by moonlight with a bag of partridges to be toasted next day before the kitchen fire. On the walls hang old English hunting and racing pictures, together with family portraits. In use today, too, at Oakland are old silver goblets from which the Carlisles and the Fairfaxes, of Belvoir, in Virginia, drank toasts to King and the ladies. These goblets are heirlooms which have come down in the family of Mrs. Charles R. Hooff, a descendant of the Snowdens, whose maiden name was Sarah Carlisle Fairfax Herbert and who, with her husband and children, lives at Oakland. Washington very likely drank from those goblets when he visited Belvoir, which was often, and as he drank his eyes probably met and held over the rim of his cup those of Sally Cary Fairfax with whom he is known to have been deeply in love.

Richard Snowden, son of Major Thomas Snowden and Ann Ridgely Snowden, of Montpelier, was the builder of Oakland.

Though he was married twice he had no sons and Oakland descended to his daughter, Ann Louisa Snowden, who married John Contee, bringing the estate into the possession of this family. The Contees of Maryland claim descent from a noble French family deriving from the royal houses of Conde and Conti and who fled to England during the religious wars against the Huguenots during the reign of Louis XIII.

The first of the Contee name in Maryland was Col. John Contee who emigrated to Charles county about the end of the Seventeenth century and, having no sons, sent for his nephew, Alexander, to join him in America and inherit his property. Alexander Contee answered the summons and settled at Nottingham in Prince George's county, taking up large tracts of land and becoming a prosperous merchant. For years he served as clerk of the county court, a position of dignity in the Eighteenth century, and when he died he bequeathed, in addition to many lands devised to his children, a guinea to the rector of St. Paul's with the request that he preach a sermon on "ye danger and folly of ye deathbed repentance."

* * *

Part of the land which was disposed of by the will of Alexander Contee received the name of Pleasant Prospect when it became the property of his son who invariably is referred to in the old county newspapers as "Colonel" John Contee. Colonel Contee is mentioned as an active participant in the various acts of Maryland citizens who met at Upper Marlborough to devise means of opposing British oppression. On June 6, 1775, he was chosen as a delegate to represent his county at a meeting in Annapolis and on July 26, 1775, he was one of the signers of the famous Declaration of the Freemen of Maryland.

Colonel Contee married, about 1744, Margaret Snowden, a daughter of Richard Snowden, "the younger," and it was their grandson, Lieutenant John Contee, who further complicated the tangled skein of family relationships by secretly marrying Ann Louisa Snowden.

Pleasant Prospect is built of frame and has been much altered within the last sixty years, or since its purchase by Jonathan Thomas Walker. A long porch has been built across the front of the house in place of the prim Colonial doorway, which was an abomination to the Victorian taste, but the Georgian door and transom are untouched. At the back a two-story portico has been constructed. A long and comfortably wide hall stretches through the house from door to door, and at one side a simple and well designed stairway rises in place of the boxed-in stair-case which stood in one of the back rooms on the lower floor.

Carving showing a considerable skill appears on the woodwork of the lower floor, with classic garlands and Greek fret cut on the friezes above the doors and on the decorations of the mantel-pieces. The moulding of the cornices also shows the Greek key carving.

Richard Alexander Contee, only son of Colonel Contee and Margaret Snowden Contee, inherited Pleasant Prospect, where he was born. He was only twenty-two when he is mentioned as having participated in a meeting of citizens held in Upper Marlborough in 1775 and he is known to have served on the committee of inspection for the Patuxent district to watch the movement of the British ships. It is said, also, that he fought in the Continental army during the Revolution.

During the life of Richard Alexander Contee and his son, the previously mentioned Lieut. John Contee, Pleasant Prospect was surrounded by more than a thousand acres of land, tilled by slaves and yielding a large income. Lieut. John Contee, at the age of nineteen, married Eliza Duckett, only daughter of Isaac and Margaret Bowie Duckett, whose father was one of the most opulent planters in the State and who brought to her already wealthy husband a large fortune.

John Contee entered the United States Navy and for gallant conduct received a vote of thanks from the Legislature of Maryland which also presented him with a sword and with medals. He retired from the Navy with the rank of lieutenant and spent the rest of his life at Pleasant Prospect. Eliza Duckett Contee, the wife taken when he was still a boy, lived only eight years after their marriage. Three years later he contracted his secret marriage with Ann Louisa Snowden who also was wealthy, and who bore him three children in addition to the four who survived from his first marriage.

Another John Contee, the only son of Lieutenant Contee and Eliza Duckett Contee, who like his father and grandfather, was born at Pleasant Prospect, also entered the Navy, retiring with the rank of Lieutenant. When the war between the States developed he was elected captain of a cavalry company known as "The Planters' Guards," but did not live through the war, dying at Pleasant Prospect, May 29, 1863. Six children survived him, the last of the Contee name to be born at the homestead where now the great-grandchildren of Jonathan Thomas Walker are busy with childhood games.

* * *

Colonial builders were privy to many secrets but to none more vital than the ability to select from the miles of terrain at their disposal the right location for their homes. Set on the crest of a hill, with a sweeping view of the countryside for miles, the Maryland house of pre-Revolutionary days derived much of its beauty and no little of its imposing effect from the felicity of its position.

Particularly is this true at Belair, the estate of the Colonial

Photo by Capitol Photo Service
RIVERSDALE, NEAR WASHINGTON

OAKLAND
First a Snowden, then a Contee Place

Photo by Aubrey Bodine

BELAIR

Photo by Aubrey Bodine

POPLAR HILL, PRINCE GEORGE COUNTY HOMESTEAD
OF THE DAINGERFIELDS

Governor Samuel Ogle who, at forty-seven, married the winsome Anne Tasker, aged just eighteen, and lived with his bride in the Georgian house which stands at the head of a mile-long lane leading from the State road which connects Baltimore and Washington with the great Bowie race track. During the regime of Governor Ogle the lane broadened out into a double avenue, bordered with tulip trees, for a distance of 500 yards from the house. The trees were planted in four parallel rows and though many are gone, thirty-two of them survive, the largest more than twenty feet in circumference. Belair will probably outrank, in the elegance with which it is maintained, any house of its period. To the original building large, square wings have been added, with low connecting wings between, the difference of more than a hundred years in the house as Governor Ogle knew it and its present aspect being rapidly concealed by the ivy which is covering the walls.

Belair is long and low, its two and a-half stories of the central portion being so disposed as to carry the eye easily along to the wings. The tall brick chimneys, with their ornamental caps, which are rather widely spaced at each end of the central building, carry up only a short distance above the hip roof broken by a triangular pediment and low, almost squatty dormer windows. The eaves overhang a cornice provided with heavy modillions and a projecting belt course between the first and second stories tends still further to bring down the apparent height of the house.

A porch the exact width of the pediment which cuts the roof and enclosed by an ornamental iron railing stands before the front of the house, that part of it in front of the doorway being covered by a Grecian canopy supported on Ionic columns.

The door opens into a small, almost square hall, well lighted by a window on each side of the door and without ornament

[87]

except for the moulded cornice and a carved stairway with a mahogany handrail. The steps themselves are rather steep but are interesting for the manner in which the moulding which outlines the top of each is carried back the full width of the step above. An arch with a keystone and panelled soffit at the back of the hall leads into the music room which has, on a line with the front door and the arch, a door leading into the garden, where the old bowling green and the terraces beyond were the rendezvous on summer evenings of the Ogles and their guests who gathered there "to take the air" or play at ninepins in the twilight.

From the music room deeply recessed doorways lead at the right into the diningroom, where two windows look out over the garden, and at the left into the drawingroom which boasts two fireplaces and runs the entire width of the house from front to back.

On the second floor some of the rooms are panelled across the ends where the chimneys are and some of them have powder closets. All of the windows are deeply recessed, the thickness of the brick partition walls being evident in the wide facing of the door jambs. Low ceilings and plain chair railings emphasize the Colonial character of the bedrooms which seem, in a way, to embody more of the pre-Revolutionary spirit than do the rooms on the first floor.

Belair was built for Governor Ogle and his bride under the supervision of the latter's father, Benjamin Tasker, who was one of the outstanding figures of his time in Maryland, and was constructed in compliance with the request of Governor Ogle who had taken his bride to England. It was not, as often has been supposed, a wedding gift from the bride's father. When the governor and his wife returned to Maryland they took up their residence at Belair for a large part of the year, spending only as much time in Annapolis as was absolutely necessary.

At Belair they lived with great pomp and ceremony. Six hundred acres of the thirty-six hundred the estate originally included were reserved as a deer park and the governor had his private race track and kennels on the place. When he or members of his family drove abroad they traveled in a heavy coach emblazoned with the Ogle arms and protected by liveried outriders.

No more enthusiastic patron of the turf ever existed in Maryland than Governor Ogle whose stables at Belair were the finest in the colony. He it was who brought to this country the celebrated Spark, a gift from Lord Baltimore to whom the horse previously had been given by Frederick, Prince of Wales (father of King George III). Prince Frederick had revived the royal stud in England and Lord Baltimore was an ardent devotee of horse flesh, as well as a close friend of the young captain of cavalry to whom, on September 16, 1731, he had given the commission of governor of Maryland. Much as Governor Ogle valued the royal gift of a splendid race horse, he was even more interested in the opportunity to introduce into Maryland a strain so excellent that some of the best race horses in the country today have in their veins the blood of this famous British animal. Governor Ogle also imported Queen Mab for his stables at Belair, becoming thereby the owner of two horses which were the envy of every man in the colony. In those days, too, he kept a private pack of fox hounds and rode like a royal prince of modern times in pursuit of the elusive brush. No man, modern or colonial, lived life to the full more completely than did this son of the old Saxons in the new world, but his idyll was short. His only child, a boy, was but three years old when the governor died. Benjamin Tasker, Sr., the boy's grandfather, and Benjamin

Tasker, Jr., the child's uncle, were appointed joint executors of the governor's will and guardians of the boy who was sent to England to be educated as soon as he was old enough and who, it seemed entirely likely, never would return to Maryland. Within a few years the deer park had disappeared but the farm land had become far more productive than ever it had been during the life of the royal governor. Fences were built, orchards and vineyards laid out and the great avenue of locusts and poplars leading to the mansion was planted by Benjamin Tasker, Jr., now become Colonel Tasker, who was far more business-like a person than Governor Ogle.

When it came to horses, however, the reputation of Belair was carried forward by Colonel Tasker at the same pace set by his brother-in-law. He, too, imported thoroughbreds from England and was the owner of Selima, still famous in the annals of the turf. When the old stables tumbled down Colonel Tasker built better ones and the Belair colts were famous all along the coast, from New York to Virginia.

Colonel Tasker died unmarried but Governor Ogle's son, whose name, like that of his mother's father and brother, was Benjamin, came back from England to take up the family tradition in America. He, too, became governor of Maryland, in 1809, and his son, Benjamin, succeeded him as master of Belair, the last Ogle of the name to live there. Later the place passed into the hands of the Bowie family which also has furnished Maryland with several governors and which was allied to the Ogle family by marriage. From the Bowies it came into the hands of the late James T. Woodward of New York, from whom it descended to his nephew, William Woodward, also of New York, who is bound to Maryland by ties of kindred and who lives there part of each year.

At some time during the tenure of the first Benjamin Ogle

an addition was made to the house by a brick structure about forty feet square and two stories high, built as an L-shaped wing, with kitchen and servants quarters. This addition long ago was destroyed but evidences of it were to be seen until recent years.

*   *   *

Governor Ogle's love of horse flesh was typical of the colony. Marylanders from the beginning have been ardent lovers of this animal. Give them half a chance, even in Colonial days, and the devil-may-care spirit which brought many of them to the new world would lead them straight away from whatever serious task might be crying for completion and out into an open field to put a likely looking filly through its paces. In the view of many a Colonial planter the paramount virtue of a fence lay in furnishing a barrier over which a two-year-old might jump, with heels disdaining the top rail, and professional men of the colony shared the same weakness.

So it happens that Dr. Thomas Hamilton, who flourished long and happily during the Eighteenth century in Prince George's county, has come down to posterity as a great horseman rather than as a physician of parts. Excellent compounder of "physicks" he may have been, expert with the lance and a wizard in his dealings with the fevers which infested the river shores in his day. These things no one knows. Instead, he has become a memory not as a genius of healing, but as one who probably knew more about the fine points of a horse than any of his neighbors for miles around.

This was the man who, in Colonial days, owned Mount Calvert, an estate on the banks of the Potomac which now serves as a hunting lodge for a wealthy Washingtonian. The old house stands on a plateau around which the river winds as if it liked the place particularly and were loath to leave, but it fails to create the spell cast imperceptibly by most of the old houses of the lower counties. There is something about Mount Calvert which seems to indicate that it mattered but little in the life of its builder.

As it stands today, the house is the result of three different building ventures. The wing nearest the river is the oldest and most crudely built, with bricks of irregular size set in mortar almost as thick as the bricks themselves, four rows of headers alternating with a row of stretchers.

Windows at once tiny and irregularly placed indicate that this wing was built in the days before symmetry was a consideration with the Maryland landholder and that it was the work of artisans of little skill. The connecting wing which joins the original to the big house has a stairway of its own, narrow and useful, but little more. Its rooms are so small and so cut up that it is difficult to see how a family of any size occupied the place without constantly getting in its own way, but those in the main structure are more pretentious. Here is a hallway of comfortable proportions, with a well made stairway to one side, mahogany railed, and, at the left of the entrance, a drawingroom, simple in design but well finished, with a view from the front windows over the terraces to the river some distance below. A great double chimney adds distinction to this wing, with windows placed between the stacks, and around the top of the walls is a cornice carved with the pattern of the Wall of Troy.

* * *

Not far distant from Mount Calvert is Bellefields, built about 1735, and once the home of Governor Oden Bowie. When Bellefields was completed it was regarded as the finest house for miles around. Now it is tenanted by negroes and going rapidly to destruction. Bats fly in at night and wasps build their nests in the corners of huge, deserted rooms. Despite its neglected state, however, traces of vanished pomp are to be seen in the fine brick walls of the main house and in the stairway which winds to the roof with a grandiloquent sweep of mahogany rail and spool spindles. The newel post is carved with acanthus leaves and what does it matter if it seems somewhat too heavy for the stairway?

At the back of the central hall a vestibule opens on a stone portico with a flight of fan-shaped stone steps leading down to the lawn where once mocking birds sang in the dawn and a magnolia tree bloomed in the spring time. The front portico is gone, but the broken brick pillars which supported it remain like fragments of a skeleton to show where once it stood. A tarnished silver knob still is on the front door and traces of the old strap fastening are to be seen, though the strap itself has disappeared, too.

Double chimneys rise at the gable ends of the house to serve fireplaces which provided heat for all the rooms in the main wing. The right wing, which is much older than the main house, takes rank as a ruin of the first water. Not a trace remains of the flooring and even the walls are giving way. Through the crevices and in at the windows a thick growth of ivy pushes its way as if to conceal the shame which has come upon the house. Two old wooden mantels of good design lie upon the raw dirt which now constitutes the only floor, face downward, lost in desuetude.

Traces remain of the once formal approach to the house though even these are almost obliterated. The feet which have worn deep grooves in the wide stone door sills are motionless now forever, but in the spring the old magnolia tree still covers itself with purple. White violets push their way up through the grass and at each end of the one-time portico a thousand-leaf rose comes into bloom to take the place of the japonica as it fades.

Originally Bellefields was known as Sims' Delight. The estate comprised more than two thousand acres which had been granted to Colonel Patrick Sims and who, surrounded by his descendants, lies buried in the graveyard on the place. Upon the slab which covered the body of this colonial warrior was engraved his coat of arms and a reference to his service to the colony. The slab is shattered now and the negro tenants have no idea what became of the pieces.

After Colonel Sims' death the land was sold in sections. The mansion and twelve hundred acres were purchased by Benjamin Oden who married successively the two daughters of Stephen West, of The Woodyard, and changed the name of the place to Bellefields. One of Benjamin Oden's daughters became the wife of Colonel William D. Bowie and Governor Oden Bowie was her son.

* * *

Near the little village which goes by the piquant name of Rosaryville in Prince George's county, stands Poplar Hill, long the home of the Darnalls and Daingerfields and now the property of Mrs. Chandler Hale, of Washington, whose husband was formerly an assistant Secretary of State.

Closely following the lines of the middle period of Georgian architecture, Poplar Hill was known, in its youth, more naively as His Lordship's Kindness and was built by Henry Darnall, 3rd, a descendant of that Colonel Henry Darnall who had much to do with the first days of the Maryland palatinate.

Today Poplar Hill remains as completely expository of the estate of a Maryland gentleman of nearly two centuries ago as Mount Vernon does in Virginia. The house derives its present sobriquet from the grove of tulip trees in which it stands and is reached by a circular driveway bordered with holly. More than thirty of the holly trees are in view from the front door, darkly green in summer, brilliant with scarlet berries in winter. A low flight of steps stands before the door, with its strictly classic frame and spider-web fanlight. Above the door a Palladian window is cut into the facade, with a fanlight in the pediment above. The hipped roof adds to the impression of dignity and represses any tendency there might have been to make the house appear unduly high. So completely does Poplar Hill convey the impression of other days that the impulse to linger before the doorway, with its suggestion of crinoline and its nicety of line, is almost irresistible. One hesitates to imperil the illusion by seeking further, but such qualms are unnecessary.

The central portion of Poplar Hill connects by low, one-story wings, with square-end wings a story and a-half high, the design being the creation of an architect sent over from England by the Earl of Shrewsbury who presented the house as a wedding gift to his niece, Anne Talbot, after she had persisted in marrying the dashing young Henry Darnall who had gone to England from Maryland to secure the same education his father had received at Stonyhurst, a stronghold of the Jesuits. The Earl of Shrewsbury, the fourteenth in line, was bitterly opposed to the match and thought to break it off completely by insisting that his niece, who was also his ward, should become the bride of no one who could not furnish a financial settlement conforming to the Earl's ideas of the amount in keeping with his position. To his amazement the settlement was agreed to almost casually by the young Henry Darnall and a record of the transaction is preserved to this day in the office of the clerk of the court at Upper Marlborough, sworn to and signed on the second of August, 1735, by Henry Darnall, 3rd.

An architect for a country house in the Maryland of that day was an extraordinary thing. Instantly the Earl's gift was assured of a distinction attainable by few other dwellings in the colony, for most of the fine houses were the work of local builders who adapted the plans contained in books sent over from England with the supervision of their patrons who studied architecture as a part of their education.

Quite obviously the architect of Poplar Hill knew his business and the result of his efforts was so pleasing to the young bride and bridegroom who went there to live when the place was finished that they expressed their pleasure in it and their gratitude to the donor by calling the place His Lordship's Kindness.

The feeling of anticipation created by the doorway is more than rewarded by the interior. The heavy panelled door opens into a hallway which equals any to be found in Maryland, if not in all the thirteen original colonies. In it are all the qualities which made dignified Georgian houses the particular fetish of the Colonial builder south of the Mason and Dixon's line,—the wide, sweeping arch, the carved doorways, the broad stairway mounting comfortably to the upper floors and finished with a carved balustrade, its mahogany handrail complemented with a half-handrail let into the wall.

The two doorways nearest the front door adhere strictly to classic lines, with fine hand carving on the frames and delicately leaded fanlights overhead. Those at the back of the hall are less elaborate, but equally sincere in workmanship. All of this work, as well as that on the mouldings and mantels throughout the house, is said to have been done by men who served their apprenticeship in England.

In the drawingroom and in the diningroom the decorations are simple. Both rooms are enormous, with high ceilings and many paned windows, some of which retain the original translucent glass which permits persons inside the house to see out, but prevents anyone outside from gazing within.

One of the interesting characteristics of Poplar Hill is the conformity of its various wings, each different from the other, to the design of the whole. The extreme right wing in the days of the Darnalls and Daingerfields was used as a chapel, for these families were devout Catholics. The Bible which rested, before the place was sold, upon the old altar of Sienna marble bore the date, 1825, and was illustrated and illuminated. The left wing is given over to culinary uses and contains a veritable carillon with bells ranging from the size of the smallest coffee cup up to that of an imperious dinner gong, hung there to summon slaves to any quarter of the house.

The plan of the second floor is identical with that of the first. The rooms are spacious and, as seldom happens in Colonial houses, the ceilings are as high as those in the rooms below. The windows duplicate those on the first floor in size, and are placed in deep embrasures. In the hall three windows admit light at each end, the arched window of each group yielding in decorative treatment to the other two which are placed between Corinthian pilasters and further adorned with beading and scroll work.

In the attic the framework of the house has been left exposed, with the resultant opportunity to observe the strength of construction, the occasional copper nails, the quality of the materials.

As so often is the case, the garden front is the more interesting of the two. The ivy grows, if possible, more luxuriantly there and the house seems to bask in the sunshine. Before the main door the lawn stretches, broad and green, to a series of terraces planted with boxwood and brilliant again with bloom after years of neglect. On the second terrace a maze of boxwood outlines the beds which have been replanted and elsewhere through the garden boxwood is used lavishly, against fences, bordering winding paths and just for its own sake. In a far corner, under the trees, is the fenced burying ground where generations of Darnalls and Daingerfields are buried.

But what makes Poplar Hill more interesting than these things is the group of little buildings which stand just beyond the lawn to the right of the service wing, covered almost completely with ivy old enough to bloom. A veritable little village is this, constructed to enable the estate to be independent of the rest of the world for months at a time. Nearest to the dwelling is a bath house with its curious tub which was filled by servants with water from two pipes. Close by is the ancient smokehouse where, each year, dozens of hams were cured over a hickory fire. The old rafters are blackened with soot and the old fire irons upon which the logs rested were in use before the second war with Great Britain.

The one-time slave hospital does duty today as a home for the overseer of the place and the brick stables are eloquent of a family devoted to fine horse flesh. The stalls in the main stables were fitted with arched entrances for the riding horses and in the section set apart for the colts, little box stalls were provided. A great space was reserved for the carriages and it was needed, for the Colonial coach was a vehicle which demanded room and the Darnalls had their exclusive "light carriages" and still other vehicles in addition to the coach.

The old carpenter shop is still standing, too, and the blacksmith shop where some sinewy smith, working in a blaze of sparks, beat white hot metal into nails for the house. Here is the old ice house and here, even, some of the old slave quarters which have disappeared from almost all of the old Maryland estates.

Twenty-seven thousand acres were included in the patent which Charles Calvert, Lord Baltimore, gave to his old schoolmate and close friend, Henry Darnall, and which included not only Poplar Hill, but the adjoining estates of The Woodyard, where stood the first Darnall home, and what are known today as the Turner and Holloway tracts. Only five hundred and thirty acres belong to Poplar Hill today.

When Henry Darnall died he left the estate to his nephew, Robert Darnall Sewall, from whose descendants it passed into the collateral Daingerfield branch of the family. Its present owner has made numerous but not serious alterations, the most conspicuous one being a remodeling of the chapel into a study, with a narrow interior balcony.

* * *

Another Prince George's estate of old established lineage is called Compton Basset. During the latter part of the Seventeenth century a young Welshman with a thirst for far places in his blood went to England where he met Charles, third Lord Baltimore, with whom he joined forces and from whom he secured a grant of land in Maryland. Then, having burned his bridges behind him, he set sail in the general direction of the sunset.

Clement Hill and Lord Baltimore arrived in Maryland on the same ship in 1662-3, and Clement Hill immediately took up his grant at St. Clement's Bay, becoming almost immediately an official of the province. From 1674 to 1676 he was high sheriff of St. Mary's county, a member of the Lower House from 1677 to 1685, a member of the Council in 1685. He died without children and his estate in America passed to his nephew and namesake, Clement Hill, Jr., who patented, in 1699, a great tract along the Patuxent river which he called Compton Basset. Two years before that he had been appointed by the proprietary deputy surveyor general for "his Lordship's Mannours, Forrests, etc., in Maryland."

A little less than a hundred years later—the evidence points approximately to 1780—the descendants of Clement Hill, grown decidedly prosperous, erected the present homestead which has descended on the distaff side to Dr. and Mrs. Reverdy Sasscer, with a large portion of the original estate still in possession of the family. The house, decidedly English in appearance, stands on a high bluff, completely screened from the road by trees and bushes massed at the foot of a terraced garden.

Large and square, with a hipped roof from which two solid looking chimneys rise, the house presents its side to the road and looks away across rolling country, with a view of several miles. The curved driveway leads to a small square portico, railed in at the sides,—the architectural impulse of a day considerably later than the one which saw the building of the house. The original doorway, however, is still there, with fluted and reeded pilasters supporting the denticular pediment above the round transom.

Small side windows are cut on each side of the front door. Above, in the second story, a large window, round at the top, is flanked by two small windows, giving a Palladian effect, and a triangular pediment, pierced by a semi-circular window, cuts the roof line at the top. Otherwise the walls are without ornament except for a strong wooden cornice. Across the back of the house runs a long veranda.

No wings ever have been added, although the position of the windows in the side walls would seem to indicate that the builder had expected, some day, to construct them. The house is built of brick, now concealed behind a coat of modern white stucco.

The hall at Compton Basset furnishes one of the innumerable instances to be found in the Colonial houses of Maryland of the

COMPTON BASSET

KILLMAIN

AUBURN

ingenuity of the early builders who manipulated their designs so that, in spite of many general resemblances among them, there are almost no exact duplicates. Here is a wide, hospitable corridor, provided with the decorative arch so extensively used, but in this case the arch has an elaborate glass fanlight and slat blinds which mark the entrance into a considerably larger hall, almost square, with an elaborate stairway occupying two-thirds of it.

On the walls of the hallway hang old English prints, bearing the imprimatures of Robert Sawyer and John Bennett, of London, and dated 1730, indicating that they must have been brought over to hang on the walls of an older house on the place and here, too, hangs one of the rare candle lamps for which collectors yearn.

To the left of the hall a door opens into the drawingroom with its high mantel and to the right is the library where stands the old hand-made mahogany surveyor's table at which Clement Hill worked out his problems in the service of Lord Baltimore. Two tables, so dark with age that it is difficult to tell whether they are made of walnut or mahogany, but which bear the stamp of the Duncan Phyfe period, are included among the antiques in the house and are said once to have stood in the home of Henry Clay.

Towering Linden trees stand on the wide terrace in front of the house. To the left, laid out in a series of terraces, is a rose garden and to the right stands a diminutive chapel, its walls almost obliterated by ivy and wistaria and its shingled roof covered with moss. Here the early Hills and their slaves worshipped in the religious freedom established by the Calverts in Maryland. Back of the chapel, on the highest terrace of the vegetable garden, a fig tree brings forth fruit.

There was a day, of course, when all the various small and

important outbuildings of a Colonial estate were to be found at Compton Basset. Many of them have vanished with the need for them, but the old dairy and the old meat house remain, with vestiges of the neat brick walks which once connected them with "the big house" to show what the old place must have looked like when every man's home was his castle.

CHAPTER SEVEN

In that part of Maryland which is somewhat remote from the Chesapeake Bay and its immediate environs, important houses are fewer and farther between than they are in the tidewater regions. Almost none of them date back to the Seventeenth century and few of them go back even to the early days of the Eighteenth. Consequently, it is interesting to discover within a few miles of each other, in Montgomery county, two houses which have considerably more than a century to their credit.

One of them, Killmain, stands on a tract which included 3,500 acres when it was granted to Daniel Carroll in 1735. Of this estate, between 1,300 and 1,400 acres were purchased by one Richard Bennett Hall and conveyed by him to his son, Richard Lowe Hall, from whom this estate was bought, with several hundred acres additional, by Ludwick Young, Jr., who also completed the old stone house begun by the Carrolls. The other estate is known as Chiswell's Manor and stands about three-quarters of a mile north of the tiny village of Poolesville.

The manor house at Killmain, as far as it is possible to judge from its appearance and from all the lore concerning it, was built about the close of the Revolution. Standing on an abrupt knoll and dominating the countryside for miles, it takes the shape of a capital "T" and, beyond question, constituted a tremendous undertaking for the unskilled artisan who built it.

The walls are of field stone, evidently the yield of the ground on which the house stands, and are of all sizes and shapes from the boulders of the foundation to the pathetically cut pieces which form the flat arches over the windows. In these arches alone there is a whole story of primitive ambition matching itself against the demands of skill and, though losing the test, going down with flying colors. The idea is there, cheerfully enough, but the realization can inspire only admiration for the workman who was game enough to tackle a problem which none but the trained might solve.

Three windows appear in the wall to one side of the front door which forms as simple an entrance to a big land owner's house as well might be. To it leads a low flight of stone steps, guiltless of railing or other ornamentation. On the other side of the door there are but two windows and on the second floor, making no pretense whatever at balancing those below, five windows appear. The Carroll family was notably independent in its thinking and in its actions and the Youngs, who completed the house, were equally unhampered by custom. Symmetry was the least of their concerns.

Nine panes of small glass, separated by broad muntins, appear in the windows on the first floor but in those on the second floor there are only six, the ceilings of the bedrooms being much lower than those of the living rooms. Many of the original panes of glass remain, despite the vicissitudes of fortune which have overtaken the place and the innumerable little fists of generations of children who have drummed against the windows in rainy weather, or used them as a backstop for ball games when the skies were clear.

Massive chimneys rise from the gable end walls which are entirely blank except for two very small windows huddled close to the roof. The roof itself derives interest from the curious heavy wooden cornice which tops the stone walls and extends outward from the house at an angle of forty-five degrees. The eaves are carried out over the cornice and the result is unique.

Within, the entrance hall is square and spacious, with a large room on each side. Back of the entrance hall is a smaller hall from which the stairway leads to the upper floors, and beyond are three large rooms of generous proportions. The great thickness of the walls, the deep recesses of the windows and the size of the fireplaces combine to provide in all of them a survival of primitive Maryland.

The purchase of Killmain by the Youngs, who paid $20 an acre for it in 1814, brought the estate into the possession of a family which had prospered exceedingly after the original immigrant reached port at Philadelphia in 1753. Seventeen days after Ludwick Young's arrival he purchased of Daniel Dulany a lot, Number 117, in Fredericktown, and Magdalin's Fancy, a tract of 595 acres, was granted to him in 1765.

The Youngs owned many slaves and the old quarters, together with the old farm buildings, some of which are still standing, were placed back of the house, to the West. The house servants occupied a wing which was torn down about twenty years ago and with it vanished the great kitchen where were prepared the feasts with which the Youngs entertained their friends in pre-Civil War days.

At the time when Killmain came into the possession of Ludwick Young that worthy had five sons to each of whom he gave a farm, all joining. Killmain had a splendid lawn, shaded by locust trees and filled with boxwood and other shrubbery of the period. The locust trees remain, gnarled and broken, but the boxwood and the crepe myrtles and the grandiflora are gone. So, too, are the Youngs, for the property passed from the possession of this family about twenty years ago and tenants occupy the place today.

* * *

Time has dealt more leniently with Chiswell's Manor which has become the summer home of Mrs. Beryl Evans Gray, of

Washington. Mrs. Gray has restored but not altered in the repairs which were necessary when she obtained possession in 1929. Chiswell's Manor has been known by this name for a great many years but old deeds refer to it as Chiswell's Delight and Chiswell's Inheritance and in Stephen Newton Chiswell's will, dated 1800, he speaks of it as Chiswell's Lodge. A brick high up in the gable end of the house, dated 1796, is marked with the initials, "C. S." an inscription which, being interpreted, signifies Stephen Chiswell, the builder.

Unlike Killmain there is to be found in Chiswell's Manor not the handiwork of unskilled artisans, but workmanship fortified with the power of expression. A modern entrance porch replaces the original portico before the front door which, in the days of Stephen Chiswell, is said to have been used as the back entrance. In the drawingroom, now entered directly from the porch, the original panelling is as perfect as the day it was put there. Built-in cupboards, with rounded doors, appear on each side of a high mantel carved with tulips in relief and enriched with small moulding. The architrave of the fireplace is finished with an eared moulding and ears appear on the decoration of the over-mantel. In the little office tiny closets were built into the panelling and are traditionally said to have contained at all times a bottle of rare wine and a bottle of "spirits" which probably served as a solace when crops failed and as an inspiration when neighbors dropped in for a game of piquet. A well proportioned triangular pediment completes the ornamentation of the over-mantel in this room.

Upstairs two large bedrooms occupy the entire front of the house. Originally this space was included in one enormous room, panelled across the chimney end and fitted with powder closets on each side of the fire place. The panelling in this room is much like that in the drawingroom below and the doors of the powder closets are swung on H-hinges. The stairway to the attic is supplied with a balustrade of Chinese Chippendale design, an idiosyncrasy which seems not to have commended itself to the builders of early Maryland homes to the same extent that it did in Virginia. Few examples of it are to be found in the State. In the attic the exposed beams show how solid was the oak of which the frame work of Chiswell's Manor was constructed and how enduring are the wooden pins which hold the rafters together.

The kitchen, which always constitutes one of the most interesting attributes of Colonial houses, is placed, together with the servants' quarters, in a story and a-half wing adjoining the south end of the main building. In it is a fireplace which measures six feet, six inches in width, and a door which still operates on a string latch. The kitchen wing is said to have been built several years after the main portion had been completed and to have replaced an earlier one of logs which stood at some distance from the house. Be that as it may, this wing of Chiswell's Manor is picturesque to a degree, with its voluptuous chimney and the great oaken beams, squared from solid trees, upon which the roof rests. The earlier designation of Chiswell's Delight would seem, through the perspective of years, to have been an appropriate name for this estate.

The brick work of the walls, which are laid up in the pattern generally called American bond, consisting of a course of header bricks to every five or six courses of stretchers, shows excellent material and sound workmanship. The floors are put together with dowel pins and are as firm as they were more than a century ago. Each of the rooms has a fireplace, showing that the comforts of life obtained to the full extent that the times afforded and the land on which the house was built is as fertile as any in Maryland.

Stephen Chiswell was only nineteen when he left London in 1734 and, after weeks on the ocean, arrived in Anne Arundel county where his mother's brother, Joseph Newton, occupied a home on the banks of West river. The uncle in question was a widower and his life was further complicated by the possession of four daughters with the comeliest one of whom Stephen promptly fell in love. Her name was Sarah and Stephen lost little time in obtaining her promise to marry him, but securing her father's consent was another affair altogether. The uncle refused to consider the matter for a moment and the flaming youth of the day did the only thing possible under the circumstances.

The elopement was carried out as decorously as possible, with a negro maid to assist Sarah in her descent of the ladder which her lover had, conforming to the custom in such matters, placed against her window, and to act as witness to the ceremony. But such concessions failed to placate Joseph Newton. When he discovered that his daughter had defied him he retaliated by ordering the newlyweds out of the house and it was a crestfallen young pair who made their way into what then was Frederick and now is Montgomery county.

Much to the probable chagrin of Sarah's father the matrimonial adventure prospered. So did young Chiswell's fortunes, for before very long he owned several thousand acres in grants from the Lord Proprietary. One of them was dated September, 1736, and another December 15, 1738. Before his house was finished, however, Stephen Chiswell died, leaving eight daughters who received substantial inheritances and the manor went to his son, Joseph. The descendants of Joseph Chiswell married into the prominent families of the neighborhood and so it was that the estate came into the possession of a branch of the same Young family which owned Killmain. The last of them has been gone from Chiswell's Manor, as from Killmain, for a generation, but the house stands firm, half covered by ivy and facing the rising sun.

Both the Newtons and the Chiswells were Episcopalians. Joseph Newton Chiswell was one of the signers of the petition to Governor Horatio Sharpe for the division of All Saints' Parish in Frederick county and he was a vestryman at old Monocacy Chapel. Joseph Newton, the stern parent unto Sarah, was owner of Pew Number 1 in St. John's Parish, Prince George's county, for which he paid four hundred pounds of tobacco.

*　　*　　*

It is extraordinary, the way houses come to be associated with the dominant personalities which inhabit them, even though such persons hold no title whatever to them, not even to the nether shingle. Such a house is Rose Hill, on the outskirts of the busy city of Frederick among the hills of Western Maryland and which has become so completely identified with Thomas Johnson, major in the Continental army and the first governor elected by the people of Maryland, that it popularly is supposed to have belonged to him.

The land on which Rose Hill was built did, as a matter of fact, form part of Governor Johnson's lands in Frederick county, but it was given by him to his daughter, Ann Jennings, in 1770 when she became the bride of Major John Grahame, from whose family came the Dukes of Montrose and whose mother was a daughter of the "Laird of Muncie." It was Major Grahame who built the big house which is visited today by virtually everyone who goes to Frederick, but those who make the pilgrimage are, in nine cases out of ten, under the impression that they are going to see the home of Thomas Johnson.

Rose Hill has been changed considerably within recent years.

[109]

The driveway by which it is reached now leads from the public road through two substantial stone gate posts, almost concealed by twining roses, in "Y" formation with arbutus trees which half screen, half reveal Colonial yellow walls and dominant brick chimneys, on the way to the front door.

Rose Hill has a double portico, fitted on the first story with Doric columns, surmounted by a row of the Ionic order supporting a triangular pediment. Two sturdy dormers, one at each end, also break into the roof line, making the house appear higher than it really is. The heavy brick walls show the workmanship of master masons and are laid up in Flemish bond capped at the top by a wide cornice ornamented with console brackets, fluting and a modified Greek fret.

Within, a wide hallway leads from door to door through the center of the house, with drawingroom and diningroom to the right and left of the entrance. Both are well proportioned and the drawingroom is well lighted by six large windows, two opening to the south, two to the north and two to the east. This room occupies the entire end of the house. In it the woodwork is simple, except for the high carved mantel, but it has served to form a background against which great men have appeared to talk seriously and brilliantly of the problems which confronted the fledgling republic which they had succeeded in bringing into existence.

Weighty affairs were discussed in this room, for Thomas Johnson, who came to Rose Hill to live after his own home, Richfields, had been burned, was a close friend of Washington. The two were born in the same year and when both were young, Thomas Johnson had assisted the Virginia surveyor-engineer in working out problems of navigation on the Potomac. He knew John Quincy Adams, the Massachusetts patriot, too, and other leaders of national policy who came to Rose Hill to talk with the man who had been courageous enough to declare when the Revolution was brewing that the first Hessian soldier who set foot on American soil would absolve him from allegiance to Great Britain.

No place in Frederick county was more noted for lavish hospitality and elegance of entertainment than was Rose Hill, though there were a number of splendid homes in the vicinity. Washington is believed to have been the honor guest on at least one formal occasion and family tradition recounts that he poured tea and coffee for the ladies in the drawingroom, while wax tapers gleamed in crystal candelabra and the heavy brasses of the fire-place reflected the brillance of the flames.

Across the hall from the big drawingroom is the diningroom, its equal in cheer. The stairway which leads to the second floor is simple and plain, with the conventional white spindles and mahogany hand rail, but given particular interest by the presence on the wall beside the steps of the framed fac-simile of a letter written by Washington to Thomas Johnson in August, 1795, and offering him the portfolio of State. Close by is a copy of Johnson's letter, written a few days later, declining the offer.

Upstairs the bedrooms are simply disposed around the upper hall from which a door opens upon the upper portico where the governor's family sat on summer evenings while the heat lifted slowly and the cool breeze from the mountains crept in to bring relief. The fireplaces in two of the bedrooms have been closed to make slipper cupboards, but the old flues are still there and could be used were anyone disposed to restore them to their purpose in life.

The kitchen and pantries are located in a wing, with sleeping quarters above for the servants, and show by their size what manner of household was the one at Rose Hill. In one of the outbuildings, not far from the house, stands a quaint contraption which served Governor Johnson as a bath tub, and was one of the few to be found in early Maryland.

Of the garden, which was one of the great glories of Rose Hill, memories are all that is left, save for a few clumps of the boxwood which formed a hedge separating the front garden from the rear. In the old days, at the back of the house, a strip of greensward ten feet wide ran the length of the garden, with flower beds on both sides. The garden reached its greatest beauty in the spring when hundreds of flowers bloomed at once and spread a natural pastel upon the ground. In the far corners were beds of strawberries and raspberries and vegetables, but they were screened from the house by bushes of lilacs and snowballs, wigelia and mock orange.

Governor Johnson was in the prime of life when he went to Rose Hill in 1794. The ink was scarcely dry on the treaty of peace with Great Britain and Johnson still was full of the fiery energy, consuming faith and implacable resolution which had made him one of the fomentors of the Revolution. It was characteristic of him during that long, uncertain struggle that, while holding the rank of major, he arrived one morning in the camp of Washington, whom he had nominated to be commander-in-chief of the Continental army, and demanded to see the general at once.

Colonel Humphreys, the aide on duty, temporized. The general had given orders that he was not to be disturbed. Major Johnson fumed. Waiting was not to his liking and finally he declared that his business was urgent and that he would brook no further delay.

"And what name, sir, shall I give of the person who wishes to see the commander-in-chief?" inquired the ceremonious colonel.

"Why, Thomas Johnson, sir, and be damned to ye," the little

man snapped out. According to the story the colonel proceeded to awaken the commander-in-chief of the American forces who was decidedly testy in consequence.

"Your Excellency will excuse me," apologized Colonel Humphreys, "but there is a furious little man outside who says that he must see you and who will take no denial."

"Who is he?"

"Well, sir, he simply says his name is 'Thomas-Johnson-and-be-damned-to-ye'."

"Oh," came the reply with a complete change of manner, "Well, well, never mind! Show him in at once, sir. A most valuable man, sir, a most valuable man!"

A portrait by Charles Willson Peale, now hanging in the rooms of the Maryland Historical Society to which it was given by members of the Johnson family, shows this man who was recognized as the foremost citizen of Maryland in his day as the center of a family group and depicts him a resolute character, with black hair, direct eyes, and a forceful chin.

A real tragedy befell at Rose Hill years after the death of Governor Johnson when all of his private papers and the whole of a voluminous correspondence he had carried on with the leading men of the colonies was gathered up from the attic where it had been stored and used as kindling for the kitchen fire.

Rose Hill passed from the hands of the Johnson family a number of years ago. It now belongs to Noah Creamer, of Frederick, who leases it for use as a tea house, but many of the Johnson family treasures which it contained during the days of Grahames have come into the possession of Mrs. Henry H. Rogers, of Riderwood, Maryland. Among them are two chairs of the Chippendale period, both of which were used by Governor Johnson during his term as chief executive.

In the foothills of the Blue Ridge, adjoining the land purchased by Lawrence Richey, secretary to President Hoover,
for a hunting preserve, and not far from Rose Hill is Auburn,
so stored with memories of vanished laughter that its name
should be amended to read, (with the permission of Mrs.
Wharton) A House of Mirth.

Auburn was erected just after the turn of the Nineteenth
century. Standing on a broad plateau, with its back to the
mountain which is terraced upward to form a garden, Auburn
looks out over a broad stretch of lawn shaded by century-old
oaks and copiously weeping willows, across the State road to
fields of grain which are swallowed up by the shadows which
hang constantly over the distant hills.

The house was built practically as it now stands, a brick
structure covered with white plaster, about forty feet by sixty,
with a connecting wing leading to the servants' quarters and
kitchens. Its construction occupied a number of years, for there
was much to be done, but it was completed before 1810. Walls
two feet thick, with cellars of the same dimensions as the house
and eight feet deep, tell their own story of sound workmanship
and indicate that but little additional earth was needed to aug-
ment that taken from the hillside when the foundations were
dug in order to build the impressive terrace in front of the house.

Two stories high, with a two-story columned portico, the big
white house with its many windows and deep green blinds
attracts instant attention from passersby. It also draws back to
itself, by some subtle pull, men and women whom the years
have scattered to all parts of the world and who recall wistfully,
as their feet touch the threshold, the gay times which have been
celebrated within its walls.

Dormer windows of recent date and modern design have
been inserted into the gable roof which is supported by bracketed

HALL AT AUBURN

AUBURN: DININGROOM DOORWAY

DOUGHOREGAN MANOR

Home of Charles Carroll of Carrollton

cornices stretching across the front and rear facades, with a return on the gable ends. Opulent-looking chimneys push their way up above the ridgepole at each end of the house and a flange, pierced by a semi-circular attic window on the servants' wing, forms a distinctive architectural *motif* of the front facade.

The front door is sturdy and solid, a tested barrier against the winter snows and the winds that blow, cold and biting, from the mountains. Over the door a transom fitted with two rows of small-paned glass permits a generous supply of light to enter the hall and additional light comes through a small window on each side of the entrance. No meagre sidelights, these, but real windows!

If ever a hallway expressed the spirit of the house to which it belongs, the hallway at Auburn is the one. Enormously wide, with doors opening to the right and left into spacious rooms, it has a stairway of unusual felicity to complete the impression of welcome.

The stairway begins its ascent on the left side of the hall, more than half way to the back of the house. The newel post is small and square, made of mahogany and a mahogany rail surmounts the white, round spindles, two to a step, of the balustrade. Straight across the entire end of the hall runs the landing, without visible means of support, and the second flight proceeds against the wall opposite the lower flight.

There is a tradition in Frederick county which maintains that one of the masters of Prospect Hill (an old Dulany mansion on the road between Frederick and Charles Town, West Virginia, and later owned by the McPhersons) once drove a four-horse team into the hall of his home and turned it around to settle a wager; and Frederick countians declare that the hall at Auburn is quite as wide as the one at Prospect Hall. There is no record, however, of the experiment having been tried at Auburn.

Ornate panelling of plaster breaks the length of the hall walls and the moulded cornice also is of plaster. The deep jambs of the doors leading into the living rooms are panelled and the wide floor boards belong to another generation. In the drawing-room the walls repeat the hall scheme of decorative panelling, though here it is less elaborate in design. Between the drawing-room and the diningroom an arched doorway has a panelled soffit and a panelled door, curved at the top, to fit into the arch.

Sandwiched between the diningroom and hall walls is a concealed stairway, the door to which opens outside the house. This stairway was used by the slaves who carried the wood for the fireplaces and the water for ablutions to the upper floors in order that they might fulfill their tasks without appearing too much in evidence.

Eight large fireplaces are to be found in the house, provided with mantels of varying degrees of beauty, the one in the dining room being the finest. The castings in the fireplaces are inscribed, "Blackford and Thornburgh, Catoctin Furnace." This firm was established at Catoctin in 1803 and in that year became the property of Baker Johnson, builder of Auburn.

This fact and the will of Baker Johnson, leaving to his son, also named Baker, the house with its furnishings and a retinue of negro slaves with "their future increase," serve to establish the date of the building of Auburn. The will was filed in 1810.

One of the early proprietors of Catoctin Furnace was John McPherson, whose daughter, Harriet, married its manager, John Brien, later received by her father into partnership. John Brien in 1820 acquired Auburn by right of purchase and when his son, William Coleman Brien, married a Miss Tiernan, the wedding party was entertained in the house, leaving the record of the occasion on one of the window panes upon which was scratched, with a diamond ring, the names of the wedding guests.

It was for Miss Tiernan, too, that the little chapel, now a vine-clad ruin on the edge of the woods near the county road, was begun, but the young wife died before it was completed. She was a frail little thing and the winters must have been extremely trying in her hillside home. At any rate the lovely old hall was divided by a partition to enable her to go from library to drawing room without encountering the drafts of the staircase well, and the scar of that partition still can be traced.

Colonel Brien died in July, 1834, at Bedford Springs and the property again was sold, this time to Mrs. Cheston Galloway, of Hagerstown, who bought it for her nephew, Peregrine Fitzhugh. Not long afterwards Auburn came upon evil days. Hard working farmers obtained possession and weeds grew up over the window sills. Walls and woodwork were whitewashed with lime impregnated with indigo. Grain was stored in the bedrooms and slaughtered beeves and hogs were hung from the stair landing and cut as needed.

Everything on the place was in a dilapidated state when Auburn was sold again in 1850 to Dr. William McPherson who took there with him a courageous young bride. In a short time the house flourished as of old. The partition which had been built to protect the delicate bride still marred the beauty of the hall and, though the sight of it irked the sensibilities of Dr. McPherson's bride, the conservative physician, who made all of his calls on horseback, with saddle bags of medicines and instruments, hesitated about having it removed. The day came, however, when his wife could stand it no longer. No sooner had her husband departed to make his rounds than she called for an ax and when the doctor returned it was less trouble to take down the remainder than to rebuild the wall.

[117]

The doctor's wife was less lucky, however, in preserving the romantic windowpane record of that early wedding party. Shortly after the Civil War she left Auburn to visit a brother in California and before her departure gave instructions concerning certain repairs she wished to have made during her absence. As a part of her instructions she left a box of windowpanes with which a faithful retainer was told to replace all that were cracked and the wedding party went the way of all flesh.

During the Civil War Auburn was on the border line. Dr. McPherson was too ill to take up arms, but he was known to be a Southern sympathizer and Auburn, no doubt, would have suffered severely had not his wife's sister, (whose husband, Robert Harper Clarkson, afterwards was first Bishop of Nebraska) had a good friend in the Union General Reynolds. This considerate officer stationed guards about the place whenever Union troops were about and though they camped in the orchard which they cut down for fire wood, and confiscated cattle and horses, they did not harm the buildings nor harass the McPherson family.

There was tension in the air, however, and the strain was increased by the visits of Dr. McPherson's nephew, McPherson Kennedy, who held a captaincy in the Confederate cavalry and who swam the Potomac on his horse whenever the opportunity presented itself in order to visit his relatives at Auburn. By night he stayed at the house but by day he was hidden in the barn to which the physician or a trusted slave carried his food. A convenient knot hole in the barn door served as a lookout through which he watched for the Federal troops and on one occasion he had hastily to be put in the grain bin and covered with oats to escape the prodding bayonets of the Union scouts.

After the battle of Gettysburg, not far distant, stragglers from both armies passed Auburn for days and the humane mistress of the estate and her sister put all their resources to the test to feed them. Two barrels of flour were made into biscuits and apple tarts in three days for the men in blue uniforms and gray who presented themselves at the door.

Open house, except during the regime of the tenants who so desecrated the place, always has been kept at Auburn. The clergy especially were honored guests, Roman Catholic and Protestant alike, and the gentry of the neighborhood commingled there. To this house came the Goldsboroughs, Maulsbys, and Ritchies, the Buchanans, the Fitzhughs and the Johnsons and many others whose names are part and parcel of the history of Maryland.

Splendid pieces of antique furniture are to be found in the house. An Empire sofa and a number of Hepplewhite chairs which once stood at Prospect Hall (where Dr. McPherson and his father before him were born) are in the hall, part of a set of four sofas and eighteen chairs which adorned the boyhood home of the physician. There is also a chair which stood in the White House during the regime of President Monroe and heirlooms which have come down to the present day McPhersons through the Buchanans and the Fitzhughs. One of these is an old clock which stands on the stair landing and which was made in London. Another is the cabinet of musical glasses brought from England by that Colonel Fitzhugh who rode up to New York State with Lord Rochester and laid out the city which bears his lordship's name. There is a story to the effect that Lord Rochester wished to give to Colonel Fitzhugh the honor of naming the city, but the colonel refused. They played cards for it and the colonel won, but still he refused.

From its earliest years a quaint custom has prevailed at Auburn in the entertainment once a year of the neighboring villagers. During the Christmas holidays they come, droves of them, in masquerade costume, calling themselves "Bell-snicklers," in unmistakable survival of their Hessian ancestry, and into the big hall they are welcomed, there to mingle in ancient square dances, with their own fiddler and "caller-off" to direct the festivities.

The present house is the second which has stood on the same site, and before its acquistion by Baker Johnson (whose brother, Thomas, played so conspicuous a part in the Revolutionary history of the country), the estate belonged to the Lux family. In 1774 the Johnson brothers, Thomas, Baker, Roger and James, built the furnace. Originally the old forge stood just outside the gate to Auburn and the water from a small pond, which was in the lower yard until about thirty years ago, fell in a cascade over a stone embankment and ran the bellows by means of a water wheel.

At this forge cannon and balls were cast for the Continental army and only a year ago workmen in digging for gate posts, unearthed a "pig" of iron and some implements used in casting. In 1793 Roger and James Johnson withdrew from the firm and in 1803, Thomas Johnson sold his interest to his brother, Baker, builder of Auburn. The original house had been the home of James Johnson, who dwelt there until 1793 when he removed to Springfield, later the home of Frederick A. Schley. Wayside, the present tenant house, also is older than Auburn and served as a distillery in the days when gentlemen could manufacture their own spirits.

CHAPTER EIGHT

Of all the numerous homes which were built in Maryland by the Carrolls, who were one of the greatest landowning families of the colonies, Doughoregan Manor is the only one which is owned today by a Carroll and in which a Carroll lives. Few places in the country can compare with it in architectural individuality as a survival of the days when the cavaliers dominated Maryland and Charles Carroll, who signed the Declaration of Independence, grew wealthy beyond the dreams of the rest of the colonists.

Doughoregan Manor is, probably, the most famous Colonial estate in Maryland. It also is one of the oldest of the important houses still standing. Situated in the picturesque rolling country which stretches between Baltimore and Frederick, it borders the historic turnpike which once formed part of the great natural highway from East to West and which was travelled precariously by all the great men of the country at one time or another.

An iron gateway marks the entrance to the manor. On each side of the gate stone pillars are surmounted by gaily painted tubs in which, the summer long, flowers bloom profusely despite the shade from the trees just inside the gates. Under the trees stands the lodge house—a quaint place and one of the few such appurtenances to great estates remaining in Maryland.

The long driveway leads straight through a lush stretch of woodland for at least half a mile and on between a double file of aspens, maples and oaks which are generations old and have been one of the great prides of the Carroll family since the first sapling was planted. No matter how hot the sun may beat down elsewhere—and the sun's rays can be brutal in Maryland in mid-summer—there is always to be found on the driveway of Dough-oregan a stimulating coolness.

Wide green lawns, formal beds of flowers, exotic trees and shrubbery, stretch away on both sides of the driveway which works around to the back of the house and then maneuvers to the front, still threading between a double row of trees. Always, for generations, the lawns at Doughoregan have been assiduously tended. The grass has become a deep and velvety carpet upon which are set masses of brilliant geraniums, red and yellow coleus, rose bushes and tiger lilies, together with native and exotic shrub-bery which blend into a tapestry. At the end of the garden is a century-old stone wall, overgrown with moss and lichens and in another direction the lawns slope down to the remains of the old quarters where the slaves who once worked on the manor ate their co'n bread and cracklins for breakfast and in the twilight of summer nights sat on rude benches outside their doors while they crooned strange racial melodies, full of mystery which no white man ever has been able to understand.

"House of Regan" is Doughoregan, being translated, though the significance of its application to the manor only can be con-jectured. It has been supposed, plausibly enough, that the Regans were Irish folk of importance from whom the Carrolls in some manner trace descent. Charles Carroll, grandfather of Charles Carroll, the Signer, was the first of the name in Maryland and was land agent for Lord Baltimore, an opportunity which he was not slow to utilize. He secured thousands of rich and fertile acres for himself in the colony, Carrollton, near Frederick, from which the Signer derived the affix to his signature was another. Doughoregan was a later acquisition. Always, since first the Carrolls came to America, has there been a Charles Carroll, and always have the various persons who have borne this name dis-

tinguished themselves one from another by adding to their sig-
natures the names of their estates or some other significant
appellation.

It has been said that the manor house at Doughoregan looks
more like a section of some great wall, with a watchman's tower,
than like a dwelling, but the comparison holds only as long as
the first impression lasts. With the additions which have been
made the house is now three hundred feet long, with an "L" at
each end, one used as the servants' quarters and the other as a
chapel. The front faces the east and is adorned by a simple portico with Doric columns, and a recent superstructure, providing
an extra room on the second floor, has been built out over the
roof of the portico. A central hall, heavily panelled in oak,
divides the house and connects with a rear portico similar to the
one in front. Extending along the house, on both sides of the
rear porch, is a veranda with a marble floor and ivy covered iron
columns. Along the cornice of the roof runs a narrow walk
guarded by a white railing.

In the hallway heads of deer, antelope and bear attest the
fondness of the Carrolls for hunting big game. To the right of
the entrance is the parlor, and beyond that, the study where
family portraits are assembled in profusion. The old Carrolls,
justifiably enough, seem to have had a weakness for having their
portraits painted, with the best artists available to do the work.
In this room the Signer conducted the business of his estate and
wrestled with the problems which beset the young country in its
difficulties with England both before and after the Revolution.

Opposite, on the other side of the hall, are a reception room
and diningroom, with a modernly appointed breakfastroom adjoining the reception room. Nowhere in the house does the spell
of the past exert itself more completely than in the diningroom
where, as in the study, the features of Carrolls of eight genera-

tions ago look down from gilded frames on a mahogany banquet table about which have been gathered men whose distinction and women whose beauty were the talk of two continents.

The second floor contains all of the sleeping apartments which were completely renovated and redecorated some sixteen or seventeen years ago and which are almost filled by poster beds so wide that often, when Doughoregan was crowded with guests, they were called upon to hold four or five persons at a time, who occupied them by sleeping crosswise. One of the bedrooms is known as the Cardinal's Room and is furnished in red and gold. During the lifetime of the late Cardinal Gibbons this room was reserved entirely for his use, or for that of some other dignitary of the Roman Church who might happen to be a guest at Doughoregan.

The second Charles Carroll in America, father of the Signer, was known as Charles Carroll of Annapolis. This Charles Carroll loved the gay, busy life of the little capital on the Severn where he had a handsome house (now owned by the Redemptorist Order) and liked to be identified with the life of that extraordinary pre-Revolutionary city. Born just beyond the bend of the century, he was sent by his father to France to be educated and to the end of his days is said to have spoken English with a French accent. While he was abroad he was received in audience by Louis XIV and during his stay in France his ingrained love of the Roman Catholic Church became so intensified that he chafed constantly when he returned to America against the oppressions to which the Romanists in Maryland had come, by this time, to be subjected. Frequently, it is told, he became so enraged on the subject that he declared his intention of going to the Southwest and founding a colony, but nothing ever came of it and he remained in possession of his estates in Maryland. He was still comparatively a young man when an accident resulted in his death. He had been standing on the portico of his Annapolis home, watching the progress of an incoming ship, when he fell and was injured so severely that he did not recover.

Ceremonies attending the departure of a young prince for unknown lands could not have been more elaborate than those which took place when Charles Carroll, the third, grandson of the land agent, sailed for Europe to carry on the family tradition of education abroad. His mother is said to have prepared him an elegant wardrobe of silks and velvets and fine linen, and his father to have presented him with purses of gold. Many tears were shed, but finally young Carroll departed with his cousin, John Carroll, then also young and high-spirited, who afterwards became archbishop of Baltimore. Upon completing his studies in France Charles Carroll sailed for England and spent several years of legal study as a lay resident in the precincts of the Temple. He did not join either of the Inns of Court, but studied from the books which had been used by his grandfather while a member of the Inner Temple and which had been sent to London from Maryland for the purpose.

In 1764 Charles Carroll of Annapolis wrote to his son in Europe, giving him an estimate of his own estate and indicated the rich property which the subsequent Signer might hope to inherit in land, although the cash revenue deriving from it at that period was comparatively meagre.

"You must not suppose my annual income to equal the interest of the value of my estate," the elder Carroll wrote. "Many of my lands are unimproved, but I compute I have a clear revenue of at least 1,800 pounds, Sterling, per annum, and the value of my estate is continually improving.

"I propose upon your coming into Maryland to convey to you my manor of Carrollton, 10,000 acres, and the addition thereto of 2,700 acres, now producing annually 250 pounds, Sterling, not one-half of which is let. Also my share of the ironworks, producing at least 400 pounds.

"On my death I am willing to add my manor of Doughoregan, 10,000 acres, and also 1,425 acres called Chance adjacent thereto, on which the bulk of my negroes are settled. As you are my only child you will, of course have all the residue of my estate at my death. Your return to me I hope will be in the next fall."

The following year did see young Carroll return to his homeland, then beginning to seethe with unrest and threats of war. Three years after his return, a charming, polished man of the world with the graces of European culture added to the resources of a brilliant intellect, he brought to the already aging manorhouse a bride, Mary Darnall, daughter of Henry and Rachel Brooke Darnall, a member of that same family from which his grandfather's wife had come.

Although he was debarred by his religion from holding public office young Carroll wholeheartedly cast his lot with the restive colonists who were arraigning themselves in constantly growing numbers against the king. He pledged them his wealth and all the resources at his command and as time went on and the tension increased the leaders of the rebellion travelled in increasing numbers out to Doughoregan to take counsel with this brilliant and practical man who had just enough imagination to make him dare greatly and so strong a love of freedom that he was willing to risk everything he had for its sake. The crowning act of his life, which was long and filled with a multiplicity of affairs, was the signing of the Declaration of Independence. Knowing that, by a stroke of the pen, he hazarded all of this vast personal wealth, for by that time he was a millionaire, Charles Carroll did not hesitate to put his name to a document which held no such significance for many of the other signers. The familiar version of this ceremony is credited to Robert C.

Winthrop in his centennial oration at Boston on the Fourth of July, 1876.

> "Will you sign?" said Hancock to Charles Carroll. "Most willingly," was the reply. "There goes two millions with the dash of a pen," says one of those standing by, while another remarks, "Oh, Carroll, you will get off. There are so many Charles Carrolls." And then we may see him stepping back to the desk and putting that addition, "of Carrollton" to his name which will designate him forever and be a prouder title of nobility than those in the peerage of Great Britain which was afterwards adorned by his accomplished and fascinating granddaughters.

A pretty story this, and one which it would be nice to be able to accept entire but, alack for romance, Charles Carroll for years had been accustomed to add the words, "of Carrollton" to his name. Hundreds of documents filed in the record offices of Maryland remain to prove that this was his habitual signature and the Signer himself failed to make mention of such an incident when the late J. H. B. Latrobe was engaged in writing his biography.

At the time of its greatest opulence Doughoregan contained fifteen thousand acres which were the accumulated results of several grants to the Carroll family between 1723 and 1734. Whether or not there was a house on it before the Signer went there to live is not known, but tradition has it that there was and that it has been incorporated in the present structure. Since the tenure of the Signer the estate has been divided sixty-four times, and now only about three thousand acres remain. Even with but one-fifth of its former extent included in its present boundaries, however, Doughoregan Manor is one of the largest estates in Maryland.

When the chapel was built it was considerably smaller and

lower than it now appears, the roof having been elevated and the interior changed a number of times in the last hundred and fifty years. Its present seating capacity is three hundred and fifty persons. Sanctuary and altar are simple and composed of rich materials and through deeply colored stained glass windows the sun filters to a "dim, religious light." In the gallery is an organ and on one of the walls is a copy of the celebrated "Immaculate Conception" painted in 1853 by a French artist.

Charles Carroll of Carrollton is buried in the chapel, near the altar, a white slab sealing his tomb. Close by is a memorial tablet of marble, with two angels in bas-relief holding a replica of the Declaration of Independence, across which lies a pen. Above are thirteen stars, representing the original States, and a cross.

Ever since the chapel has been built masses have been said there for the Carroll family, the Catholic tenants, slaves and servants. About half a century ago it became a mission of the Clarksville parish, so that even when the Carrolls are not in residence at Doughoregan, masses are said in the chapel.

After the death of Charles Carroll of Carrollton the next master of the Manor was the Signer's grandson, Charles, who was known in Maryland as "the Colonel" and who married, in 1825, Mary Digges Lee. Their son, Charles, inherited the estate in his turn and married Miss Caroline Thompson, of Staunton, Virginia, whose lineage was as distinguished as his own, one of her ancestors having been Colonel Ball, grandfather of George Washington. No children were born to them and, consequently, no strong ties bound them to the soil of Maryland so they determined to live in Europe. Some years after they had left America they sold Doughoregan Manor to John Lee Carroll, brother of Charles.

John Lee Carroll, unlike his brother, was a Marylander to the bone. He had no desire, even, to carry on the family tradition of education in Europe and, instead, went to Harvard. After his marriage to Anita Phelps, of New York, he lived in New York for several years, returning to Maryland and Doughoregan finally to stay for the rest of his life. His wife died in 1874, a year too soon to see her husband elected governor of the State. Two years later he was selected to represent Maryland at the great centennial exposition held in Philadelphia to commemorate the country's birth. Two years later he married again, his second wife being Miss Mary Carter Thompson, of Staunton, a sister of his brother Charles' wife.

Many children survived Governor John Lee Carroll when he died in 1905. Among them was another Charles, who inherited the estate, and lived there for a number of years, finally relinquishing to his son, Charles, who also lived there only a short time. It now is owned by Philip Acosta Carroll, a member of another branch of the Carroll family.

The tourney, which still survives as a vestigial remainder of feudalism in Maryland, was practiced for years at Doughoregan Manor and was the central interest of many notable entertainments which have taken place there. One of these events, described by J. D. Warfield, author of the "Founders of Anne Arundel and Howard counties," is said to have been unique in the annals of tilting in Maryland.

> "The gentry of the neighboring counties with their families were present," says Mr. Warfield. "The joust was out of the ordinary way of such entertainments. Instead of the conventional ring suspended in the air, through which the knights at full gallop were to thrust the spear, the object of their skill was a lay figure of wood, representing a man life-size, caparisoned as a knight, and so nicely balanced on a pedestal that a blow in the face from a well poised spear would unhorse the figure, while a stroke against the body

was calculated to shiver the spear or unhorse the knight.

"Against this figure each knight, handsomely attired and mounted with heavy spears about twelve feet long and one to three inches thick, with a strong brass point was to dash himself at full speed. One knight was dismounted and another had his spear shivered, but no injury occurred to man or horse. The victor who overthrew the lay figure three times and so won the right to crown the queen of honour, was an officer in the United States cavalry, but his name, with that of the queen, I have forgotten. After the joust followed the crowning of the queen and then the menu and the departure of the many guests."

Tournaments no longer are held at Doughoregan, but elaborate hospitality is dispensed at the Manor when the Carrolls are there. Hunting parties frequently are held as they were in the days of the late Governor Carroll when the men attended in their pink coats, fitting into the picture formed by the ancient manor house with its trophies of the chase adorning the walls and the painted scrutiny of generations of Carrolls who, in their own day, had ridden madly to hounds, fixed upon the guests in understanding and, perhaps, in envy.

*　　*　　*

Adjoining Doughoregan Manor is Burleigh. Not more than two or three families in Maryland before the Revolution had greater wealth or owned more land than the Hammonds whose holdings covered a large part of what now constitutes Anne Arundel, Howard and Frederick counties and who also had vast acreages on the Eastern Shore. They were powerful numerically, leaders in social life and influential in politics. No important event of the early days of Maryland and Virginia took place without the participation of a Hammond.

[130]

Essentially they were a race of builders, these men whose far-off ancestor helped to place William the Conqueror on the throne of England and whose kinsmen in Britain included bishops and abbots, soldiers and statesmen, two officers who accompanied Sir Walter Raleigh on his gold-hunting expedition to Guinea and whose family name is to be found on a list of twelve gentlemen to whom James I granted a charter to found a colony in Virginia.

The Hammond-Harwood house in Annapolis (of which more anon) has become known throughout the country as a monument to the family genius for architecture, but of this other house in Howard county, about five miles from Ellicott City, few persons ever have heard, though it nearly approaches in beauty the house in Annapolis.

Burleigh was built by Col. Rezin Hammond, a brother of Col. Mathias Hammond, master of the Hammond-Harwood house. The exact year of its completion is not known, but it was soon after the Revolution. Surrounding it was a tract of 2,345 acres of rolling, well wooded land.

To reach the house a driveway leads about a quarter of a mile under over-hanging locusts and maples to the barred fence which encloses the lawn and makes almost a complete circle to the front door. Much of the driveway now is overgrown with grass but its outlines are clear as ever. From the gate there is an excellent view of the house, a large structure of brick with one wing, solid and well proportioned. The effect of age is accentuated by the peeling of a coat of yellow paint from the old red brick.

Before the door is a small, open porch, with benches on each side. A panelled arch, carved with garlands and fluting, with a keystone above, frames the door which swings wide into a hallway so large that it would make an admirable ballroom. A good fourteen feet wide, it runs directly through the house and is broken about two-thirds of the way by an arch literally covered with elaborate carving. Its rounded pilasters are reeded and banded close to the wall with tambour fluting in the herring-bone pattern. Tambour fluting covers the soffit of the arch and its face shows the same device applied diagonally with a lace-like carving on the edge. Fastened into the carved keystone is the hook where the old candle lamp, with its hurricane shade, once was lighted at dusk.

At the far end of the hall, through the archway, the garden door appears in perspective, set in a framework of carving so delicate that it, too, seems almost like lace, with a fanlight over-head and the old brass lock gleaming dully in the half-light. The stair hall opens "L" fashion into the main hall from the left and from an unusually long scroll step at the bottom the stairway swings upward with a mahogany hand rail finishing a balustrade of square white spindles. A half-hand rail is set opposite it into the wall. The little sunburst carvings at the corners of the step ends add to the lightness of the stairway and recall an age when man drew a fine line of distinction between decoration and ornateness. The little sunbursts are exactly the right size!

From the hall panelled doors, with carved cornices showing the sunburst design, lead into the drawingroom at the left and the library at the right, with the family sitting room beyond the library. In the drawingroom the mantel over the fireplace in-stantly attracts attention by virtue of the elaboration of its carving and the boldness of its relief. Around the fireplace opening the carving simulates a chain and the narrow architrave is com-pletely covered with a band of guilloche. Two slender, fluted columns, with a single entablature, appear on each side of the mantel, with a repetition of the chain design, instead of the

Photo by Aubrey Bodine

DRAWINGROOM FIREPLACE, BURLEIGH MANOR

Photo by Aubrey Bodine

BURLEIGH MANOR

STAIRCASE AT BURLEIGH MANOR

BURLEIGH MANOR: GARDEN DOOR

usual reedwork, set into the fluting. Across the chimney breast the sunburst carving appears again, surmounted by bands of elaborate fretwork under the mantel shelf. The old brass fixtures for shovel and tongs still are fastened into the woodwork and the crumbling bricks of the fireplace tell mutely the story of the fires which have roared up this chimney, of Yule logs which have blazed on brass andirons rubbed until they gave back the brilliance of the flame, of love songs sung in the firelight and powdered heads which nodded sleepily in the heat.

Around the room the walls are wainscoted below the low chair rail which is decorated with fluting and stars and over the door the cornice is decorated with rope and sunburst carving. The windows are treated in a similar manner, making the drawingroom at Burleigh a room to be included among the fine Colonial interiors in Maryland.

Less elaborate is the decoration of the library, but this room has the old brass locks on the doors, a built-in cupboard and a mantel show sunburst carving and tambour fluting. All of the rooms have open fireplaces and undoubtedly were as comfortable in winter as Colonial rooms ever could be made, but what a scurrying of dusky-skinned house servants there must have been on February mornings through those enormous halls which could not be heated and into the rooms of family and guests to build the fires and bring the hot water!

The rooms in the wing are one step down from the main house, with the original floor boards, laid with handmade nails, still doing valiant service. In the kitchen a modern range mocks the old fireplace, with its deep hearth upon which many a succulent pone was baked on the coals. And no one who cares at all for old houses could fail to find interest in the attic, where the stout oak lintels rest over the windows and the chimneys form a "Y" curve which brings them out at the right place through the roof; or in the cellar with its thick foundation walls of stone and funny little oval windows, rimmed with brick, peeping out into the garden at the back. The garden now exists in name only, but until a half a century ago it was kept up with old-fashioned flowers in ordered parterres.

For years after the Civil War a group of stone cabins stood at a short distance from the house—the old slave quarters. All of them have tumbled down, or been torn down, except one which remains to show how the others appeared. In those days, too, enormous beetlebacked barns housed the grain and hay which were grown on the place, for the fields at Burleigh were very productive, but the barns also have vanished as the place has dwindled in size. Some things are gone from Burleigh in the lost barns and the old slave quarters, but there is left the old wooden pump close to the kitchen steps. And a knock at the front door summons to undo the fastenings old "Uncle Billy" who claims to have been born in 1830 and a few steps around the corner of the house brings into the picture a flock of pickaninnies tumbling out of the kitchen door.

The builder of Burleigh, Col. Rezin Hammond, was a Revolutionary character, but had come into public notice considerably before that when, with his brother, Mathias, he served on all the important patriotic committees of the colony. He was a direct descendant of that Maj.-Gen. John Hammond, a Royalist commander who died in Annapolis in 1707 and who left to St. Anne's Protestant Episcopal Church a sum of money which was expended in the purchase of a big brass-bound Bible that is cherished today among the archives of St. Anne's. The donor's tombstone stands in the churchyard, but his body was taken to his estate north of Annapolis and buried on a bluff overlooking the Severn river.

Col. Rezin Hammond was a bachelor and was regarded as

the benevolent philanthropist who took pity on the problems fate bestowed upon his "Brother Philip" in the form of seventeen children and offered to look out for the future of at least one of the sons. Denton Hammond was the recipient of Colonel Hammond's bounty and Burleigh Manor was the expression of his generosity.

There were many brothers in the Hammond family but it was the Benjamin of the lot, his brother Mathias, who was closest to Rezin Hammond and with whom he was most intimately associated all through life. At the beginning of the Revolution Col. Rezin Hammond was in command of the Severn Battalion but afterwards he was appointed to lead the Maryland troops in defense of Philadelphia. When the war was over the intimacy of the brothers was resumed, but not for long. Within six years after the peace Mathias Hammond died. Within a month their mother, who had lived to bury all her family save one, followed him to the grave, but Rezin Hammond lived on for twenty-three years, his closing days made cheerful, no doubt, by his interest in the three children of Denton Hammond, all of whom were born at Burleigh Manor and who were married there before deserting the big house to go to homes of their own.

Before his death Colonel Rezin Hammond liberated many of the slaves who worked for him on his various plantations and when he died, in 1809, he was buried in the Hammond family burying ground at Gambrill's, Md., where the original Hammond homestead was located, beside the body of Mathias. Carved on his tomb is this prophecy:

A sweet remembrance of the Just
Shall flourish when they sleep in dust

From Denton Hammond the Burleigh estate passed to the

possession of his son, Mathias, who also won the rank of colonel in the military forces of his country. He, however, had no sons and at his death Burleigh (minus the "Manor") became the property of his only daughter who married a cousin, Richard Craigh Hammond, who perpetuated the family name on the estate. It now belongs to the heirs of the late Miss Grace Hammond.

CHAPTER NINE

An estate which has grown through the years to be something more than the home of a dominant family and which has become almost a national institution, not merely because of its survival of a day that is done but because of the memories which envelop it, the traditions it has served and the associations it has preserved, is Hampton, home of the Ridgelys through eight generations.

Here are not, as at similar great houses in Europe, tales to be told of armies which have stormed its walls or dangerous men gone in secret ways to sudden deaths. Rather does Hampton embody the story of peace and gentle living which are, at bottom, the history of Maryland. Mellow and benign, still basking in a "befo' the wah" atmosphere which has vanished almost entirely from Maryland and the South, the century-and-a-half old house stands in the center of the picturesque Dulany's Valley, twelve miles to the north of Baltimore, close to civilization but completely apart from its jangled notes and discords.

Hampton was built by Captain Charles Ridgely. Dominating the park-like lands which surround it, it looks beyond them to acres of rolling farm country which border on the lovely lake, now the source of Baltimore city's water supply, known as Loch Raven.

Its dimensions are on a grand scale, one hundred and seventy-five feet long and seventy-five feet in width. With the interior laid off into rooms of generous proportions, it is strikingly in contrast with the constricted interiors of such notable houses as Arlington and Mount Vernon.

Rough stone, quarried on the place, forms the material of the walls, overlaid with plaster. Broad belt courses divide the stories, with a cornice of heavy modillions and Greek key carving. Foliated dormers, with carved consoles framing them at the sides, look out from the pitched roof and the high chimneys, two each end, have crenelated caps. On the garden front, which is the finer of the two, a wide, two-story portico, enclosed at the sides and topped by a heavy pediment pierced by a Palladian window, marks the entrance and is overhung with a luxurious wistaria vine which almost completely obscures the Chinese Chippendale railing along the upper floor of the portico. Ornamental urns stand at each corner of the roof to accent each angle of the pediment above the portico.

Towering above the roof is a great, octagonal cupola which has been the subject of much controversy. The cupola is much like the one surmounting Howard Castle in England, the ancestral home of the mother of that General Ridgely who was the builder of Hampton. Howard Castle was apparently the inspiration of Hampton and it is but natural that the cupola should have been included in the building plans of its Maryland prototype. There are those who insist, however, that the cupola was not a part of the original structure and was added many years after the house was built to gratify the whim of a quondam mistress of the estate.

The front portico is flagged with black and white marble and a further note of elaboration appears in the triangular pediments which crown the doors and windows. The front door opens into a dim hall, twenty-one by seventy feet, with stained glass windows at each end. Carved tables, sofas and chairs covered with brocades, were provided by the builder for its furnishing and stand there yet, a bit faded and blurred with the beauty of old things. On the walls hang masterpieces of the Seventeenth and

Eighteenth centuries, the works of Sassoferrato, Carlo Dolce and Thomas Sully, with the latter's portrait of the lovely Eliza Ridgely, daughter of the builder, painted in the artist's happiest mood, the focus of them all. Glowing in youth, for Eliza Ridgely was only fifteen when she posed for the great painter, the young girl stands in white muslin, a deep blue scarf around her shoulders, radiant against a golden harp. Her picture easily dominates the room and seems to smile encouragingly at the doughty colonials who bear her company.

Characteristically, the builder of Hampton loved the light and the flashing prisms of cut glass on the chandeliers recall the days when candles glowed in them every night, bringing out hidden fires in deep red mahogany and illuminating the highly bred faces of men and women who went to their graves a century and more ago. At the right of the entrance is the drawingroom, twenty-four feet by twenty-five, a very jewel of a room. For it the cabinet makers of the Chippendale, Hepplewhite and Sheraton periods were called upon to contribute the products of their handiwork. Great mirrors reflect the colors of Oriental rugs in this room and rare brocades and brilliantly painted blinds, deplorably unsigned—for they are unquestionably the work of a gifted artist—attract instant attention.

The drawingroom is wainscoted and provided with a light, denticular cornice. The chimney breast is panelled, with a wide, eared moulding framing the fireplace and an eared frame for the portrait which hangs above the mantel shelf. At the top of the frame a plain frieze is crowned by a triangular pediment ornamented with dentils. Eared mouldings also frame the windows and doors and ornamental cornices, showing a coat-of-arms, appear at the tops of the windows.

The music room beyond is festive with old and very lovely chintzes and is filled with ancient musical instruments of great

[139]

intrinsic value. Instantly the eye comes to rest upon that gilded harp beside which Eliza Ridgely stood to have her portrait painted and from the strings of which she drew decorous, plaintive melodies for the edification of the young blades who came, in the parlance of the day, to woo.

Down a flight of steps from the music room, in one of the wings, is the office where the Ridgelys keep their books and administer the affairs of Hampton. In use today as they were a hundred years ago, are chairs from the famous Belvedere, once the estate of the Howard family, and which were painted by Angelica Kaufman. None of the work of this inimitable artist is finer than these chairs which are priceless to the Ridgely family and which are, in every way, similar to those for which collectors of antiques willingly pay, upon occasion, a thousand dollars apiece.

At the left of the entrance is the family sitting room, another well proportioned apartment, homelike and inviting. Across another hall, sixteen feet wide, is the diningroom with a splendid portrait of George Washington, painted by Gilbert Stuart, and one of General John Eager Howard, hero of the battle of Cowpens. Over the mantelpiece hangs the portrait by Hesselius, a pupil of Sir Godfrey Kneller, of the builder of the mansion and there is one, also, of his wife, the only being in the world of whom the valiant gentleman is said to have been wholeheartedly afraid. And truly reason enough for Captain Ridgely's reputed state of mind appears in the flashing black eyes and set, determined expression of the erstwhile Rebecca Dorsey.

Many and peppery are the stories told of this strong-minded and willful woman, and many an uncomfortable hour did she inflict upon the gay, easy-going husband of hers who rode constantly to hounds, who could quaff a glass with the best of them, who took life as he found it and liked it well. When Hampton had been completed and the furnishings installed the captain determined to give a great party. There were many arguments on the subject between the host-to-be and his wife, and bitter scenes, but the captain was firm. He would celebrate the opening of the mansion and that right royally. He won the day and to Hampton his boon companions of the countryside were bidden to a magnificent stag party.

Men in red coats and hunting breeches were there, adding color to the assemblage, and others came in more sober array. Lights blazed in the crystal chandeliers and slaves poured bottle after bottle of imported wines into glasses which seemed to be always empty. Toast upon toast was drunk with expansive gestures and much oratory. No woman was present, however, to add to the gayety of the party for the excellent reason that the redoubtable Rebecca, a psalm-singing Methodist, had remained adamant to the end and, instead of presiding as her husband wished her to do, held a prayer meeting in the room above.

Rebecca, fortunately, was childless. Four years after the foundations of Hampton had been laid the builder of the house made his will, leaving to the termagant who bore his name her choice between the old home (built by his father on the estate—and where, they, too, were living at the moment) "with eight acres thereto adjoining for a garden"—or the new home then slowly moving forward to completion. In case she chose the latter he made—no one can say whether in retaliatory mood or not—no provision for any ground to go with it.

Only a few months after the rip-roaring party which opened the house took place Captain Ridgely died, the upper story of the house being still unfinished. His principal heir was his nephew, Charles Ridgely Carnan, with whom the captain had been on excellent terms and who changed his name, by permission of the State legislature, to Charles Carnan Ridgely in order to comply with his uncle's will and inherit the property.

Charles Carnan Ridgely wanted the new house and wanted it acutely. So did Rebecca—and she was in possession, the proverbial nine points of the law being obviously in her favor. Its large, well-appointed rooms were so admirably suited, from her point of view, not to the fine art of entertaining, but to the holding of prayer meetings. The nephew tried every means he could think of to induce his aunt-in-law to change her mind. He flattered and wheedled and begged without making the slightest dent in the resolute Rebecca's determination to keep the place. He even tried to bribe her to give it to him by promising to build her a house and surround it with a sizable number of acres which would also be hers if she would yield him the big house. But this ruse failed, too. Rebecca remained entrenched.

The young heir was defeated but he was also resourceful. He granted the new house possession of three hundred acres of cleared land "to the westward" and so circumvented the possibility that Rebecca might obtain possession of the gardens, directly south of the house. Having accomplished this much he turned his attention to the development of the terraces which had been planned by that easy-going cavalier, his uncle, who had located his home with special reference to a situation which so patently called for their beauty at the back of the house.

Directly in front of the vestibule on the southern facade of the house Charles Carnan Ridgely built a small, red-bricked court and then laid out a broad stretch of lawn which, with the constant care of generations, has become as deeply sodded as any to be found in England and which is girdled round with enormous evergreens. Splendid cedars, although obviously planted at a period much later than those in the garden below, cast dark, impalpable shadows over the walk of the upper terrace.

In his plans for the development of the gardens Charles Carnan Ridgely was lucky enough to enlist the services of one William Booth, a competent gardener of English birth, who flourished in the environs of Baltimore about the year 1810 and who had a splendid reputation among the earlier botanists of the country. Booth lavished all the skill at his command at Hampton and created a garden which has been celebrated by experts as the finest thing of its kind in the United States and which stretches away, terrace after terrace, from the big white house in diverting panorama.

On the first terrace, below the house, is a series of formal garden beds separated by low hedges of box. This terrace, with its solid ramp, bears mute evidence of the engineering skill and splendid workmanship in which the Revolution had trained many experts who passed on their knowledge to successive generations. The second terrace was laid out as a rose garden, with hundreds of varieties, many of them imported from Europe, blooming every June. With the development of the art of horti-culture and the consequent appearance of monthly roses, many new specimens have been added from time to time so that now, from May until the frost blasts the last bit of outdoor vegetation, roses bloom constantly in the gardens at Hampton.

Peonies in masses of color, blended from the faintest pink to a red so deep it seems almost black, cover the terrace below while the succeeding terraces, dotted with white marble urns, carefully spaced, stretch beyond.

Charles Carnan Ridgely came of a line of men who have been prominent in the affairs of Maryland ever since that pic-turesque little boat, the Assurance, arrived with a passenger list of "gentlemen" a few months after the landing of the Ark and the Dove. In the Assurance came Robert Ridgely, who settled in St. Mary's county and immediately became a person of distinction and influence in the affairs of the Colonial government. His honors culminated in his appointment by Charles Calvert, third Lord Baltimore, to be deputy secretary of Maryland.

Charles Ridgely, grandson of Robert, served with distinction in the Colonial wars, pushing his way rapidly upward to the rank of colonel. In all the important affairs of the colony his advice was sought and his counsel frequently prevailed.

Both Colonel Ridgely and his son Charles, then captain, were members of the Committee on Observation in 1774 and 1775. Both had seats in the constitutional convention of 1776 and contributed a wisdom born of experience to the unravelling of the tangled interests of the embryo nation. In all their counsels they had the association of John Eager Howard, maternal grandfather of Captain Charles Ridgely, who, during his life, held every office within the gift of the State and at whose funeral great men of the State and nation, led by President Adams, mourned.

Always, from the time when, as a wide-eyed youngster, he had curled up in the corner of the great fireplace of his father's home in St. Mary's and listened to glowing tales of the English countryside, that first Charles Ridgely had dreamed of reproducing in the New World an estate which would embody the glory and the spirit of the great manors his father described so graphically that the boy could see them without closing his eyes. In 1758 he acquired by patent from the Lord Proprietary four thousand acres of splendidly rolling, well-watered and excellently wooded land beyond Baltimore which was, at that time, a miserable, straggling huddle of scarcely a hundred houses.

To the original grant to his father Captain Charles Ridgely added two thousand acres more, so that he was able to drive twenty-seven miles in one direction on his own property. He then began the erection of the manor house. The exact date of its erection is a matter which has never been determined definitely, though the queerly formed leaden figures, 1783, set into the wall of the west wing, near the eaves, indicate that preparations for building must have been begun just after the Revolution.

For many years, though various persons had sought unsuccessfully to penetrate the secret, the identity of the builder or architect of Hampton was unknown. It was only a short while ago that an old account book unexpectedly came to light and revealed that one "John Howell designed and built Hampton and that as early as 1784 he and his family were established in a wing of the house while the rest of it was being built." This succinct statement indicates a complete reversal of the usual order of Colonial building in Maryland, for it was the custom of the early lords of the land to put up the central portion of their houses first, adding a wing or two later as the family increased or fortune permitted. Not infrequently a single wing was found sufficient and was all that was built.

Three years after the entry in the old account book had been made Howell died. Another entry shows, with the meticulous nicety which the Colonials bestowed upon their financial affairs, that the builder had received for his work by cash in kind £3,483, 3s. 6½d. With the costs of houses remotely resembling Hampton in magnificence running, in this year of grace, into hundreds of thousands of dollars the outlay upon Hampton seems extraordinarily meagre, but it was a big sum for those days.

According to tradition which has been handed down in the Ridgely family and which seems to be substantiated by both internal and external evidence, much of the work on the house was done by English prisoners got together in gangs from the Colonial government and by slaves and indentured servants. So strong and firmly knit is the joinery and so thoroughly British in spirit is the workmanship of the house that there is every reason to believe that Captain Ridgely found in the employment of this type of labor not only an advantageous business arrangement, but additional opportunity to secure verisimilitude to the English manor house of his desire.

At the time when Hampton was built the country side was virtually a trackless wilderness. The laborers went to work soon after daylight, but early in the afternoon they put down their tools because of the dangers from wolves which menaced on the way home. Not a man of them but must have heard that blood-curdling howl during the time he worked on the mansion, not one who did not picture himself a potential sacrifice to these rapacious beasts. But nothing of the sort, apparently, happened. Certainly there is no record of blood shed that this great house might come into being.

During the year which Charles Carnan Ridgely spent in developing the gardens at Hampton he found time to dabble in politics and make a successful campaign for governor of the State. In consequence of his activities in this direction the work on the gardens lagged. A few years later he died, but the unflinching Rebecca had preceded him to the grave.

Governor Ridgely's son John, who had married a wealthy girl of the same name but no traceable connection with the family, succeeded as the owner of Hampton. With the resources which the new Mrs. Ridgely's income provided, the place assumed new life. Distinguished persons from Europe as well as from America were entertained there, for the Ridgelys travelled extensively and were, incidentally, entertained by the Marquis de Lafayette at La Grange, on one of their trips to the continent, renewing in France an acquaintance begun during the French general's last visit to the United States.

Mrs. Ridgely was unsparing in her expenditures at Hampton

and was particularly interested in the gardens. As the result of her European impressions, however, some of the beauty of the upper terrace was destroyed when the box garden on the right was removed to make way for beds of coleus. The one on the left, luckily, was left undisturbed. One mistake she made, later to be rectified, was the planting of Norway spruces. It is evident now that Mrs. Ridgely had no idea of the growth to which these trees would develop, but as years passed they achieved immense proportions, cutting the garden in two. The remedy was found in cutting an archway through the lower branches of each pair of spruces, so that vistas of color and shadow were revealed, increasing the atmosphere of antiquity.

Today it seems extraordinary that Mrs. Ridgely should have been able to resist copying the marble balustrades of English gardens and should have preferred the effect obtained by the white marble vases, now gray with the rains and suns of a hundred years. On either side of the front portico Mrs. Ridgely placed orange and lemon trees in tubs, giving an exotic flavor to the place, and to this day, citrus trees grow there in the same position.

The road leading to Hampton drives straight north from Baltimore. Out past rows of ugly, two-story houses, past baroque "developments" through the village of Towson it runs until, of a sudden, the rolling fields of Hampton come into view. Decades drop away in a moment. An unpretentious gateway, a mile beyond Towson, marks the entrance to another world.

Turning sharply to the right from the smooth road which has replaced the old Dulany's Valley pike, the lane to the house leads between tall hedges of cedar, interspersed with stone pine. On one side of the road cattle graze in a green meadow. A colt maneuvres on unsteady legs and a couple of dogs, bound on some secret quest, hasten towards the woods.

There is an unwritten law in the Ridgely family by which the old house and a certain portion of the estate pass in unbroken line of succession from father to eldest son, making it in effect the only entailed estate in the country. Much of the six thousand acres which Captain Charles Ridgely owned has passed into other hands. Some of it has been sold to the city for development of the municipality's water supply and some has been divided among members of the family. Here and there a farm has been sold, but the Ridgelys still number their acres by the hundreds.

Today the family in residence at Hampton is headed by Captain John Ridgely, whose wife, Mrs. Helen West Ridgely, was the author of several books on Colonial Maryland and who, before her death in the spring of 1929, did much to preserve the beauties and traditions of the place. With Captain Ridgely, whose military title was bestowed for service in the State militia, lives his widowed daughter, Mrs. Clarence Fontaine Maury Leidy.

Five or six years before the death of Mrs. Ridgely a great celebration took place at Hampton when Captain Ridgely and his wife observed their golden wedding. Notables came from many cities to congratulate them upon the occasion. Foreign diplomats were present and the rooms were filled with throngs of men of affairs and women of fashion. Many of them were relatives, some of the fourth and fifth generation (for Americans are proud of even a remote connection with the Ridgelys of Hampton and seldom fail to mention the fact in their discussion of family trees) but most of them had come to pay tribute to a hospitable host and hostess upon an occasion so strongly in contrast with the first party ever held in the house.

In the graveyard at Hampton there is a brick and marble vault where rest six or seven generations of Ridgelys whose names are inscribed on a wall of marble slabs visible through the

HAMPTON

THE STEMMER HOUSE

Photo by Aubrey Bodine

iron grating of the door. In her description of this burial place of her husband's family Mrs. Helen West Ridgely, whose own grave was the last to be made there, wrote in her "Historic Graveyards of Maryland":

> "Periwinkle overruns the whole enclosure, and with the ancient ivy on the walls, enables the spot to retain its beauty through the changing seasons of the year."

A lovely picture!

* * *

Across the country, bordering another artery of travel from Baltimore, is the Stemmer mansion. There is little about the Philadelphia road as it makes its way, under the guise of Fayette Street, out of the eastern limits of the city and turns toward the north to invoke suggestions of hidden treasure. A more commonplace environment would be difficult to imagine as the road leads from a thickly populated section through a busy trucking country occupied by hardworking folk of foreign extraction, to the Golden Ring road, with here and there, at distant intervals, glimpses of the waters of the Patapsco to break the monotony of gingerbread houses and unimaginative surroundings.

The last place in the world is this where one might think of looking for a survival of the best building period in Maryland, and it is a fact that one might travel that way for years and never notice the old house standing within calling distance of the road. Between it and the road is a screen of trees and undergrowth, isolating the house completely from the mushroom community which has grown up around it. But turn from the macadamized road and cross the bridge which spans the narrow Stemmer's Run, and it is evident at once to the initiate that something unusual is not far distant. There is a hush in the air, a dignity about the little stream which makes its way between the lane and the public road. Then the old house appears, looking just as it did more than a century and a-quarter ago when it was built by the robust seaman who has come down to the knowledge of posterity only as "old Cap'n Stemmer."

The salmon brick walls are laid in American bond and worn by sun and rain to a color impossible to reproduce. In the main the house follows the three-part construction of a central building with wings which was so greatly favored by Marylanders of the late Colonial era, but certain modifications of this formula endow it with the personality which is the possession of houses not built in a day, and which could not have been "standardized" had anyone wished to do so.

Generous proportions characterize the square, central portion, the interest of which lies not merely in the unusual color of the brickwork, but also in the doorway reached by a single stone step mounted on a flagged terrace, almost obliterated by moss and grass. The doorway itself is not pretentious, but it does embody some of the most pleasing characteristics of the classical design. Fluted pilasters are set close to the walls of the house and crowned by Ionic capitals supporting the entablature and a triangular pediment with its ornamentation of dentils. The semicircular transom is simple, though not plain enough to be severe, and the width of the doorjambs betokens walls fully eighteen inches thick. The door itself is panelled to face the weather and reinforced on its inner surface by five-inch boards applied diamond-wise to the main axis. Massive brass locks with swinging handles provide security which is further augmented by a substantial iron bar swung directly across the door, an effective deterrent to the most determined of intruders.

One of the most interesting characteristics of the house is the size of the windows which are just enough smaller than those which present day architects would design for a house of this type to bring them instantly to the attention of the beholder. Twelve panes compose each of the upper and lower sashes— three rows of four panes each—and solid outside shutters, swung on wrought iron strap hinges, are there to provide additional privacy though, from all indications, many years have come and gone since these shutters were closed. The windows are arranged at well-placed intervals, two on each side of the doorway, with others to correspond in the second story, the space directly over the doorway also being occupied by a window like the others. From all appearances the glass in the windows all over the house is original, the quality of it being identical in each pane and totally different from the glass of today. One or two panes are cracked in the windows at the back of the house but not badly so, the slight flaws, like freckles on the nose of a pretty woman, adding to rather than detracting from the effect.

The roof is low and pitched, covered with split shingles put on with handmade nails and sloping down to a broad cornice over which it extends protectingly front and back. At the sides it stops short with the gable ends, where wide chimneys rise from inside the walls and betoken fireplaces which will take a cord stick with ease.

At the back of the house the facade differs markedly from the front and suggests an English dwelling rather than a Colonial American home. Straight and sheer is the wall, the ridgepoles of the wings being flush with the rear wall of the central portion of the house, so that the roof planes of the wings, which parallel those of the main roof in front, have no counterpart at the back. A thick growth of English ivy covers all of the right wing at the back and spreads over a large section of the main portion, encroaching here and there over the corner of a window. Over the doorway leading to the garden twines a wistaria vine.

A wide hallway, broken in middle distance by a wooden arch

with a keystone in the center, divides the house from front to back and opens through the rear door on a formal garden. No stairway breaks the line of the hall or offers rival interest but, on the other hand, the stairway has a room all to itself and rises in spindle balustrade and mahogany handrailings from the first floor to the attic. The room directly behind the diningroom and to the right of the hallway has no other reason for being than to serve the stairway.

Five steps constitute the first flight and lead to a landing floored with wide, ancient boards, directly under a window. There the stairway turns at right angles and ascends to another landing where it turns and reverses itself to the second floor. The flight to the attic duplicates that from the first floor in every detail and a narrow mahogany railing has been engaged into the wall parallel with the railing on the balustrade to provide comfort in descending as well as in ascending the stairs.

To the left of the hallway, on the first floor, is the drawing-room with a deep fireplace and a white, painted mantelpiece carved just enough to keep it from absolute plainness with a conventionalized star and groove design which is used on much of the woodwork throughout the house. As on the front door massive locks appear on the doors between the hall and drawing-room and the livingroom directly behind it. The square flags on the hearth have never needed to be replaced, although they have been warmed by the fires of more than a century.

Upstairs, in two of the bedrooms which are of a size to frame adequately the vast four-posters of our great-grandfathers, there is to be found a survival of the tastes and habits of the builder in strong iron rings imbedded firmly into the ceiling. "Cap'n" Stemmer was a seaman in the West India trade. There was salt in his blood and the tang of the spume in his nostrils. His step was accommodated to the pitch of a rolling vessel and he could find no rest in the smug, stationary beds of the landsman but must needs, even in his own home, swing himself at night into his hammock. And, apparently, his restlessness would not let one bedroom suffice, for the telltale rings are in adjoining rooms and have been allowed to remain there from generation to generation since the estate passed into other hands.

In the attic beams and joists of seasoned timber, now almost impregnable, are meticulously fitted together and fastened with a myriad of handmade nails. "Cap'n" Stemmer was prodigal with those nails in a day when they were as scarce as genuine Georgian houses are now. Today, to be sure, there is urgent need of a new roof to replace the present one which "lets in the sunshine and the rain," not to mention the skits of snow which sift through in winter and settle down on discarded maple and mahogany beds and broken, spindle-legged chairs which have been cast off and stored there, with bits of patchwork quilts and queer little brass-studded trunks which the Howards, who succeeded Captain Stemmer as owners of the place, carried with them when they went forth.

In the right wing is an old kitchen. The deep fireplace, sealed up within recent years but not otherwise disturbed, still holds the old fireirons which were built into it and whch served in the preparation of the first meal ever cooked in the house. The crane and pothooks are all ready for use at an instant's notice. The left wing, once completely detached, now is connected with the house by a doorway cut through from the livingroom.

No hint of the use to which this wing was put during Captain Stemmer's tenure is available, but later it served the late Robert Howard into whose possession the place came during the year 1800, as a store from which he supplied the considerable number of workmen whom he employed in the iron furnace on the place, as well as the laborers on his plantation, for his holdings at one time included some two thousand acres and necessitated the maintenance of a great number of slaves as well as ironworkers.

In front of the house spreads a broad lawn, shaded by locusts and Paradise trees. The lane leading from the road borders it on one side, curving to a semicircle in front of the house and out again on the opposite side of the lawn. Years ago the approach led straight, for almost a quarter of a mile, through the double avenue of locust trees with the house at the end of the vista. The grandfather of the present owners, however, succumbed to the vaunted charms of the Paradise tree, uprooted most of his locusts and cast them out to make room for his new passion. Many of the Paradise trees died, but the few which lived grew to a great size and add their shade to that of the remaining locusts.

When Robert Howard died, the estate descended to his children and still is in the family, although his great-grandchildren who recently inherited it do not live on the place. A tenant family of hardworking Poles occupies the house, to be removed, brick by brick, during the autumn of 1930 by a recent purchaser to another site.

*   *   *

The lone survivor within the city limits of Baltimore of the splendid houses which were threaded along the banks of the Patapsco river before the Revolution is Mount Clare, once the home of Charles Carroll, Barrister, who figured both in the civil and political development of the country and who used the affix, Barrister, to distinguish himself from his contemporaries of the same name.

Mount Clare stands in the center of well kept grounds, maintained now by the city as a park, which are bordered on one side by Columbia avenue, laid out on the line of the old post

Photo by Aubrey Bodine

STEMMER HOUSE: THE HALL DOOR

MOUNT CLARE
Home of Charles Carroll, Barrister

road between North and South and which, before the cavaliers landed in Maryland, was an old Indian trail. Six terraces, traversed by a file of poplars bordering a brick walk, stretch from the rear of the house in stately succession, terraces of which John Adams wrote after he had been the guest of the Barrister, "There is a beautiful garden and then a fall, another flat garden and then a fall, and so on down to the river." The aspect of the place as it appeared then is preserved in an oil painting which hangs in the hall of the old house. Three horsemen are represented, the figures being those of General Washington, commander-in-chief of the American forces, his aide-de-camp, the Marquis de Lafayette, and their host, Charles Carroll, Barrister. The three stand with their mounts near a group of elms, some of which still are in existence.

The front of the house, which was built in 1754 and is the oldest Colonial structure in Baltimore, is distinguished by a portico which has a flagged floor of gray and white marble and round, smooth columns supporting an entablature adorned with classic triglyphs and the nails of the Parthenon. The double entrance doors show eight panels and open into a hall interesting for its well proportioned arch and wide stairway adorned by a heavy mahogany rail and a half-handrail let into the panelling of the wall. Two landings break the flight of the stairway between the first floor and the second, where the balustrade makes an arc at the end of the upper hall before continuing its way to the attic.

On the lower landing is a tall grandfather's clock, with a brass dial and flame finials, which stood there in the day of the barrister. At the second landing, against the end wall of the house, there is a door the purpose of which can only be surmised. There is no sign on the exterior of the house of a doorway on this spot, though such an aperture may well have been there only to be closed later and completely obliterated by the successive coats of paint which cover the bricks. The most reasonable explanation of this apparently blind door seems to be that it once connected with an exterior stairway used by slaves as they came and went to their duties on the second floor and so were prevented from being too much in evidence in the living rooms of the house.

To the right of the entrance hall is the little office and opposite the front door is another opening into the drawing room on a line with a third door which afforded a view, when all of them were opened, through the house and over the garden to the river, now entirely filled in at this spot and occupied by factories. Another door, panelled and provided with a round, foliated transsom, is cut into the end wall of the drawingroom and formerly gave access to the side lawn. This door now forms the entrance to a modern wing. The walls of the drawingroom are finished with wide, bevelled panels in perfect condition and over the fireplace is an Adam mantelpiece showing a classic urn in the center panel, with festoons on each side and a line of honeysuckle down the end panels. The narrow shelf rests upon two courses of denticular moulding.

In the diningroom the panelling is similar to that of the drawingroom, the fireplace being slightly smaller but provided also with an Adam mantelpiece. Beside the fireplace two china closets are built in, with arched tops and wing doors, but examination of one of them will disclose that its back, instead of being plastered, is composed of rough boards, painted over. Probably, when the house was built, there was a doorway here instead of a china closet, opening out upon a brick walk which led to the kitchen in its own building a short distance from the main house.

On the second floor the most beguiling of conceits is to be found in the shape of the powder closet which is reached from one of the bedrooms. Into its recesses the Carroll ladies and their feminine guests retired to have their hair besprinkled with the white dust which was necessary to a fashionable coiffure and there the application could be made without having the dust applied also to all of the furniture in the room.

From invoices which have come down from the day of the "chyurgeon" Dr. Charles Carroll, father of the Barrister, who built the house and furnished it, it is evident that the Carrolls lived in great luxury at the Georgia Plantation, as they called the estate. Imports were made of Turkey carpets, looking glasses in gilt frames, dressing tables of mahogany, "one four-wheeled Post chariot made light and fashionable without a box, but strong and neat, with plain, simple strong springs—lined with green cloth, painted and ornamented fashionably with the enclosed coat-of-arms, and strong good harness for a pair of horses, the crest on brass plates for the harness, not for travelling into the country, but for town use, as they answer much better than heavy chariots as our horses are but small and the ground deep and sandy." Dr. Carroll himself went about in "a London suit of blue cloth, made in the French fashion, lined with double gold lace" which cost "about ten guineas."

At some time after the house was built a wing was thrown out at one side, contrasting incongruously with the central building. When the house came into the possession of the city this wing was torn down and two others, conforming to the architectural plan, were built. The Maryland Branch of the Colonial Dames of America, under the leadership of the late Mrs. William Reed, was permitted to take over the trust of preserving the house and has succeeded in restoring to it many of the actual furnishings which were there before the Revolution.

Dr. Carroll's family, unlike that of Charles Carroll, the Signer, was Protestant in religion. Like the Signer, however, Dr. Carroll was a patriot and when the serious uprising of 1738 took place against the British rule, Dr. Carroll was a representative of the city of Annapolis in the Maryland Legislature.

But it was Dr. Carroll's son, the Barrister and not the "chyrurgeon" himself who engraved the family name deeply into the history of the country. Educated in Spain and at Eton and Cambridge, he entered for the law at the Inns of Court, (occupying the Middle Temple Garden Court, Library Staircase Number 2) and returned to Maryland, one of the ablest and most brilliantly educated men in the colonies. Immediately he assumed a position of leadership in the imbroglio which already was beginning to seethe. He was chosen to serve on innumerable committees which called for the ability to think clearly and forcefully to express public sentiment. He wrote the Declaration of Rights adopted by the Convention of Maryland held on the third of November, 1776. He also wrote the greater part of the first constitution and framed the form of government for Maryland. He served as a member of the Convention of Delegates which met at Annapolis in May, 1776, and was a member of the Council of Safety to which he was elected three times. When Maryland became a State he was elected a member of the first Senate and declined the appointment of first chief justice of the General Court. A family tradition accounts for the omission of his name from the list of signers of the Declaration of Independence by the fact that he was confined to his room at the time of the signing by an attack of gout.

Almost to the moment when relations between the colonies and Great Britain definitely were broken Charles Carroll, Barrister, refused to believe that separation from the mother country was to be the final goal and when Sir Robert Eden, the last royal governor of Maryland, who shared with him a keen desire to perpetuate friendly relations, accepted the Barrister's invitation to a notable dinner at the latter's Annapolis home, the two discussed the future over the last feast at which the erstwhile friends ever sat together.

But when the Revolution finally was declared no more ardent supporter of the Colonial cause could have been found than this former loyalist who spent his days and nights in council and committee meetings convened to devise ways and means of repelling the British men of war which constantly menaced from the Chesapeake. George Washington frequently was his guest at Mount Clare, the room in which he slept being furnished today almost exactly as it was during the Revolution.

There still exists at Mount Clare a long, subterranean way which formerly led to the Patapsco. An old story has it that this was one of the exits which were used by the townspeople of Baltimore when, by order of the town authorities, they placed their women and children on board the ships in the harbor after Braddock had been defeated by the French and Indians. There was stark terror among the little population of Baltimore town that day, for the savages had come within thirty miles of their homes after devastating completely the northwestern part of the State. Within recent years the entrance to this little passage has been walled up for safety's sake, together with a mysterious little chamber, twelve feet by ten, near the house, the use of which, probably, never will be known.

The Carrolls of Mount Clare trace descent from the old kings of Ireland and the "chyrurgeon" corresponded constantly with Sir Daniel O'Carroll who had retained the prefix to his name and had, apparently, shared in the expatriation of Dr. Carroll. The physician referred frequently in his letters to Ballebrit, Leap and Castletown, declaring that he did not expect to inherit a foot of this land or, for that matter, of any other part of Ely O'Carroll, which was an age-old possession of the clan.

[159]

But if he was disinherited at home Dr. Carroll had little cause to repine. After emigrating to America he became exceedingly wealthy. He acquired title to immense landed estates which included in addition to Mount Clare (the Georgia Plantation) tracts on the Eastern Shore, others in Anne Arundel county and still others in and near Baltimore Town. Mount Clare he had purchased to obtain the iron ore which was abundant there in that day and which, after it had passed through the furnaces of the Baltimore Company Iron Works, formed a fruitful source of revenue. In addition to this, the land along the Patapsco was put to use as a shipyard and there several ships were built for Dr. Carroll.

* * *

Across the city from Mount Clare, in what is now a fetid and sordid slum, stands another fine old house, eloquent of the last days of Charles Carroll of Carrollton, and of the famous Caton sisters, his granddaughters, whose international marriages, together with their beauty and charm, made them known in both Europe and America as "the three Graces." Like a monarch deposed and discredited, but lordly still, the old house rears three stories high, with an attic, at Lombard and Front streets where it was built in 1800 by Charles Carroll of Carrollton for his daughter, Mary, when she became the bride of Richard Caton. Not long after their marriage the Signer went there to live with the Catons, and there he spent the greater part of the last thirty years of his life. From this house he went out in 1824 to meet Lafayette when the French patriot landed at Fort McHenry on his second visit to Baltimore and on Washington's birthday, in 1832, a great civic parade passed the house to be reviewed by the aged Signer, who stood at a front window on the second floor for the purpose. In this house, on November 14 of that same year, he died. The house is of the double type, fronting fifty feet on Lombard street, with a depth of one hundred feet on Front street. From the center hall, to the right of the entrance, a mahogany-railed staircase sweeps to the top floor, all that is left of the once splendid finish of the interior. In the cellar are the remains of a splendid wine cellar and tradition says that here, also, was a small arsenal which the provident Signer had prepared for use in case his British majesty should overstep the line beyond which the vigorous rebel had vowed he would not permit the king to go after the Revolution. The old man is said to have kept a sharp eye on all incoming vessels, which he could observe easily from the house, and to have had also in readiness an underground passage to the river through which to escape should flight become necessary.

Most of the social traditions of the place, however, revolve about the Caton girls who were born in the house and grew there to womanhood, rather than about Charles Carroll of Carrollton who already was growing old when he went there to live and preferred to sit in the shade of a sycamore in the garden rather than to take part in the gayeties which are associated with the mansion. In the drawingroom Robert Patterson, brother of the famous Betsy who married Jerome Bonaparte, became the husband of Mary Caton, eldest of "the three Graces" who, after his death, became the bride of the Marquis of Wellesley, brother of the Duke of Wellington. The American marquise, the story goes, made such excellent use of her wit in her English home that she was more than able to hold her own with the British nobility who found frequent occasion to deride her American birth. Another of the Caton "Graces" became Lady Harvey and, later, the Duchess of Leeds; a third, Elizabeth, became Lady Stafford. The fourth sister, Emily, married a MacTavish.

Upon the death of the Signer the house became the property of the MacTavishes. The last of the line, Miss Emily MacTavish, in 1856, turned it over to the Sisters of Mercy who occupied it until 1871 when it was sold to Jacob Seeger. Many years before that, however, the neighborhood had ceased to be fashionable and gradually it degenerated into a place of swarming tenements. Heedless, uneducated immigrants, ignorant of the significance of the house, took possession. Unkempt babies sprawled in the doorway and the memorial tablet, which had been placed by the Daughters of the Revolution on one of the side walls, was so mutilated that it had to be removed.

Even then, however, a number of Baltimoreans concerned with the history of their city did not wholly lose interest in the place but, in 1910, sought to have the State, through the Legislature, appropriate an amount sufficient to restore the house and maintain it. The bill was passed, but the governor vetoed it. Still the antiquarians persisted in their efforts to save the house from destruction and finally succeeded in inducing the Baltimore city fathers to buy it. For a number of years afterward it was used as a school for vocational training but the school subsequently was removed to larger quarters and now the old house is alone with its cobwebs and its memories of vanished pomp.

* * *

In the northern reaches of the city, on the new grounds of the Johns Hopkins University, stands still another Carroll mansion, known as Homewood and unquestionably the most beautiful of the various houses built by Charles Carroll of Carrollton. It, too, was a wedding present, built for his son Charles, who married Elizabeth Chew, daughter of Chief Justice Benjamin Chew, of Philadelphia. The wedding took place in 1800, but the house, which is celebrated among architects as one of the most gracious examples of the Georgian manner in America, was not completed for a number of years afterward.

Homewood crowns a steep terrace and stands at an angle to the wide, busy boulevard to which its grounds slope down. Its

HOMEWOOD
Built by Charles Carroll of Carrollton

Photo by Aubrey Bodine

WHITE HALL

softly colored walls, with deftly placed marble panels above the windows, and its worn stone steps speak the language of an age when laced and furbelowed ladies sat on stiff, unyielding sofas and graciously permitted the attentions of young men whose long, delicate hands toyed with jewelled snuffboxes; when people had manner as well as manners and when suavity was an excellent thing.

A perfectly proportioned portico, with slim Ionic pillars reaching to the eaves, and a frail looking iron railing outlining the wide steps, appears before a doorway surmounted by a beautiful fanlight. A wide hallway extends through the house to the rear door under its fanlight of tracery, which is distinctly more delicate than that over the entrance door. On one side of the hall is an enormous drawingroom, with windows from floor to ceiling, and at the left is the diningroom, eloquent of hospitality. Behind each of these rooms is a passageway separating the diningroom from the music room and the drawingroom from the bedrooms.

Corridors connect the central portion of the building with wings so proportioned that they lend an air of graciousness as well as of dignity to the building. One wing contained the culinary apartments, for by the time Homewood was built the kitchen no longer occupied a separate building in Maryland, the other being used as a library and office. A curious little cupboard is placed in one wall of the latter, high above a man's head. The use for such a contrivance is not instantly apparent. It may have been merely a repository for old account books, or it may have been a convenient place in which to keep a bottle of spirits.

The most radical departure from the usual Georgian house of the Homewood period is to be found in the absence of an ornate stairway leading to an upper floor. All of the living rooms and

[163]

bedrooms are on the first floor and only a tiny, ladder-like stair, concealed between the walls, leads to the second floor.

In its scholastic environment the old Homewood house seems just a little lonely. True, its erstwhile occupants were men of learning and culture, but they were, more particularly, lovers of a certain insouciance of life, a quality which has little place among the cloisters. Some magical touch is needed to bring it back to life, though sometimes, at night, when the moon is right, shadowy forms seem to the imaginative to flit airily up the worn steps, through the panelled door and into the stately rooms,—forms that seem to smile quietly to themselves as if, in death, they had learned the secret of life,—and found it all very amusing.

CHAPTER TEN

A real triumph of Colonial building is White Hall, the most pretentious house erected in Maryland before the Revolution. Nor has any other house in the State a history more interesting than this overseas home of the royal governor, Horatio Sharpe, who presided over the fortunes of the Free State in the days when the fields sprouted with gold in the form of tobacco and men of wealth vied with each other to excel in the magnificence of their homes and splendor of their retinues.

Only a few miles distant from the incessantly travelled road which leads from Baltimore to Annapolis, White Hall is as remote from the hurrying populace as if it were walled in by high mountains instead of being separated from it by a short stretch of cultivated, level land. Few who pass along the boulevard, unless they know the secret, even suspect its existence.

Governor Sharpe spent his winters in Annapolis which had become the capital after St. Mary's had been abandoned, but his dreams, almost from the moment of his arrival in the Palatinate, were of a country house which would form a worthy background for the representative in Maryland of His British Majesty. To such a house, it is said, he hoped to take as his bride, the winsome Mary Ogle, who became the heroine of a romance for all the world like the storied wooing of Miles Standish. And between the years 1750 and 1760 Governor Sharpe proceeded to bring at least a part of his dream to earth in White Hall.

For its setting he chose the green peninsula which pushes out into the waters of Meredith's Cove and White Hall creek at the place where they unite to flow into Chesapeake Bay above Annapolis. A thousand acres were included in the tract Governor Sharpe purchased from the widow of Nicholas Greenbury but, bit by bit, the land has been sold until there remains only about sixty acres.

From the landward side the approach to the house leads through a long lane laid out at right angles to the public road and bordered during the regime of Governor Sharpe by a double row of poplars. These trees gave to the driveway an air of stateliness and formality, and though many of them have been laid low by the storms which sweep up the Chesapeake Bay and its tributaries, those that are left serve to suggest a picture of the days when Governor Sharpe rode out in his coach, with six outriders galloping ahead.

The driveway stops short about two hundred yards from the house, giving way to a broad and still closely clipped lawn. From the grass a low flight of steps leads to the wide portico, with four enormous Corinthian marble columns, painted white, supporting a plain entablature surmounted by an ornamented triangular pediment. The portico, in all probability, was added years after White Hall was built, for entrance porches of this type were rare in the colony before the Revolution.

The doorway is massive. A semi-circular transom tops the door, with its broad panels and brass lock into which the great key often was turned by the governor's negro body servant after a party which had lasted until the candles burned down to their sockets and the host's supply of wines had been seriously and generously sampled.

The back of the house is more interesting architecturally than the front. The doorway is similar, but leads to an open porch with steps descending on each side to a landing from which they proceed at right angles to the ground. No windows appear on the second floor above the doorway, but in the ends of the main

THE DRAWINGROOM AT WHITE HALL
The cornice repeats the decorative note of the fireplace

WHITE HALL: ENTRANCE HALL,
LAND FRONT

"GREATE ROOM," WHITE HALL

Photo by Pickering

structure are curious bull's eye windows, and in the connecting wings on the first floor a row of white bull's eyes look out over the gardens. Particularly well disposed is the low, hipped roof, conforming with hipped roofs on the end wings, each of which converges to a central chimney. A modern covering of tin, painted a bright red, is the only incongruity anywhere apparent.

The interior of White Hall is but one room deep in the main portion. The front door opens into the state reception room, beyond question one of the most elaborate Colonial interiors in the country. The door frame establishes the decorative note for the room, with fluted pilasters ending in boldly carved Corinthian capitals and supporting a triangular pediment enriched with modillions, dentils and small foliage carvings, the whole in relief against an apparently wider background which it seems almost, but not quite, to cover. The white walls are carried up to a cornice which fairly drips with carving, enriched modillions and Lesbian leaves in relief. Above the cornice the coved ceiling flattens out and hideous, satyr-like faces, carved in black mahogany, are set into each of the four corners, grinning interminably down on the foibles of the mortals who pass beneath them.

In the centre of the ceiling, in a square panel, is a carved golden eagle. Four lofty windows furnish the light for the room, two in front and two at back, deeply recessed and set in frames carved with small foliage, egg and dart and bead and reel designs. Lateral consoles, carved with acanthus leaves, rest on the chair rail.

Beneath three of the four windows stand armchairs said to have been there since the days of Governor Sharpe. Portraits darkening with age and curious old prints hang against the walls. Ancient tables and chairs, a grandfather's clock and a spinnet, all survivals of the regime of Governor Sharpe, preserve an authentic picture of a cavalier Maryland house.

The doorways from the state room into the diningroom and into the drawingroom are the last word in Colonial decoration. Each has an architrave with ears outlined with rococo and bead-and-reel carving. The frieze is entirely covered with foliage and scroll *motifs,* alternately placed, and surmounted by a denticular cornice which is both light and graceful. The doors themselves are of panelled mahogany, with the bevelling outlined in egg and dart moulding.

In the diningroom, at the right of the great salon, carved window frames provide the decorative interest, together with the deep recesses of the doors which show how thick and sturdy are the walls of the house. The small fireplace in the right wall seems to modern eyes a pitifully inadequate means of providing against even a moderate chill but, since Governor Sharpe spent his winters in Annapolis, it probably was used only on cool days in the spring and fall. Within recent years the diningroom woodwork has been happily freed of the paint which obscured much of the carving for at least a century.

Governor Sharpe's portrait hangs in the same room, showing that astute person, who is said to have had much to do with the famous Stamp Act, in the costume of a cavalier with lace ruffles covering the strangely effeminate hands. The portrait is believed to be from the brush of Hesselius.

To the left of the salon is the withdrawing room, also achieved through a deeply recessed door and duplicating the proportions and decorations of the diningroom, with the exception of the fireplace, which is much larger. An elaborate cornice also offers an opportunity in this room for the display of more carving of the same character as that which appears in the salon.

The stairs at White Hall are useful rather than ornamental. They have been hidden away in the wings like unpleasant necessities rather than as possibilities of architectural interest, one flight going up beside the diningroom and one beside the with-drawing room. Beyond the stairs the remainder of the right wing is given over to pantries and kitchens, but in the left wing the arrangements are more formal. When the stairs have been passed a small connecting wing has been given over to a hallway from which a door, placed about midway its length, opens upon the front lawn. On the walls of the corridor hang yellowed prints and historic documents stained with years.

There is a quality in the decoration of White Hall which indicates to the student of such things either the overwhelming absorption of the artist in his work or else the motivation of some vital force, some great end to be gained through the minute, sharply defined leaves and scrolls which appear everywhere it is possible, within the dictates of good taste, to use them. Both of these qualities, it is conceivable, were combined in the decoration of White Hall, for the story goes that all of its carving was done by a proud young redemptioner who had been shipped out to Maryland to expiate some untold crime and who instantly at-tracted the interest of Governor Sharpe because of his youth and artistic appearance.

The boy, according to the legend, would tell nothing of him-self but the governor who, like many another crusty bachelor, seems to have been an arrant sentimentalist, took him into his household and kept an eye on him. When he discovered his protege's talent at wood carving he set him at once to the task of decorating White Hall and promised him his freedom when the work was done. The young redemptioner agreed to the bar-gain and worked from daylight until his eyes burned at night, enriching doors and windows, baseboards and chair rails, cor-nices and mantelpieces, with designs adapted from those he found in the architects' guides sent over from England. The work took several years and during that time Governor Sharpe conducted

[169]

from Maryland an inquiry into the crime for which the boy had been transported. But life, as so often happens, was ironic and when the work was finished and freedom within the grasp of the artist, whose name never has been revealed, the boy died from tuberculosis. A few days later proofs came from England that he was innocent.

None but the best of materials went into the building of White Hall. The window frames and sills are of solid walnut and the floors of native pine are laid with hand-wrought nails. Every bit of timber was hewn out at the saw mill and the bricks were moulded in the brickyard which the governor maintained for the benefit of himself and his friends at Annapolis. As was usual on large plantations, the house was built with dungeons for the solitary confinement of offending servants and slaves.

Governor Sharpe seems to have been both hospitable and generous. Several times a week a boatload of young people would set sail from Annapolis by way of Greenbury's Point for White Hall and there would celebrate to the queen's taste. The governor's cellars were filled with Maryland Burgundy and good Madeira and there is a tradition that, upon one occasion, Mary Ridout, the comely young sister of the governor's secretary, danced with George Washington in the withdrawing room while Benjamin Franklin played the tune on the musical glasses. Washington often was a guest at White Hall, although the time came when relations were considerably strained between the young Colonial and the royal governor, and though none of the recognized biographers of Franklin refer to any visit from him to Annapolis, the tradition maintaining this story persists.

Governor Sharpe delighted in the life of a country gentleman. His gardens were his special pride. In them he grew not only the trees, flowers and shrubs which were indigenous to the country, but sent abroad constantly for seeds and scions of shrubs and rare flora. A neat white bar fence made a semi-circle around the garden from which the Locust Walk, the Willow Walk, and the Crepe Myrtle Walk led down to the water.

From the time he came to Maryland until 1768, when he was replaced by Sir Robert Eden, who had married the sister of the Lord Proprietary, Governor Sharpe was on the most intimate terms with Lord Baltimore. Constantly from White Hall went consignments to his lordship of homemade wine, smoked hams, quail, partridges, and wild turkey. Indian scalps and rattlesnakes in which Lord Baltimore seems to have been much interested also were included in the gifts shipped to him overseas. The Lord Baltimore, in his turn, was equally generous with his deputy and is known to have sent him, in response to the governor's expressed wish, "some dogs and hares" which had been "ketched" by the steward. In acknowledging the gift Governor Sharpe wrote that "unluckily all the Hares, except a Leash, died at sea, and one of them, also, the day after they were brought hither, I am much afraid the surviving brace which I have turned out at my farm are affected with some disorder."

The province of Maryland prospered exceedingly under Governor Sharpe's rule. He governed, according to a letter written by William Eddis in a voluminous correspondence from Annapolis where he was collector of customs during the pre-Revolutionary period, "with honor to himself, satisfaction to the people and fidelity to his sovereign."

Every day or so he held conferences with Judge Borflet (Bordley?) at Annapolis on the best methods of improving agriculture and developing home industries. When there was no further use for the old saw mill he converted it into a loom and spinning factory where wool from his famous flock of

South Devon sheep and cotton and flax were spun and then woven into clothing for "my people."

When he returned to private life he went to White Hall to live permanently and devoted all of his attention to the estate. In 1769 the aforesaid William Eddis wrote to a friend in England, "Colonel Sharpe, the late governor, possesses a most delightful retirement . . . his house is on a large scale, the design is excellent, and the apartments well fitted up and perfectly convenient. The adjacent grounds are so judiciously disposed that utility and taste are everywhere united. . . . This gentleman does not seem to have any idea of returning to his native land but appears inclined to spend the residue of his days in Maryland."

But William Eddis was wrong. In 1773 Governor Sharpe went back to England and never returned to his home in a land which changed so greatly after his departure. Before he died in 1790 he sent from London to his one-time secretary and constant friend, John Ridout, his power of attorney, with orders to sell White Hall. The sale took place as directed and the estate was purchased by Benjamin Ogle, father of John Ridout's wife, whose hand the governor had sought in marriage soon after coming to America and for whom, it is said, he built his pretentious house. Two days later the estate was reconveyed, in consideration of the identical sum he had paid for it, from Benjamin Ogle to John Ridout and it remained in the Ridout family until 1895 when it was purchased by the late Mrs. W. G. Story, wife of General Story, U. S. A., to whose son it descended.

CHAPTER ELEVEN

A city as sophisticated as Paris, inhabited by men whose wit and learning recalls the scholars of Athens, replete with luxury and the sole center of what little art there was in America was Annapolis before the Revolution. The scene was curiously theatric. Aristocrats in elaborately curled perukes walked the streets laid out by Sir Christopher Wren, their jewelled swords clattering by their sides and threatening to trip them at every step. The stiffened skirts of their coats stood out like sails in the wind and their silken hose disappeared beneath velvet breeches fastened at the knee with jewelled buckles.

When they had a distance to go they travelled in sedan chairs painted in cyphers, festoons of flowers and embellished with coats-of-arms, the motive power being supplied by negro slaves in livery. Or, if their journey were longer, they rode in coaches drawn by four or six horses, with outriders to clear the way and afford protection.

Social distinctions were rigidly drawn, centering about the person of the royal governor and the "court circle." Among the aristocrats there was scarcely a family which was not allied by ties of blood to the ruling class in England, families of great wealth whose cultivation of mind and discrimination of taste equalled that of their kindred across the Atlantic. Men had their coffee houses and their clubs, their portrait painters and silver-smiths. They sent their sons to schools such as King William's, established by royal patronage in 1696, and the forerunner of the present St. John's College; or placed them under the tutelage of the county clergy, the Rev. Thomas Cradock at Garrison

Forest, the Rev. Thomas Bordley of Cecil, or the father of Charles Willson Peale at Chestertown in Kent. Later the graduates of these schools went abroad to study at Oxford or Cambridge, or to read law at the Inns of Court in London.

Social intercourse among members of the exclusive "set" was free and delightful, but the barriers were high and rigid. No menial or person of low degree was permitted to set foot within the confines of the area about the State House Circle and the waterfront, when the aristocrats promenaded streets which bore the names of King, Prince George, and Duke of Gloucester—names by which they are called to this day. On Duke of Gloucester street stood the Ball Room, built in 1764 from the proceeds of a lottery and described by an early commentator who added "when it is illuminated it shows to great advantage."

"The walls are decorated by full length likenesses of Charles, Lord Baltimore," he continued, "and portraits of several of the former governors. At the lower extremity is the supper room which was formerly the revenue office of the province. At the upper end is a card room for use of the gentlemen who may choose to enjoy the 'circulation of the party-colored gentry' without having their attention diverted by the sound of the violin and the evolutions of youthful performers."

Balls were a favorite diversion among the early Annapolitans, most of whom spent the summer months on their tobacco plantations in the country and came to the city for the winter, determined to pack into a scant half-year all the gayety which their resilient natures demanded. Such affairs afforded the women opportunities for a display of feminine vanity and magnificence which never failed to astonish visitors from other colonies or from over the sea, and the toilettes they made were the result of hours of preparation. Their hair they wore built up (by the aid of French barbers retained at 1000 crowns a year) into pyramids, upon which they placed a turban of silk or flowers or a great feather headdress. Jewelled stomachers and tightly laced "stays" compressed waistlines into incredibly small compass and trains of taffeta, sometimes as much as fifteen yards in length, could be turned only with the assistance of a maid.

The second theatre building in America was erected at Annapolis in 1752 for the entertainment of its citizens and the wealthy planters who had no town houses but came to Annapolis for the Assemblies. The plays of William Shakespeare found high favor, but the crowds were considerably larger when the bill was "The Beggars' Opera," "The Orphans," or "The Lying Valet." Concerning the performances William Eddis wrote to a friend in England, "My pleasure and my surprise were therefore excited on finding performers in this country equal at least to those who sustain them at home."

Races were held in Annapolis from the time anything is known of the town, but the first one to be publicly advertised was announced in the *Maryland Gazette* "to take place on the 30th and 31st day of May, 1745, to be run at John Conner's in Anne Arundel county. First day's purse, £10; second, £5; to be run for by any horse, mare or gelding (Old Ranter and Limber Sides excepted) to carry 115 pounds, three heats, the course 2 miles, entrance money 15 shillings the first day and ten shillings the second day."

Within two years the first full-fledged jockey club in the country had come into existence, including in its membership, according to an account in the *Maryland Gazette* of its organization, "many principal gentlemen of this and in the adjacent provinces, many of whom, in order to encourage the breed of this noble animal, imported from England at a very great expense horses of high reputation."

Meets were held spring and fall. Subscription purses of one

hundred guineas constituted the maximum rewards to the winner and the race course was located "in that part of the city just beyond Mr. Severe's blacksmith shop, embracing a circle of one mile, taking in all that portion of the town now built up." The races lasted a week and were attended by the wives and daughters of the club members, as well as by the members themselves. The courts were adjourned and schools dismissed when the racing season arrived, in order to give everyone an opportunity to attend, and frequently fine gentlemen from Virginia arrived after spending a week or more on the way and were known, in more cases than one, to have staked their negroes on the result of a single race.

Washington frankly delighted in Annapolis. He came frequently, stayed a week or more at a time, and spent money with a lavish hand. He records among his diary notations for the year 1762 an expenditure of £2, 10 shillings, 11 pence, with 17 shillings as expenses for his servants. He bought "sundry tickets" for the play and "sundry tickets for the Ball." He paid £25 for two boxes of claret and £50 for a horse. He lost £1 6 shillings on the races and made numerous other expenditures, including £4, 4 shillings for a hat for his stepdaughter, Miss Custis. As an offset to all this extravagance he deducted the sum of £13, "won at cards."

The following year the races took place two weeks earlier than usual but Washington was there despite the change in schedule. The trip from Mount Vernon was made in his postchaise, with four horses and a retinue of servants. This time, however, he was more restrained in his expenditure of money, the result, probably, of the presence of young "Jacky" Custis who accompanied his stepfather for the first time to the track.

Nothing, not even the most biting winter weather, served to depress the ebullience of the carefree gentry of the city. The rigors of such a winter as that of 1765, which was set down in the *Maryland Gazette* for that year as one of the most severe ever known in the colony, served only to stimulate them to new hilarities and "on Monday, February 5, a very merry set of gentlemen had a commodious tent erected on the ice between the town and Greenbury's Point where they had an elegant dinner, &c., and in the afternoon diverted themselves with dancing of reels on skates and divers other amusements."

Constant participants in this brilliant social life were the Brices who lived in the great house fronting on East street, with grounds extending the entire block from King George street to Prince George street, and with whom Washington frequently stopped when he came to Annapolis. This house is palatial in its proportions and remarkable in its effect of arrogance. Its pitched roof has a slope of 40 degrees, with two huge, daringly high chimneys rising flush from the gable ends of the central portion to dominate completely the entire section of Annapolis in which the house stands. Thin, bold chimneys rise from the gable ends of the wings, at right angles to those on the main entrance.

The Brice house is one of the oldest of the sturdy old mansions to be found still standing in Annapolis. It either was built or purchased almost as soon as it had been completed by Thomas Jenings, who was a brother of Sarah, first Duchess of Marlborough. In 1745 Jenings presented it to his daughter, Juliana, as a wedding gift when she became the bride of Colonel James Brice.

As if to emphasize its superiority the house stands high on a terrace above the street, with a high basement making the central portion appear still more disdainful. The facade of the central portion is built entirely of header bricks, the kind which measure four inches by nine—except for the flat arches over the windows, which are formed of brick as thin as those the Romans laid at York in England—and are even and smooth in texture. The jointing is very fine. It is evident that the work was done by trained artisans who employed a fine tool and deployed their cement of sifted sand and pulverized seashells so well that it forms a line scarcely more than a quarter of an inch wide between the bricks. A moulded water course outlines the basement story and four rows of headers in projection make the belt course. At the top of the walls a wide and richly carved cornice with ears rests at the corners upon consoles of moulded brick, and a triple window with fluted and reeded columns separating the sections and displaying the same decorative motifs, appears above the carved door frame.

The rococo decorations of the interior assign the house definitely to the first half of the Eighteenth century. The entrance hall has a stairway of San Domingo mahogany rising opposite the door, its lightly moulded handrail glowing with deep fires and curling on the lower step about a finial scarcely larger than a fine walking stick. The spindles of the balustrade are square and the end of each tread is carved with a rococo scroll under which runs a line of continuous Greek fret. The wall opposite the balustrade is wainscoted and finished with a half handrail of mahogany.

The walls of the "greate" room and diningroom are wainscoted above the chair rail with plaster panelling, said to be the finest in the country. The panels in the "greate" room are large and raised, of equal dimensions, while those on the diningroom vary in size. The cornices, too, are of plaster, the one in the "greate" room being provided with modillions showing an acanthus ornament alternating with rosettes, enriched mouldings with dentils appearing above and below. A pulvinated frieze

BRICE HOUSE

Photo by Pickering

PARLOR, BRICE HOUSE

Photo by Pickering

Photo by Pickering

DOORWAY, HAMMOND-HARWOOD HOUSE

Photo by Pickering

KITCHEN, HAMMOND-HARWOOD HOUSE

has a decoration of oak leaves and acorns in high relief and above is a heavy, plain moulding.

The chimney piece is of wood. An eared architrave outlines the marble facing of the fireplace and a carved shell appears in the central block on the high frieze, with small cartouches and scrolls on each side. Exceedingly ornate lateral consoles, carved with foliage and rockwork, appear on each side of the architrave and the mantel shelf rests on reversed consoles carved with foliage. The overmantel is finished with a raised panel outlined with carved mouldings, and a carved rosette is placed in each of the ears. The rococo design of the fireplace presents some of the decorative elements to be seen at Mount Vernon and was adapted from Swan's "British Architect," published in 1745 and widely circulated in the colonies.

The small, very deeply set windows in this room are provided with interior shutters fitted with H-hinges, and a line of continuous Greek fret appears below the chair rail.

Directly opposite the entrance a door leads from the "greate" room to the high *stoep* from which a flight of steps goes down into the garden. Another and far more elaborate door, balancing the fireplace, opens under a triangular pediment carved with dentils. In the sitting room, to the left of the hall, is a built-in wine closet from which, it is said, both Washington and La-fayette have been served.

In the diningroom the decorations are less elaborate than those of the drawingroom but show a strong fondness for the rococo decoration. The cornice is lighter, with a flat frieze decorated with airy scrollwork, and the lateral consoles of the chimney piece are much less florid. The paramount charm of this room is a recessed china closet with each of the shelves carved in a different profile, and edged with paper-lace carved in wood.

[179]

The Brice house, together with three other fine old Annapolis houses, the Hammond-Harwood house, the Peggy Stewart house and the Pinkney house, has come recently into the possession of St. John's College which will use the lower rooms for social gatherings and the upper floors and wings as living quarters for members of the faculty.

The only memory which seems to have come down of Juliana Brice, first mistress of the house, is that she was famous for dispensing a confection known as Naples biscuit. But to her home came notables not only from Maryland, but from colonies to the North and to the South, making it in its day a veritable American *salon*. At one time the house belonged to William Paca, signer of the Declaration of Independence, and at another it was the residence of Thomas Johnson, first governor elected by the people of Maryland, and whose name also is identified with Rose Hill, in Frederick county.

No one, however, has lived for any great length of time in this splendid old house. No sooner have families moved into it than they have moved out again, declaring they simply could not stay in the place. Starts and shivers have been the portion of virtually everyone who has sought to occupy it and they have left vowing never to spend another night under a roof where the steps leading from the second floor to the attic creaked with an unearthly sound and the scuffle of feet mingled with a blood curdling shriek at midnight. Many persons have had no notion concerning the source of such disturbances but older denizens of Annapolis declare that their grandparents have told them the reason.

Thomas Jenings Brice, they say, who inherited the house when his father died, was a man of unusual generosity and was known to have made provision in his will for his household servants. One of them, greedier than the rest, is said to have murdered his benefactor by going to his room in the night and striking him over the head and the spirit of the victim, re-enacting that gory tragedy with the ghost of his murderer, is said to terrify occupants of the house.

As Thomas Jenings Brice was a bachelor the Brice house descended to his brother, Judge John Brice, from whom it passed to the ownership of Nicholas Carroll Stephen of Bladensburg and Charles W. Stephen of Baltimore. In 1873 it was purchased from them by Thomas Ennals Martin, then Mayor of Annapolis. His daughter, Mrs. Louise Martin Robb, was the next owner. From her it was purchased in 1911 by Carvel Hall Hotel in Annapolis and held until it became the property of St. John's.

* * *

On August 10, 1708, the community of Annapolis received from the royal governor, John Seymour, its charter as a city. The document bestowed by Governor Seymour was granted in response to "the humble peticion of the Corporation of the Citty of Annapolis and the greater parts of the inhabitants of the same" and on the list of "peticioners" appears the name of Thomas Boardley, who came to Maryland from Yorkshire about 1694.

Together with the other "peticioners," Thomas Boardley was named by the Charter an alderman of the newly created municipality. He also held office during his life as a member of the House of Assembly and as attorney general. And he it was who built the first unit of the house, half hidden by magnolias and shrubbery from the street which circles about the old State House where Washington resigned his commission as commander-in-chief of the Continental army.

Delightful glimpses of the house, which was built about 1727, may be had from the street. Through the glossy green leaves of the magnolias and evergreens tantalizing suggestions appear of old brick walls, benign dormer windows with rounded tops, a captain's walk. Winding paths lead to the front door, where a deep portico, surmounted by a built-out projection from the second story, replaces the original entrance where a row of columns supported projecting eaves and rested on a porch typical of an architecture which had a greater vogue in the far South than in Maryland. The portico was added about 1860, when the house was enlarged, and is interesting from the fact that its flagged floor is made of marble from the old State House which also was undergoing repairs about the same period.

The house consists of a big, square central portion with wings. The oldest wing where the kitchens and pantries are placed, is but one story high and has the small windows of the period together with a hip roof of particularly pleasing pitch. The wing at the other end has a gambrel roof, its "hip," like the old entrance door, having been sacrificed during the 1860 rebuilding and replaced by a gambrel roof which fits with remarkable felicity into the picture. Climbing roses run with little or no restraint over portico and walls, with clematis mixing in to mingle the results of the various alterations and additions to the house into a congruous whole.

Utter simplicity characterizes the interior. A central hall, with a plain stairway at the right, divides the house a little off center with the main axis and bends to form an "L" back of the diningroom. To the left of the hall are front and back parlors and to the right the diningroom, interesting particularly for the built-in china cupboard painted brown and dull red, with the edges of the shelves flecked in gold, a combination of color which seems to have been frequently used and much liked by early Maryland householders.

But though Thomas Boardley built the house, its chief interest centers about his son and heir, Stephen Bordley, who was a member of that brilliant coterie of lawyers who foregathered at Annapolis during the quarter of a century preceding the Revolution. Stephen Bordley studied law in London, having been admitted to the Inner Temple of the Inns of Court on November 5, 1729. He spent a number of years in London, happy years apparently, but not sufficiently so to eradicate the strong love of home which brought him back to Annapolis in 1733.

Hardly had he set foot in America again before he sent back to England for a great list of law books and before long he was the owner of one of the best libraries in the colony. In less than a year after his return to Annapolis he had become involved in a law suit with Lord Baltimore, who had sought to vacate a grant of land for two hundred and thirty acres to Thomas Boardley and to another person, and so fiery was he in his determination to maintain the rights of his family that he immediately returned to England to prosecute the suit.

Stephen Bordley, like most of the Annapolitans of his day, appears to have been possessed of an extraordinary buoyancy of spirit. His attitude toward life was entirely carefree and, from all accounts, he regarded every day as a holiday. He lived luxuriously, entertained constantly and his table was the talk even of an Epicurean community. Particularly did he seem to delight in rare wines, ordering from Hill and Company, in London, "a pipe of your best Madeira wine, cost what it will. As I do not stint you in price, I hope you will not slight me in the wine." From French merchants he ordered a cask of champagne at a time, and two of Burgundy.

Liberality was a fetish with this brilliant Colonial who dispensed largesse with a lavish hand but never permitted himself to be imposed upon. And stories are still current of his powers of satire and the biting quality of his wit which prevented his enemies from giving battle without looking well to the fortifications of their own position. No man ever crossed Stephen Bordley in an unjust cause who did not have reason to regret it.

He was a member, too, of Ye Ancient South River Club, which met regularly every Thursday with a curious melange of pomposity and hilarity and on July 15, 1746, took special occasion to express, as the *Maryland Gazette* said afterwards, "their loyalty to His Majesty on the success of the inimitable Duke of Cumberland's obtaining a complete victory over the Pretender and delivering us from persecutors at home and popery and invasion from abroad, have appointed a grand entertainment to be given at their club-house on Thursday next."

Magnetic as Stephen Bordley must have been and desirable from many standpoints as a husband, he failed in his suit to win the Philadelphia belle, Peggy Shippen, who apparently enjoyed the attention he lavished upon her but refused him to marry a wealthy Bostonian. No one ever replaced her in Stephen Bordley's affection. He remained unmarried but continued to live the life of a carefree bachelor, indulging in all manner of sport, fastidious in dress, courtly in manner. In 1750 the Assembly passed a tax bill to raise a sinking fund to protect the colonists from border ravages by the Indians. In the taxables were bachelors. Those assessed more than three hundred pounds were taxed twenty shillings each and Stephen Bordley, together with William Stuart, John Ridout, John Gilliss, Daniel Wolfstenholme and Charles Carroll, Barrister, paid the impost for six years.

Public works found a practical supporter in this erudite barrister. In 1744 he conveyed to the then royal governor, Thomas Bladen, four acres of land adjoining his home as a site for a governor's palace and an architect, a Mr. Duff, was sent for from Scotland to draw the plans and superintend the work, but after the walls were about two-thirds completed the work was stopped and the project was dubbed "Bladen's Folly." In 1750 Stephen Bordley was appointed one of the commissioners of Maryland to settle the disputed boundary between the province and Pennsylvania, an undertaking which was finished in 1768. In 1754 he was elected to represent the city of Annapolis in the Assembly of the following term. Two years later he became attorney-general and from 1757 he served as a member of the Council. In addition his public offices included the post of Commissary of Maryland, Naval Officer at Annapolis, and he was constantly in the consultation of Horatio Sharpe when he was royal governor. Later, he was the legal preceptor of Thomas Johnson, who has been mentioned before, and of William Paca, champion of the people in their refusal to pay the clergy tax of tobacco, and later governor of the State.

After the *debacle* of Bladen's Folly, the land was granted by the Legislature to a group of men who petitioned for a charter for St. John's College, the third oldest liberal arts college in the country. Stephen Bordley was one of the first supporters of the project. He was a great letter writer and kept up an enormous correspondence with friends in England and the other colonies, but his "Sister Bett" was his confidante and most intimate friend. She, too, was the victim of a blighted romance, having been "in love with an amiable and exemplary young man" who died in England and whose verses, together with some little tokens of affection he had given her at parting, she kept to the day of her death. Together the brother and sister were seen at all of the important entertainments and assemblies given in Annapolis, a striking pair with Stephen Bordley in wig and velvet and "Bett" in stiff brocade and lace ruffles.

After the death of Stephen Bordley the house upon which he had lavished wealth and attention passed, together with its furniture and plate, to his sister. There she lived alone for many years, willing the place when she died to her half brother, John Beale Bordley, of The Vineyard, Wye Island, who had made a fortune in raising wheat and who, as war with England was seen to be inevitable, voluntarily deprived himself of all luxuries and substituted things "which could not be traced to any common source of gratification."

John Beale Bordley died in 1804 and the house, with its lawns in front and diverging walks bordered with box and flowerbeds behind, was sold to John Randall who settled in Annapolis after the Revolution and in whose family it remained for more than a century, becoming known as the Bordley-Randall House. It now is the home of Mr. and Mrs. R. T. H. Halsey, the former of whom directed the creation of the American Wing of the Metropolitan Museum in New York.

* * *

Almost in the shadow of the State House, which it antedates by more than a decade, unnoted by most authorities on Colonial affairs and seldom receiving a glance from devotees of the antique, stands Kentish House, oldest and most historic brick building in Annapolis and the home of King William's School, first institution of learning in the province.

Until recently the location of this immediate ancestor of St. John's College has been entirely a matter of conjecture. Elihu S. Riley, writing of "The Ancient City" in 1887, places it "very nearly if not on the site of the DeKalb statue," but, in the light of investigations made by Arthur Trader, keeper of the land office records at Annapolis, it has been established beyond shadow of doubt that King William's school stood at what is now 76 Francis Street. At present it is the home of James A. Walton, president of the Annapolis Banking and Trust Company, and his sister, Miss Agnes Walton.

So greatly has it been changed by the vicissitudes of years and the fancy of its occupants that there is little about the aspect of Kentish House to suggest the building in which the quaintly garbed youngsters of two and a-quarter centuries ago gave themselves over more or less assiduously to the pursuit of "Latin, Greek, Writing and the like," but the rear view, completely hidden from the street, is but little altered.

Originally the structure consisted of a large central building, gambrel roofed, and with two low, gambrel roofed wings, one at each end. The exterior was covered with plaster and coated with a wash of deep chrome yellow, vestiges of which still are to be seen on the rear walls.

The south wing, which constituted the ballroom after the house ceased to function as a school, was removed a number of years ago and some time after that, so completely had the plaster disintegrated, the present owners had the street front coated with gray cement. The bow window, which projects from the drawingroom over the street, was added a generation ago for use as a conservatory. About the same time the pillars which supported the original portico with its latticed window, and which had become so weatherbeaten that they had almost rotted away, were removed and a small, modern porch was built before the main entrance.

Completely altered, too, is the upper structure of the remaining north wing, for the gambrel roof was removed and a frame outer wall was built flush with the wall on the first floor. The antiquity of the house is better observed within.

One of the most charming and at the same time one of the most extraordinary things about the structure is the arrangement of the chimneys—two of them at diagonal corners built outside the house, after the familiar manner of Colonial architecture, and the other two at diagonal corners inside.

In one of the rooms is to be found some of the oldest wood panelling in the country. Comparatively recent coats of dark paint fail to conceal the fine simplicity of the work of some early Maryland craftsmen and on the long, narrow doors to the cupboards by the mantelpiece are hinges of hand-wrought iron. Rooms of excellent proportions occupy the lower floor and upstairs the arrangement of sleeping rooms and bathrooms follows a pattern which is a compromise between the ancient plan and present day comfort.

Black walnut and oak, poplar and pine were used in the interior construction of the house and when, during one of its periods of alteration, an effort was made to strengthen the floor of one of the upper rooms, it was found that the trouble lay not in the joists which supported the floor, since they were discovered to be as hard as flint, but in the bricks, which were so soft that the joists had worn them away. Many of the original floor boards remain, scarcely worn by the tramp of the hundreds of schoolboy feet, notoriously hard on floors, and those of the subsequent occupants of the house. As it stands today, the north wing is cut off completely from the main dwelling, the connecting doorway having been removed years ago when it was sold as a separate entity by the then owner of the property whose identity seems to have been forgotten.

Kentish House was built during the regime of Governor Nicholson, having been begun in 1696. That it was the most pretentious building of its day, next to the State House which afterward was burned, is attested by an account of the province made by a very ingenuous man who was in Maryland in Governor Nicholson's day and who wrote:

> Col. Nicholson has done his endeavor to make a town of that place (Annapolis). There are about forty dwellings in

it, seven or eight of which can afford a good lodging and accommodations for strangers. There are also a State House and Free School, built with brick, which make a great show among a parcel of wooden houses, and the foundation of a church is laid, the only brick church in Maryland.

The faculty of the school in that early day consisted of "One Master, One Usher and One Writing Master." Its trustees were "the governor, Sir Thomas Lawrence, Col. George Robothan, Col. Charles Hutchins, Col. John Adison, the Reverend Divine, Mr. Peregrine Cony, and Mr. John Hewett, Robert Smith, Kenelm Cheseldyne, Henry Coursey, Edward Dorsey, Thomas Ennals, Thomas Tasker, Francis Jenkins, William Dent, Thomas Smith, Edward Boothby, John Thompson and John Bigger, Gentleman," all of whom were named in the act of Legislature establishing the school.

Not mentioned in these formalities, yet the single figure who made King William's school a fact instead of an iridescent dream was a man quite unknown to this generation, laymen and scholars alike. This was Anthony, alias William, Workman, who came to Maryland as indentured servant and died one of the richest men of Annapolis. Around his lowly person, however, there forms a picture of swashbuckling romance, with cavaliers and smugglers passing in review across the screen.

Workman was the second son of William Workman, butcher, of the town of Colford, County of Gloucester, England, and was born there on the 20th of May, 1646. His alias he acquired upon the death of his elder brother, which made him direct heir to his father's small estate.

It is stated of him in a deposition filed in the testamentary record of Maryland by a number of inhabitants of Colford that Anthony, alias William, Workman went from that place to

Virginia. He was about twenty-two when he came to Maryland and began his service of five years as an indentured servant in St. Mary's county.

When he was freed he proved his right to fifty acres of land in 1674 and from that time onward, for a number of years, he was an active landholder on Kent Island. He was even more than that, apparently, for Anthony, alias William, was not a man to neglect his opportunities and his Pascos Adventure tract of a hundred and fifty acres at the Wading (Waiting) Place was good harbor and offered the brethren of the coast, who infested the shores of the Chesapeake in the early days of Maryland, excellent opportunity to unload contraband and evade the customs tax.

Workman undoubtedly did a thriving business in "ingots of gold and silver and sundry rich furniture of Indian aspect, better fitted for the cabinet of the virtuoso than the trade of a new province. Then, also there were occasionally costly stuffs and tissues, cloth of gold, velvets of Genoa arras, tapestry and even pictures which might have been hung in churches," landed under protection of darkness and defended in blood if necessary.

Customers saw the goods charily exhibited, "and when the bargain was made supplied in greater bulk by unseen hands from secret magazines, concerning which the customer was not so rash as even to inquire."

And, in addition to the noble hoard Workman made as "fence" for smugglers, he unquestionably put away some tidy sums as the result of his enterprise in furnishing spirits aplenty for the sailors in the service of these followers of the profligate arts. As soon as he acquired sufficient funds he added to his land holdings on the island and ultimately became possessed of thirteen various tracts with a total of 1,630 acres.

As Annapolis grew and flourished, Workman turned his practical eyes in that direction. He opened "an inn or ordinary" there and it was more than likely in his capacity of host to the thirsty that he became acquainted with Francis Nicholson, governor of the province at the time, and other high officials of the Colonial government who dropped in to forget the cares of state and chirk up their spirits with a drop of toddy.

There was one matter, however, that was constantly on the mind of the governor and which he discussed in season and out with anyone who would listen,—and there were not many who found it inexpedient to listen when the governor spoke, including Anthony, alias William, Workman.

And no doubt the governor, over his mug of ale, told Anthony, alias William, about a certain sloop which had been seized for violation of the Trade acts, and told it in such fashion that the doughty innkeeper was left in no doubt that the governor knew exactly what was going on at Pascos Adventure and other points on Kent Island.

It is quite likely, also, that the illiterate Anthony, alias William, well as he knew his way among the evil doers, was deeply impressed by the evident learning of the Governor, the easy flow of language with which he told his stories and the importance of his place in the community in contrast with his own ignorant self. Governor Nicholson, apparently a shrewd individual, evidently lost no opportunity to impress Anthony either with the precariousness of his position as a go-between for smugglers, or with the desirability of an education, although the former probably had the greater weight.

At any rate, when the time was ripe, the governor launched his plan to Anthony, alias William, his success being recorded in this fashion in the Acts of Maryland, Lib. 11, No. 4, Fol. 120, which states that

[191]

the Honourable Francis Nicholson, Esq., his then Majesty's Captain-General, and the Governor in Chief in and over this Province, excited by a laudable zeal and pious inclination of promoting a Free School within the Town and Port of Annapolis, and being possessed of three Lots of Land in the said Town, lying to the foot of the Stadt-House Hill, on the Eastward therof, did not only freely give and bestow one of the said Lots lying to the Southwest side of the said Lots, but also the sum of Ten Pounds Sterling for and towards an House to be built thereon, but did also prevail with a certain Anthony, alias William, Workman, formerly of Kent Island but then of Annapolis, Inn-holder, to advance, give and bestow One Hundred and Fifty Pounds Sterling more, for and towards the Building of the said House or Tenement on the aforesaid Lot: And together with the said Workman, and a certain William Freeman, of Philadelphia, Bricklayer, entered into Articles for the Building and Erecting the said House, to be held and enjoyed by the said Workman during his natural Life and afterwards to the Use of the Free School.

Workman, in return for his philanthropy, "by Ordinance of the General Assembly, had Liberty and License granted to him to keep an Ordinary in the said House, during his natural life, free and discharged from the Payment of the Fine (Tax) then imposed by Law Therefore."

Workman died in 1708, twelve years after the creation of King William's School, but there is nothing in his will, signed with his mark, to indicate that he ever enjoyed the privileges conferred upon him by the act of keeping an inn in the school building. As a matter of fact, there is nothing in his inventory that would lead any one to believe that he was an innkeeper, as he had gone back to his plantations on Kent Island and had become a gentleman farmer in the cultivation of tobacco.

His personal estate was valued at 1,461 pounds sterling, quite a fortune for those days, to say nothing of his holdings in real estate. Comparative values of today would put him in the millionaire class.

Just how long Kentish House was used for King William's School is unknown. As late as 1773 the school was advertising, over the signature of John Duckett, register, for instructors, announcing that "any gentleman who is qualified to teach the 'classicks' would be treated on the following terms:

> His annual stipend to be fifty-five pounds sterling certain and five pounds currency to be paid by each scholar in the Latin school; to a person who shall be capable of discharging the office of usher will be given thirty pounds per annum certain and two pounds ten shillings currency paid by each scholar as above mentioned; to a scribe who can teach English, writing and arithmetick will be given six pounds sterling certain per annum, with every advantage arising from the scholars he instructs, and liberty to make his own bargain with their parents.
>
> There are very good apartments in the house, beside those appropriated for the use of the scholars, with a good kitchen and cellar, these being entirely for the use of the master, will render it a very comfortable place of residence.

After this, however, there is no documentary evidence to show anything of the life of King William's nor to fix the date at which the school closed its doors. The act of Assembly which created the institution provided that the house and ground on which it stands "shall, in all Times to come, be deemed, reputed and taken, to be and remain in the aforesaid Rector, Governors and Visitors of the Free Schools, and their Successors, as in an indefeasible estate in Fee-simple, for ever, to the Use of the Free

School in the City of Annapolis, and to no other Use, Intent or Purpose Whatsoever."

Many of the material possessions of King William's, including 400 rare old volumes sent from England by the crown for the library, passed to St. John's College, but there is nothing to show that the college ever occupied Kentish House and much to indicate that it did not.

CHAPTER TWELVE

A museum piece of pre-Revolutionary building is the Hammond house at Annapolis, full of years, dignity and serenity. Most famous of all the seventeen Colonial houses in the mittened city on the Severn river, it is known today as the Hammond-Harwood house and stands in the fullness of its centuries as it stood two hundred years ago in the glow of youth.

Pure and unalloyed Americana is the Hammond-Harwood house, owing nothing to Sir Christopher Wren or to Inigo Jones or other famous British architects whose planning is read into so many Colonial houses with, in most cases, a somewhat questionable justification. Its owner was an American and an Annapolitan. It was built by an American builder and none but American materials was employed in its construction.

Recently purchased by St. John's College and restored, after months of study, by some of the finest architects in the country who even went to England in their search for accurate data on the Georgian period, the Hammond-Harwood house stands as something much more significant than a splendid bit of Colonial architecture. It is a symbol in an age of change of the taste and culture of the early Marylanders who quoted from the classics without affectation and sent their sons abroad to be educated in the days when most of the rest of the country still was fighting out the struggle for existence.

The house was erected for Matthias Hammond, a young barrister of enormous wealth and irreproachable social position, who always wore his rapier and lace cuffs. Its planning he entrusted to Matthew Buckland, a Philadelphian who undoubtedly derived from the published works of Swan and other English architects some of his inspiration for the creation of the house, but who brought to their adaptation an enthusiasm which makes his production completely his own work of art.

No more perfect setting could have been found for such a house than Annapolis at the time when the Frenchman, de Tocqueville, praised it as "the only finished city" he had discovered in this country. In the midst of its sophisticated society moved Matthias Hammond whose entire life was one long romance and who derived a lordly revenue from fifty-four tobacco plantations.

Hammond was a handsome fellow, brilliantly educated, and when he won from a proud Philadelphia girl (whose name has been so carefully guarded by the Hammond family from generation to generation that it has been completely forgotten) her promise of marriage he determined to build as a wedding gift to the bride a home which would reflect not only the social sphere to which both of them belonged, but the art of architecture at its apogee. Into the construction of his house he wove dreams of beauty. Over each detail he hovered, intent upon perfection. And when it was finished he went to Philadelphia for the furniture which was to complete his masterpiece, only to be told by his fiancee when he sought her advice concerning some minor detail, that his love story had ended.

The young girl apparently did not mince matters. Her explanation was spirited and vivid. Mr. Hammond had lavished more of his thoughts upon the house than he had bestowed upon her and, since he had chosen, he might keep the house. From that day forward she would have none of him and she had no interest in the furniture he had come North to buy. The astonished cavalier besought and, on his part, explained but his lady was firm. There was no house in the world, not even one which was to be her own, to which she would play second fiddle. There was nothing to do but accept his rejection. Matthias Hammond returned to Annapolis and to the house which had come between him and his love but to the end of his life he remained a bachelor.

This was the setting, this the master of the Hammond-Harwood house. The date of its erection can be fixed definitely between 1770 and 1774, the ripe years of Colonial building in Annapolis. The lines are low and long, the plain facade of the central portion being crowned by a triangular pediment and adorned by a doorway which is conceded by architects to be unsurpassed by anything of its kind in America.

Built of salmon-colored brick of a tint to be found only in Maryland clay, the house is two stories high, with walls five feet thick at the foundations, a circumstance which gives color to the story that the builder's plans called originally for a three-story structure without wings. But when the walls had been completed almost to the second story, according to the tale, Col. Edward Lloyd, who lived opposite and cherished his rights and privileges as only a Colonial could, realized that the addition of a third story to Mr. Hammond's house would obliterate completely his own view of the Annapolis harbor. This was a circumstance not to be thought of. Another man in the Annapolis of that day of fiery tempers and personal privilege would have had quick recourse to the law. Suits of restraint and injunction, bitter words and life-long animosities ordinarily would have resulted, and the building of the Hammond-Harwood house would have been indefinitely postponed.

But Colonel Lloyd, apparently, was cast in a cannier mould. Formally and in his most affable manner he approached the ceremonious Matthias Hammond and laid the case before him. Mr. Hammond grasped the point immediately, pooh-poohed all thoughts of so injuring his neighbor-to-be and agreed to build no higher than the second story if Colonel Lloyd would pay the cost of constructing wings to the house. The colonel agreed and so the matter was settled.

As far as the Hammond-Harwood house was concerned the arbitration was a piece of good fortune, for upon the two wings, extraordinarily enough if the story of their origin be true, depends a great deal of the charm of the house. These wings are by far the finest and are said to be almost the only examples of semi-octagonal additions of this character in the country. Without them the house would lack much of its distinction.

The left wing is wholly detached from the central portion of the house. This wing was used by Mr. Hammond as an office and to it came a constant stream of Marylanders from all parts of the colony seeking legal advice, not to mention those who met with him to plant the seeds of political freedom and revolt from the economic system which England was building up in America during the middle years of the Eighteenth century. The right wing forms an integral part of the house and contains the kitchens and pantries. Each wing has a second floor in which bedrooms are located.

A short flight of sandstone steps, taken from the old Alexandria quarries which furnished the stone for the coping on the porches at Mount Vernon and Monticello, with a slender iron handrail leads to the doorway which has drawn architects and lovers of past delights from all over the country to Annapolis "for to admire and for to see." The steps, which reproduce exactly the original approach to the house, replace an unsightly porch which stood before the doorway during the greater part of the last century and which was torn away when St. John's College came into possession of the property. During the removal of the porch, foundations of the original steps were uncovered, with some of the original stones.

The handmade bricks of the walls are laid in Flemish bond, broken at the line between the first and second stories by a belt course. The plainness of the facade adds to rather than detracts from the effect of the doorway with its tall Ionic columns supporting an entablature with a triangular pediment and a frieze of ribboned laurel. The heavy mahogany door and the simple fanlight over it are outlined by an egg-and-dart moulding and the keystone of the arch over the fanlight is decorated with acanthus leaves. Festoons of roses, expertly carved, adorn the spandrils.

From the doorway "the eye of the beholder" is drawn upward toward the roof by the bull's eye window in the pediment which, like the doorway, has been praised lavishly. Simple, triangular pediments appear over the doorways of the connecting wings to conform with the lines of the central portion of the house and the first floor windows are longer by one row of panes than those on the second floor.

The restraint which characterizes the exterior of the house is evident also in the decoration of the interior. In the entrance hall only the well-designed cornice and the door at the rear, which leads into the diningroom, attract attention. The other four doorways, which are placed at balanced intervals and which lead into the rooms which flank the hall, are simply "of the period." The diningroom doorway, however, the diningroom itself and the ballroom above it constitute perfect examples of the finest architectural decorations which have come down from Colonial days. Who the woodcarver was who did the work in these two rooms, whence he came or whither he went, no one knows. He may have been one of Matthias Hammond's indentured servants or, more likely, an obscure cabinet maker.

In the Hammond-Harwood drawingroom and diningroom the unknown craftsman has utilized, with the deftness and discrimination which seemed to be intuitive with some of the Colonial decorators, all the richness and the resources of the Renaissance. Mouldings, doors, shutters and baseboard, chair-rail and chimney piece are decorated with gadrooning, egg and dart and small foliage mouldings. Each of the three doors and the three windows (Matthias Hammond had a passion for symmetry) has architrave, frieze and cornice supported by reversed consoles decorated with acanthus leaves. Grotesque bird-heads end in leafy scrolls. The mantelpiece has been treated like the doors and windows, with the addition of a classical urn in the center between the grotesque heads.

A broken scroll pediment ornaments the overmantel and the frame is decorated with loose acanthus scrolls. Lovely mouldings appear on wainscoting and baseboards and the shutters have recessed octagonal panels, alternately plain and carved with rosettes of leaves, which showed their beauty to the world only when it was time for candlelight or when Matthias Hammond had business of political importance afoot which brought to his home visitors who wished to conceal their presence as much as possible.

The Palladian window over the staircase is a perfect reproduction in design and detail of the original drawings of Palladio and is, with the exception of the sill, moulded entirely of French plaster. In the ballroom on the second floor, which extends over both the diningroom and the drawingroom and which measures nineteen by twenty-seven feet, the decorations show the unmistakable influence of Robert Adam and complete one of the few really perfect Colonial rooms of this character. Wainscoted with panelled wood to a height of about three feet, the artistic effect is evident not merely in the graceful proportions of the room, but in the carved mouldings, the shutters which repeat the decoration of those in the diningroom, the light and elegant cornice supported by a frieze on which Greek urns appear with classical draping alternating with heavy fluting, every other shaft of the fluting being beaded. Over the mantelpiece roses, so realistically carved as to seem almost natural, are caught up in garlands with ribbon bowknots. Oval medallions are carved in blocks at the end of the mantel. A room to dream about is the ballroom in the Hammond-Harwood house and so compelling is its suggestion of past splendor that it calls for only the faintest trick of imagination to see Washington or Lafayette bowing there before some Maryland belle and dancing off with her in a ghostly quadrille.

One of the luxuries of the house is a withdrawing room to which Mr. Hammond's feminine guests retired while the gentlemen remained in the diningroom over their Madeira and tobacco. When the house was restored by St. John's College the overmantel for this room was found in bits in the attic and restored to its original position. Only seven of the original doorlocks, some of which were of silver, remained intact. The quest for others to match them led to junk shops and all manner of out-of-the-way places in Maryland and Pennsylvania and even into Colonial houses which were being torn down, resulting in the acquisition of twenty-nine old locks for doors from which the originals had been removed.

No screws are to be found in the hinges of this house. All of them are mortised and fastened with pins. No tongue and groove boards are in the floors which are fastened together with dowels and must have taken months to lay. None of the mortises are more than a foot apart and in many places they are only six inches.

One of the most interesting facets of the house as it stands today, completely and minutely restored to its original form, is the old oven next to the huge fireplace in the kitchen. Years ago, when "modern convenience" was just beginning to become a household phrase, the primitive cooking paraphernalia which had served generations of Maryland aristocrats who succeeded Matthias Hammond to the ownership of the house, was cast into outer darkness, the old fireplace walled up and a "range" installed with all its works.

When the restoration was undertaken the range in its turn was cast into limbo, the old fireplace uncovered and refitted with its time-honored appurtenances. While this work was in progress the vestigial remains of an old oven were discovered. It was obvious from the traces on the walls that the old oven had had a squirrel tail flue, and a long search for such an oven immediately ensued, a search which led all over Anne Arundel county and across the Chesapeake to the Eastern Shore. One finally was discovered in the Ridout house in Annapolis and after that the way was easy. The measurements of the surviving oven were taken and found to correspond exactly with those of the foundations in the Hammond-Harwood house and with the brickwork in the kitchen wall. The restorers then went ahead and reproduced the oven of the Ridout house.

While this work was in progress an incident occurred which gave rise to tremendous excitement among the college officials and the restoration committee and set them frenziedly to work in an effort to unravel a mystery which, it seems now, will remain forever insoluble. Dr. James E. Bordley, chairman of the restoration committee, while walking across the cellar discovered a loose brick in the floor. The others about it were tight and firm. Here, undoubtedly, was a spur not to be resisted. Quickly Dr. Bordley maneuvered and twisted the brick until he had succeeded in removing it. Underneath were two large keys. One was tagged in faded ink, "To the Secret Chamber." The other was labelled, "To the Secret Burying Place." Dr. Bordley's amazement waxed the more for the knowledge that he had of the graves of the departed Hammonds and Harwoods, who were among the few Colonial families completely accounted for. Instantly the house was searched for some hidden door or secret wall panel which might have been so well concealed in the walls that it had been overlooked. Measurements were taken inside and out, the proportions corresponding, as it had been anticipated that they would, exactly. News was permitted to leak out that the key to a secret chamber had been found, but a complete silence was preserved concerning the second key.

The response to the rumor of a secret chamber was immediate. An old lady in Annapolis recalled that Miss Hester Harwood, who had been the last of the name to occupy the house, had, shortly before her death, confided to her upon one occasion that with Miss Harwood there would die a secret which, she said, the world would give much to hear. What the nature of the secret was Miss Harwood had not intimated. A second response to the rumor was more definite, though nothing ever came of it, either. It was embodied in a letter to Dr. Bordley from an old resident of Baltimore who recalled that as a child she had been a frequent visitor at the Hammond house and was thoroughly familiar with the secret chamber which, she said, was reached by a flight of stairs either leading up from the cellar or down from it—she could not be positive which after an absence of almost eighty years—and she was certain she could find it if she were to visit the house again. This, however, was a physical impossibility. She added that the chamber was connected with the house by a long passageway which ran down toward the creek and that to reach it one had to pass a sarcophagus.

Proof that the old lady knew something whereof she wrote is to be found in the fact that, years ago, a creek did run past the grounds at the rear of the house, though it long since had been filled in and now is the bed of an asphalt street. Immediately upon the receipt of the second letter workmen were put to digging. A few arch bricks were the result, indicating the possible location of a vaulted passageway, but no trace of a secret chamber or of a hidden sepulchre was to be found. Nor has anything been discovered which might reveal the identity of that mysterious person whose last sleep is so carefully guarded except a legend that, before her death, Matthias Hammond's fickle and wilful sweetheart had expressed a wish to be buried in her lover's home.

At the death of Matthias Hammond the property passed by the terms of his will to his nephew, John Hammond, who sold it to Phillip Hammond from who it was purchased by Ninian Pinkney, a brother of that William Pinkney who was one of the most brilliant of the young republic's statesmen in the period immediately following the Revolution and who served variously as United States Senator, minister to Great Britain, minister to Russia and attorney-general of the United States. In 1811 Mr. Pinkney sold the house to Chief Justice Jeremiah Townley Chase who bought it as a wedding gift for his daughter when she became the bride of Richard Lockerman, a scion of the old New York Knickerbocker family of Loockermans who played so conspicuous a part in the early annals of New York city. Richard Lockerman, as many of the Colonials did, Anglicized the spelling of his name.

The only daughter of Richard Lockerman inherited the house from her parents and married Judge William Harwood who, during the Civil War, was an ardent sympathizer with the Confederacy and who, to the end of his life, remained unreconstructed.

During the war and for some years afterward he taught school in Baltimore and, rather than take the oath of allegiance to the United States, which a ride on the train would have necessitated, he tramped thirty miles each week, over bad roads, between his home and the school. Judge Harwood's daughter, who survived her brother and sister, became the next owner of the house. During the last years of her life she lived exclusively in the office wing, leasing the main portion of the building to strangers. When she died it was sold to St. John's, money for the purpose being subscribed by a group of New Yorkers and Marylanders who are trustees of the college and who also financed the movement for its rehabilitation and its present use as a museum.

When the beautifully carved doorway had been washed again and again with paint remover, a skilled carpenter spent four days picking out the bits of paint which still impaired the beauty of its festooned roses and acanthus leaves. The floors were scraped with a sanding machine and then waxed. In order to secure exactly the right shade of paint for the woodwork in the various rooms an artist was sent abroad by Dr. Bordley to study Georgian houses in England. Innumerable artists and decorators in this country also were consulted before the final decisions were made and then corroboration of their choice was obtained through the discovery in the attic of old window cornices showing the exact colors as those selected for the repainting.

Then began a keen and diligent search for furniture which, by virtue of its own right, might find place in the house. One of the happiest acquisitions was a set of eight side chairs which are believed to have been placed in the house when it was built for Matthias Hammond, and which had come into the possession of a Baltimore collector. Pure in design and splendid in construction, they were made in transitional style between Chippendale and Hepplewhite and are upholstered in old brocade.

In the center of the diningroom stands a table which the

[205]

trustees of St. John's and connoisseurs of antiques have declared to be the only pure Chippendale dining table in America.

The cellarette in this room was made by John Shaw, of Annapolis, who flourished for a number of years after 1760, when he first attracted attention, and who was considered as one of the best cabinet-makers in the colony. It contains his business card.

Another lovely piece of furniture is a ball and claw table, made by Goddard, and a mahogany highboy of the Philadelphia school. In one of the bedrooms there is a folding bed of the oldest type. Its wood is pine and it was brought to light in an attic in Maine just before being brought to Annapolis.

Several invaluable bits of furniture and hardware were found scattered about in the house itself. The escutcheon to the front door lock was discovered under the steps when the wooden porch was removed and locks and hinges found buried in the dirt. Under several feet of ashes the original crane was unearthed and rehung in the kitchen which has been completely furnished as it stood when the house was made ready for the bride who never came.

*   *   *

The only three-story house which stood in Annapolis before the Revolution is the Chase House, directly opposite the Hammond-Harwood house. Distinctly a city dwelling is this, elegant and sophisticated, too self-absorbed even to be condescending to houses which do not pretend to its height or its attributes of luxury.

Withdrawn behind a high white picket fence, which has acorns carved atop the posts where it curves like a crescent to the steps of the front porch, this house stands on land which was included in the original plot of Annapolis when it was laid out in 1695. Tall, flowering bushes, planted more than a century ago, hang over the fence, and the limb of a great tree which had

CHASE HOUSE   *Photo by Pickering*

Photo by Pickering

CHASE HOUSE: UPPER LANDING OF STAIRWAY

Photo by Pickering

CHASE HOUSE: DRAWINGROOM MANTEL

Photo by Pickering

CHASE HOUSE: FAMOUS DOUBLE STAIRWAY

stood over riotous scenes in the ancient city hangs protectingly above the porch.

Chase House is a massive structure, somewhat too large for the grounds which surround it to be sure, but as impressive as any dwelling this country has produced. The walls are about eighteen inches thick and laid in the Flemish bond of alternate headers and stretchers so greatly liked by the builders of the more pretentious houses of early Maryland.

Abundance and good taste, which form the outstanding characteristics of the house, are indicated at the threshold. From the street a broad flight of steps leads to a wide, open porch which stands before a fanlighted doorway framed by smooth, round pillars, with a triangular pediment overhead. A heavy brass Medusa knocker must be used to announce the arrival of a visitor, for Chase House knows not the electric bell.

This knocker is interesting, for in its day it hung upon the front door of White Hall, the home of Governor Sharpe, and it was sounded often by Colonial patriot and unswerving loyalist in the days when Governor Sharpe's move to promulgate the Stamp Act brought a whirlwind down about his ears.

The windows, like the doorway, seem expansive. Unusually wide for a house built in the days when glass was scarce and costly, they appear to indicate a superb disregard of expense in the building which was once the envy and the discontent of lesser establishments in Annapolis.

Through the center of the house, from the street to the one-time garden, runs the hall, with a hanging stairway at the far end appearing through a vista of slender Ionic columns which support the gallery on the second floor. A single flight of steps, each a solid block of wood with each step arched in profile, leads to a broad landing which is lighted by an enormous Palladian window set in a carved frame. At the landing the stairs divide and two flights lead from each end to the second floor gallery, where carved niches were placed to receive pieces of statuary imported from Europe. Carved archways at each end of the gallery introduce the corridors leading to the bedrooms from which, in the early days of Chase House, an uninterrupted view could be had of Annapolis harbor and the Chesapeake Bay.

A magnificent stairway is the one at Chase House and one full worthy to be admired. In recent years it has been necessary to provide pillars to support the steps between the landing and the gallery, which had begun to sag as if no longer able to endure their own weight. In doing so some of the effect of the stairway has been destroyed, but it is still a prideful thing.

Around the walls the hall is wainscoted and at the ceiling line there is a cornice, strong and substantial. In the old days a large fireplace occupied the center of the right wall, but this has been removed in the interests of a modern heating plant. Tragic associations inhere for the Chase House in that one-time fireplace for there, one autumn night, when the wind blew chill, Miss Matilda Chase hovered close, so close that her dress caught fire from a spark, and before the members of the household who heard her scream could reach her she had burned to death.

Sudden death has been the portion of another of the Chases, too, and prevented the "destitute, aged and infirm women" who live there from having the comforts their benefactress intended them to enjoy. The last of the Chases were all women. One of them, Mrs. Hester Ann Chase Ridout, in her will devised the house to the Episcopal Church for the purpose for which it is now used. Mrs. Ridout had intended to add to this bequest an endowment fund of $200,000 through a codicil to her will. According to her directions, the codicil was prepared by her attorney and brought to her for signature. It happened, however, that the arrival of the lawyer coincided with the visit of a friend and the matter was postponed "until morning." Morning never came for Mrs. Ridout as she had expected, for she died at 7 o'clock while the hour she had set to sign the codicil to her will was 9. And the money which would have maintained the splendor of Chase House was diverted to other channels.

Into the drawingroom to the left of the hall and into the state diningroom to the right mahogany doors, with handles of wrought silver, open through classic doorways. The pronounced Roman influence which is found in so many Colonial houses in Maryland is strongly apparent in the decorations of the drawingroom, a large, square apartment with an Adam ceiling of ornate plaster and recessed window shutters elaborately carved.

In this room the mantelpiece is of Italian marble, carved on the center panel with a bas-relief of Shakespeare receiving from the Goddess of Wisdom the three golden keys. Carvings of classic honeysuckle and Lesbian leaf, with classic urns in relief on the panels at each end, are subordinated in interest to the central panel and around the opening of the fireplace is a line of small foliage carving.

Far more elaborate than the drawingroom, however, is the state diningroom, which also has a carved mantel of Italian marble and silver-handled mahogany doors to which, as well as to the pantries, the first mistress of the mansion carried a silver key. In the diningroom the decorator has permitted his talents full play. Cornice, window frames, baseboard and chair-rail overflow with carving. Lines of rope, small foliage and bead-and-reel moulding almost cover the window frames with their projecting ears and lateral consoles, and in recessed panels underneath are festoons of carved ribbon from which hang clusters of grapes and roses.

On the mantelpiece the central panel shows a classic urn, with a design of foxgloves, poppies and narcissus in such high relief as to seem almost real. On the chair rail and on the baseboard there is the same lavish use of ornament. Scroll work, Greek fret, fine rope and rococo carving have been used wherever it is possible to place them without violating the dictates of taste. Over the door a broken pediment rests on reversed consoles carved with acanthus leaves and on the frieze appears a scroll design of acanthus leaves.

This room now serves as a regular diningroom for the occupants of the home, but in the great days of the Chase House it was used only on formal occasions and the family dined in the smaller breakfast room directly behind it. A rear staircase which mounts from the little hall by the breakfast room was a tremendous extravagance for the day in which it was built. In the basement is a great wine cellar, with a barrel vault of brick above, running the length of the house.

From all indications the house was designed for wings, but these were never built. The only evidence of them to be had, in fact, exists in a low, rambling structure on the northeast side which once was used for kitchen and pantry, but which, within recent years, has been refinished for use as a separate dwelling.

The foundations of Chase House were laid in 1769 by Samuel Chase, known for his anticipation in the events of July 4, 1776 as "the Signer." The land upon which it stands was in the center of the fine residential district of Annapolis as originally laid out, and was known as Lot 107. For it Samuel Chase paid £100 to Denton Hammond, who had acquired title to it.

Immediately the owner began to build but, for some reason which never has been disclosed, he sold it to Edward Lloyd, known as "Collonel" Lloyd of the Wye House, in July, 1771. Colonel Lloyd obtained for "five hundred and four pounds sterling of Great Britain, and two thousand, four hundred and ninety-one pounds, seventeen shillings, and seven pence current," the ground and "all houses, edifices, buildings, improvements, waters, easements, privileges, commodities and advantages whatsoever." For many years a controversy existed concerning the identity of the actual builder of the house but the vast difference between the amount of money paid for the lot by Samuel Chase and that involved in the acquisition of the property by Colonel Lloyd seems to indicate beyond question that the house must have been standing as it is today when Colonel Lloyd acquired it. An interesting point in this connection is that the silver drop handles on the door of Chase house appear in brass replica on the doors at Wye. Evidently those at Wye were copied from Chase House.

During Colonel Lloyd's lifetime Chase House was known to the most brilliant society of America. To it came men and women of the court circle in Annapolis as well as the intellectual giants of other colonies. Of old baronial stock, he established a tradition for hospitality which was carried on by his son, Edward Lloyd, V, during whose regime the house became the governor's mansion by reason of the election of its owner to the highest office of the State.

With the Revolution most of its glory departed but Chase House still was the abode of wealthy and cultured people. In the drawing room, in 1802, Colonel Lloyd's daughter, Mary Tayloe Lloyd, became the bride of Francis Scott Key, author of "The Star Spangled Banner."

On May 11, 1826, Edward Lloyd, V, sold the house to his son-in-law, Henry Hall Harwood, for $6,500, the first mention in the deeds by which the house had changed ownership of the currency of the United States. On November 5, 1847, it was acquired from the heirs of Henry Hall Harwood by Miss Hester Ann Chase, daughter of Jeremiah T. Chase, who willed it in 1875 to her nieces, Misses Matilda (the victim of the fire-place tragedy) and Frances Chase who died unmarried. From them the house passed to the possession of their sister, Mrs. Ridout.

Since its erection many of the fine details of the house have, perforce, been sacrificed. Originally the state diningroom boasted a ceiling equal to that of the drawingroom, but when repairs were necessary, funds were lacking to provide them and a plain ceiling was installed. The garden has disappeared, too, but still the old house maintains its dignity and draws itself up with the air of a courtier conscious of race.

CHAPTER THIRTEEN

So completely unknown to the majority of Marylanders, even to those who are more than fairly well initiated into the topography of their State, is the Rhode river that it might almost be called "a river of doubt." Ask almost any native son, outside of Anne Arundel county, where it is and the answer immediately will be forthcoming to the effect that he never heard of it. Yet the Rhode river is one of the large water courses of the Western Shore, and on a steep, wooded bluff above the spot where it receives the waters of West river, stands a late Eighteenth century plantation house, the home of a Maryland family which has had much to do with shaping the course of the State's affairs.

The estate is known as Ivy Neck, a name which seems particularly *apropos,* for the old house is almost buried under the thick growth of the green creeper in some places and because of its luxuriance the walls seem to be years older than they actually are. So carefully have the family documents of the Galloway-Cheston-Murray clan (who own the place) been preserved that there is to be encountered at Ivy Neck none of the difficulties which frequently beset the attempt to fix the date of a house within a quarter of a century. These records show definitely that it was in 1787 that James Cheston made contracts with Leonard Harbaugh, carpenter, and Andrew Green, bricklayer, to build him a house thirty-seven feet, five inches, by thirty-five feet nine inches, of brick to be laid in Flemish bond, with plain arches, "the whole of the work to be done in as good form as the house of Captain Noel near Howard Hill

[213]

Market House in Baltimore Town" and "to be complete in three months of good weather from the time it begins."

The plans and specifications included a captain's walk, removed during the Eighteen-sixties in favor of the tall, square cupola which now surmounts the roof. The piazza, which stretches across the garden front of the house, passages and kitchen, all were provided for down to the last detail. The nails and locks were mentioned, too, some of them being imported from London, some bought in this country. Nothing, in fact, was overlooked by the astute James Cheston, who was one of the wealthy planters of Anne Arundel county and was as careful a business man as any to be found in America today. All of his account books show him to have been a man who spared no expense to secure the best and who could not be hoodwinked into accepting anything less. When he furnished his house he recorded expenditures to Gerrard Hopkins, a fine Baltimore cabinet maker, (paying, among other things, seven pounds for a pair of mahogany card tables) and noted the importation of a desk and bookcase from England and a Spanish cedar bookcase.

In its general arrangement Ivy Neck follows the plan of the Brice house at Annapolis and Ratcliffe Manor in Talbot county. The front door opens into a square hall, with the stairway to one side, and the drawingroom is so contrived that the door leading from it to the long piazza overlooking the garden is in direct line with the front door.

The stairway, although altered somewhat from its original effect, is decidedly striking with the newel and landing posts extending to the ceiling instead of stopping short with the balustrade. When Ivy Neck was built it boasted a hanging stairway, but the wear of many feet had weakened it and, a number of years ago, the strain was diminished by replacing the slender posts with columns. The stairway no longer can, in consequence, be classed among the hanging, but it retains its Colonial character.

A small office occupies the space to the right of the hall and the entire garden front of the house is taken up by the drawing-room and diningroom. To one end of the drawingroom a wing has been added in recent years for use as a library, with carved bookshelves built in and polished to the color of honey. In the drawingroom the illusion of other days is enhanced by carved window and door frames, by heirlooms of American Chippendale, some of the chairs having their original needlepoint covers, and by dim old portraits of Revolutionary figures looking down on the possessions they knew in life. One portrait preserves the features of that Capt. Samuel Morris who commanded the first city troop of Philadelphia through many a hard campaign and another represents Levi Hollingsworth, an aide on the staff of Washington.

In the diningroom the old family sideboard still holds the silver which has descended intact through generations, most of it bearing the hallmarks of English makers. The echo of the past comes down too, at Ivy Neck in an old white satin muff, elaborately embroidered, which was carried by a great-grand-mother at her wedding; in queer old stays and the ghost of a shoe, scarcely large enough for a child of twelve, which is one of a pair brought over from London for Mrs. Cheston. All are preserved as mementoes of family life, instead of the museum pieces they easily might be.

Still more stirring reminders of the country's beginnings are to be found in bundles of old letters recounting the intimate story of war privations incident to the Revolution and of the famous Peggy Stewart tea party which did not altogether find favor in the eyes of some of the writers. During the Revolution

James Cheston, who never had taken the oath of allegiance to the Colonial government, returned to England, landing first in France where he was arrested on the charge of being a spy and was rescued from the shadow of the Bastile only through the intervention of Benjamin Franklin, then in France. Others of his Anne Arundel neighbors went over, too, and it was to them that the story of the hardships found in these old letters was told.

Twelve hundred pounds, the exiles were informed, had become the price of a small plough horse, and one hundred dollars the toll for a dozen small chickens. "Very bad veal" cost the Revolutionary consumer in Anne Arundel county fourteen dollars a pound and the price of lamb and beef was equally high. "To live at all takes all the money we can possibly get" wrote one "E. Scott from Belvoir" wryly to Upton Scott in London. In London, too, James Cheston continued his custom of keeping accounts, recording alike small expenditures for "gum elastic" and six shillings "for my brother Dan and myself to hear the oratorio."

The effect produced upon the colonists by the burning of the Peggy Stewart is reflected from two opposing extremes in letters from John Galloway and from Thomas Ringgold, Jr., son and son-in-law, respectively, of Samuel Galloway, father of Mrs. Cheston, and which are kept at Ivy Neck.

Writing from Chestertown Thomas Ringgold, member of the Continental Congress, declared that the owner of the brig had premeditated the affair of the tea to satisfy the ministry, but John Galloway denounced the burning of the boat as "an infamous and rascally affair" of which "the ringleaders begin to be ashamed themselves." These men, he added, asking that their names be kept secret, were Charles Ridgely, son of John,

Dr. Howard, Dr. Warfield and Walter Buier (Bowie?) of Prince George's county.

Nor, apparently, were the young women of the day fully persuaded concerning the wisdom of the Annapolis "tea-party," if the tone of these yellowed missives be taken as an indication of their feelings. "Last night I saw the brig Peggy Stewart burned" wrote "Alice Lee" to Ann Galloway (who later was to become Mrs. James Cheston) while the latter was visiting in Philadelphia with her father and Henrietta Maria Chew, who became the wife of Ann's brother, Benjamin, attorney-general of Maryland during the Revolution. "It was," she added, "a spectacle that shocked me much. I begin to be out of love with patriotism."

There is much more. Days could be spent in deciphering these faded pages of Revolutionary correspondence in which the figures of the early owners of Ivy Neck appear constantly and which serve to show that Maryland families were divided then as they were many years later during the Civil War over problems of allegiance.

From the river front of Ivy Neck there is a view of a picturesque little island which played a long forgotten part in one of the most famous love affairs of Maryland and which bears the significant name of Bachelor's Retreat. This island, then covering about two acres and shaped like an oyster shell, was granted in 1762 to John Ridout by the then Governor Sharpe, who was so madly infatuated with Mary Ogle, later the bride of Ridout. In consideration of the grant Ridout was to pay a rental of "one penny in silver or gold at the two most usual feasts of the year, the Feast of the Annunciation of the Blessed Virgin Mary and St. Michael and All Angels." The wedding of Mary Ogle and John Ridout took place in 1765, three years after the grant was made, but young Ridout's hopes for the success of his suit probably were at low ebb at the time he secured title to the little island. His position in the colony could not compare with that of his rival, and here was an ideal spot to which to retreat and nurse his wounds in silence. The little island was bought from Ridout by James Cheston in 1790—for Ridout had no need of it then—and still belongs to the Ivy Neck estate, though erosion has reduced its size to less than one acre.

The earliest records of Ivy Neck go back to 1688 when a grant of 690 acres was made to John Watkins, Roger Cross and Ferdinand D. Battee. In 1765 it was sold by one John Watkins, Jr., evidently the son or grandson of the original owner, who had acquired possession of the whole tract, to Samuel Galloway, of Tulip Hill. There was no house on the place at that time and the land, apart from its fertility and its picturesque scenery, was remarkable chiefly for the series of "Points" and "Landings" to be found there. Upon the death of Samuel Galloway the property descended to his daughter, Ann, wife of James, the builder.

At Ivy Neck life assumed, with the establishment of the Chestons in their big house, the characteristics which became traditional south of the Mason and Dixon's line and which are maintained on the plantation, almost unchanged, to the present. Negroes worked the land and performed the household tasks. Hams were cured over hickory fires in the old smokehouses and became as famous on Maryland tables as the more widely known Smithfield hams did in Virginia—and today hams are cured at Ivy Neck by the same recipe. Guests came when they pleased and stayed as long as they liked, certain of their welcome.

Since the day when Leonard Harbaugh packed up his tool kit and left Ivy Neck with his contract to build a house "in as good form as the house of Captain Noel" being fulfilled, the house has undergone various changes which have altered its original contours markedly, but it is not difficult to trace the outlines of Leonard Harbaugh's handiwork. The modillioned cornice still shows across the south front below the eaves and the tops of the chimneys, visible through the trees, could belong to no modern structure. No outside shutters have been provided for the original windows which look out from the drawingroom upon the brick-flagged portico and no modern doors will show cross panelling of the type of the doors at Ivy Neck.

The present owners of the place are descendants of the builders. Mrs. C. M. Colhoun, Mrs. Robert Cheston, Mrs. Robert Murray, Miss Emily H. Murray and Miss Anne M. Murray, live on the land which nourished their parents and their grandparents' parents, and are as absorbed as their ancestors were in the cultivation of tobacco, the swarming of bees, smoking hams and the old-fashioned flower garden between the house and the river.

* * *

The only one of all the ancient manor houses of Maryland to bear the architectural imprint of the reign of Queen Anne is Cedar Park, on West River, in Anne Arundel County. None seems more completely to disdain the new ways, none seems more completely self-sufficient.

Through some of the most diverting farming country to be found in Maryland, the country road which branches off to Cedar Park from the macadam speedway linking Annapolis with Washington makes its way past the somnolent little village of Owensville, between high hedgerows until, abruptly, the country which has been reminiscent of Devon all the way becomes so completely like that older land that it is difficult to believe an ocean lies between them. The change is significant. The visitor has reached the old deer park which never has known the touch of a plough or the imprint of a harrow since the limits of Cedar Park were set by "metes and bounds."

Skirting the edge of this ancient preserve, from which the last deer fled long ago, the lane to the house is bordered for some distance on both sides by forest trees and when the alignment fails, individual survivors of the old wooded corridor indicate the way to the entrance. A short brick walk, greened over with moss, leads from the lane to the porch, a curious little square structure with stiff benches and a line of carving pendant from the eaves like a wooden frill, similar carving was turned out many years later by jig-saw contortions to take the country by storm. This same decoration extends all the way around the house, attached to the low, sloping roof which overhangs so far that it seems literally to put the walls "into the shade."

Wide chimneys, distinctive of design and provided with ornate caps, are heavy enough to balance walls containing brick sufficient to build a short row of small city houses and broken at rare intervals by windows. The result of this type of construction makes the living rooms at Cedar Park cool and dark, even on the hottest day. Only the most determined shafts of sunlight penetrate the shadows in some of the rooms, but when they do find their way in they serve to light up some rare heirloom of mahogany or an old portrait rather than to betoken a scorching heat.

In the arrangement of its interior Cedar Park follows its own inclinations. No one can say how many building episodes resulted in the present house, but the oldest part is known to be at least two hundred and fifty years old. A coat of dull brown painted plaster which has covered the walls for a great many years is peeling off now and exposing the brickwork made especially interesting by the manner in which it is com-

CEDAR PARK, SHOWING HOLLY HEDGE

Photo by Pickering

TULIP HILL

HALL AND STAIRWAY AT TULIP HILL

bined with the weatherboarding on parts of the house which have been added since the first of it was built.

The kitchen and pantry are housed in a frame wing of comparatively modern origin, but when the house was built the kitchen occupied a little house of its own at some distance from the main dwelling. A retinue of pickaninnies carried the food to and from the pantry from which it was served by a trained negro who would not have dreamed of calling himself a butler.

The entrance hall, the oldest part of the house, leads through a square opening into the stair hall provided with a stairway extremely simple in design but built entirely of mahogany, steps, risers, balustrade and handrail, black with age. To the right of the stairhall is the diningroom, also one of the oldest rooms in the house, panelled about the fireplace and filled with early American mahogany.

At the end of the stairhall is the drawingroom with a bay window opening through long glass doors upon a tiny porch from which there is a view of twelve miles straight across the Chesapeake Bay to the Eastern Shore. From the porch a steep flight of steps leads down into a garden which is unique in Maryland. To one side is the old green where now only "a ghostly batsman plays to the bowling of a ghost," prolonging their measured revels until the moon comes up and the waters of the Chesapeake gleam phosphorescent at the end of the garden.

Two sides of the garden are enclosed by a hedge of holly, high as a tall man's head, and around the other two sides stretches a border of roses, more than a century old. Not far from the house a great white pine spreads curiously contorted branches decoratively upon the ground and at the far end of the garden gigantic tulip poplars, centuries old, blot out the world at dusk. Beds of bright perennials make daubs of color in unexpected places and in the old floral border are shrubs so old and so rare that many of them are unknown to modern gardeners.

The history of Cedar Park can be followed back to less than fifty years after the arrival of the Ark and the Dove at St. Clement's Island, bringing the first settlers of Maryland. In an old Bible printed in Edinburgh in 1726 and cherished by the Mercer family which, at one time, owned the place, it is stated that the estate was "located" in 1665 by Charles Calvert, Lord Baltimore. Three years later it was bought by Richard Ewen and called "Ewen and Ewenton."

The land, however, remained in the possession of Richard Ewen only a few years and was sold in 1671 to "Joseph Burgess, a transient trader who went to England shortly afterward and died." In 1672 John Kane, executor for Joseph Burgess, sold the farm to Benjamin Lawrence of Wiltshire, England. He, in his turn, disposed of it in 1689 to three men in England, Thomas Curtis, Samuel and Thomas Smith who sent to Richard Johns in America their power of attorney.

This legal step was the beginning of the real development of the estate, for Richard Johns employed as tenant Richard Galloway "who," the old Bible sets forth, "wishing to purchase and being unable, prevailed on John Taylor, a merchant of London, to buy the land and retain the title until he could get the money to pay for it." On the sixth of February, 1690, Cedar Park became the property of John Taylor and a little more than seven years later, on November 19, 1697, Richard Galloway came into possession of the land for which he had served so long.

At some time during his busy life Richard Galloway acquired a knowledge of architecture and when he made ready to build the house at Cedar Park it was erected after his own design. The house was tiny enough at first, but as his family grew and his worldly goods increased Richard Galloway added to his home, appending his additions so skillfully that the rambling effect of the interior only adds to its interest.

Richard Galloway died in 1736, leaving the place, which then was called West River Farm, to his son, Richard Galloway, Jr., who survived his father only by five years. Richard Galloway, Jr., had no sons so his home became the property of his daughter, Elizabeth, who married Thomas Sprigg in 1746. Their only child, Richard Sprigg, became the next owner of the estate which passed, after his death, into the hands of his daughter, Sophia, who married John Francis Mercer.

The Mercers owned the place for many years. At one time a girls' school flourished there under the tutelage of Miss Margaret Mercer, who turned out highly accomplished "young ladies" but was not enough of an ogre to prevent a stolen courtship and a dramatic elopement of one of her pupils. Before that, however, romance had encountered difficulties at Cedar Park for when the aptly named Thomas Sprigg came wooing Elizabeth Galloway his suit found little favor in the eyes of the demure Quakeress who refused to countenance such a worldling.

Argument after argument culminated in a violent quarrel and Sprigg rode away in a tantrum, swearing never to return to his straight-laced sweetheart. It is a decided tribute to the charms of the little Quakeress, however, that a month later he was back again, soberly garbed in "plain" clothes and equipped with the Quaker dialect. To his Elizabeth's inquiries concerning his religious convictions, he replied that he had become a Friend and shortly afterward they were married by the Quaker ceremony.

In 1893 Cedar Park was purchased from the Mercer family by Dr. James M. Murray, whose son and daughter, Miss Elizabeth

Murray and Mr. James Murray, still live there, with their Lares and Penates of Chippendale chairs and Duncan Phyfe tables, old Maryland chests and curious escritoires, handed on from one generation to another and which never have known the interior of an antique shop.

* * *

Very early in the history of Maryland Quakers were seated near Annapolis. Among the Friends who came at this time to Lord Baltimore's civil and religious sanctuary were the Galloways who became in less than a century after their arrival in the colony, both wealthy and influential. Possessed of fertile lands and frugal minds this family ruled over many slaves and indentured servants, developed a taste for horses and fine houses and, in spite of the traditional pacifism of the Quaker sect, became fast friends with the young fighting blood of the country.

On September 22, 1771, the meticulous George Washington wrote in his diary: "Dined at Mr. Sam Galloway's and lodged with Mr. Boucher (the clergyman to whom he later sent "Jacky" Custis to school) at Annapolis."

The dinner in question took place at Tulip Hill, the Galloway home on West river which Samuel Galloway built in 1756 and which then was the finest dwelling in the entire countryside below Annapolis. The house has been estimated to contain at least half a million brick in its central portion and wings, in spite of an entry in Quaker Galloway's account book of April, 1756, noting:

> By making and laying in my house 124,938 bricks at 20 shillings,
> By making 18,000 bricks at 4 shillings as per agreement.

This entry must have referred to the foundations and inner walls!

Pierced and vaulted chimneys, together with a classic entrance portico, give this house a decidedly worldly appearance from its land approach. Decorative panels appear in relief at each side of the circular window in the front gable and a decorative Cupid appears in the pediment of the portico. From the water front the facade is distinctly unusual, seen through the vista of enormous tulip poplars, with the doorway distinguished by a carved, hooded canopy and low wings balancing the main building.

The hall extends from door to door through the house, with a staircase rising behind two arches which meet in the center of the hall over a fluted canopy. Few finer Colonial staircases are to be found in the country than this one at Tulip Hill. Its proportions are entirely happy. The ends of the steps are finished with a bold carving of classic scroll and Greek fret and the spindles are set three to a step, each of the three simply carved in a different pattern. The lowest step extends widely beyond the others and is curved to receive the scroll of the banisters ending in a carved newel post. The handrail which finishes the balustrade is made of selected San Domingo mahogany, the painted panelling of the back part of the hall throwing it into high relief.

Samuel Galloway's wife was an invalid and it is said that consideration for her ill health prompted her husband to see that the risers of the steps were low and easy of ascent. Close inspection of the steps in the stairway at Tulip Hill will disclose a number of gashes in which may be traced a likeness to the prints of a horse's hoof. In explanation of the gashes there is a tradition to the effect that Samuel Galloway's son, a flaming youth if ever there was one, returned one night from an elaborate celebration and rode his horse up the steps to say goodnight to his mother.

In the hall, at the approach to the stairway, is a built-in corner cupboard, with its door swung on H-hinges of wrought iron, beaten out by hand. The drawingroom, to the left of the hall from the land entrance, is large and square, with a high ceiling, and deeply cut windows provided with built-in seats. The fireplace has a well-carved mantel repeating the decorative quality of the staircase. Connecting the drawingroom with the library, which occupies the left wing of the house, is a narrow passageway lighted by a curious, diamond-paned window and in this passageway the floorboards run crosswise.

The diningroom is placed to the right of the hall and from it another passage leads to the kitchen and servants' quarters in the right wing. On the second floor the bedrooms are of good size and, of course, provided with open fireplaces.

A fairly well authenticated story maintains that in the old days an underground, secret passage led from the cellar to the lower terraces of the garden by the river. This story is substantiated in part of an advertisement which appeared in the *Maryland Gazette* of March 22, 1753:

"Just imported from England in the Brigantine Grove, Capt. Robert Wilson, to be sold by the subscriber on board the said brigantine in West River for sterling or current money, a parcel of healthy indented servants; among whom are tradesmen and husbandmen. Samuel Galloway."

In business of this kind Samuel Galloway merely was following the accepted methods of the day. The underground passageway may or may not have existed. At any rate there is no trace of it now.

The gardens at Tulip Hill always have been as famous in Maryland as were the great trees by which the sailors on West river in Colonial days were accustomed to steer their course. Straight, prim paths were laid out on the terraces which dropped

TULIP HILL: SHELL PORTICO OVER GARDEN DOORWAY

LOTHIAN

from the house to the water's edge. Beside them grew lilacs and snowballs, then called the golden rose, though no one knows why; privet and holly and box made the hedges and borders to keep in bounds the larkspur and wallflowers and hollyhocks and candytuft which grew there. Lilies of the valley grew in a damp, shady corner and beds of chamomile, for "tea" and lavender and sweet basil.

There was balsam there, too, called lady's slipper; and rocket known as dame's violet. Pansies appeared by the name of ladies' delight or hearts' ease and there must have been pasque flowers and meadow-sweet and loose-strife and monk's hood as well.

Equally well known in his time was Samuel Galloway's delight in fine horseflesh. His animals, both work and carriage horses, were rivals of the best in the county and his riding horses were the best to be had. During his lifetime there hung on the walls at Tulip Hill a replica of D. Murrier's painting of the Godolphin Arabian.

When Samuel Galloway was gathered to his fathers he was buried in the little plot reserved for the dead at Tulip Hill. The estate descended to his eldest son, John Galloway, who, dying left it to his only child, Mary, wife of Virgil Maxcy, at one time minister to Belgium. At Mrs. Maxcy's death it descended to her daughter, Ann Sarah Hughes, wife of Colonel George W. Hughes, who sold it in 1876 to Henry M. Murray whose wife was a descendant of Samuel Galloway. It now is the summer home of Mrs. Henry H. Flather, of Washington.

* * *

A house which doubled itself is Lothian, typical in every way of the homes erected by the Englishmen who settled in the West river section of Anne Arundel county. Rectangular in form, serene in aspect, it stands in a grove of giant locusts and

[227]

maples a short distance from the road leading from Annapolis to Washington, but it is completely invisible to passersby when the leaves are on the trees.

Originally Lothian was but half its present size, but even then it was a large house and in its complete form its outlines suggest an ease of life and a not-too-insistent concern with the affairs of the world at large which was thoroughly characteristic of the true West river planter.

Built while Thomas Jefferson was struggling with the problems of an infant republic and seeking to evolve from "the mud flats along the Potomac" a city worthy to be called the capital of the United States, Lothian reveals none of the concern which agitated the leaders of the young country, but is, instead, the expression of a builder whose interests were bound up with the well-being of a small circle of country gentlemen who were his neighbors, who preferred to sit at the head of a long table gleaming with hall-marked silver rather than to grow choleric over politics, and who deferred the naming of his home until he discovered in the "Midlothian" of Sir Walter Scott limpid syllables which seemed to fit.

Lothian was built in 1804 by Philip Thomas and has descended through the feminine line to his great-granddaughter, Miss Sally Hall, who occupies the house and superintends the management of the farms which surround it. The approach from the State road leads through rolling, cultivated fields and over a wide lawn where buttercups scatter like gold dust through the grass in June. Tucked into a sheltered corner where the servants' wing adjoins the main portion of the house is a mimosa tree, rare in this climate, which blooms in a tentative way.

The doorway at Lothian supplies the keynote to the house. Designed on classic lines, it presents against the deep red brick of the walls the contrast of fluted pilasters and a triangular pediment, ornamented with dentils. The enframement is constructed of wood, hand carved and painted but, though the paint is in excellent condition some curious corruscation gives it, seen from a short distance, the look of stone. At the roof line a plain white, wooden cornice completes the effect of simplicity. Ivy is only just beginning to encroach on the front facade, but one of the end walls is almost completely hidden by it. Even the outline of the chimneys, which rise two by two at each end of the house, is scarcely discernible under its thick festoons.

A double door, panelled and solid, opens into the central hall which is about fifteen feet wide and leads to a corresponding door at the opposite side of the house, where a short flight of steps descends to a terraced garden. The hall is divided midway by an arch supported on pilasters carved with tambour fluting. From the center of the arch hangs a hurricane lamp of etched glass, a century old.

Back of the arch the stairway is placed against the right wall and is the most pronounced architectural feature of the interior, with broad steps rising with the ease of the day when no one ever was in a hurry. An exceedingly light handrail surmounts a balustrade of square spindles which curl about themselves like the poet's chambered nautilus, instead of terminating in the usual newel post. A single landing breaks the flight to the second floor and another landing divides the flight which continues the ascent to the attic. A conventionalized scroll carving appears on the end of each step and the posts which mark the turn of the stair have carved finials. A half-handrail set into the wall runs parallel with the balustrade.

Into the hallway of Lothian comes a subdued half-light let in through a semi-circular transom which permitted little enough illumination in its palmiest time but which was further throttled many years ago by a strong-willed ancient-of-days who was given to sitting in the hall with her head wrapped in a thick green veil, her hands encased in gloves and complaining bitterly of the glare. To placate the lady the transom was painted green and, though some of the paint has come off since then enough remains to consign the hall to an apparently permanent twilight.

The drawingroom, to the left of the hall, is high ceilinged and square, with a low wainscoting. Its mantel shows a rope carving and tambour fluting and from the walls the features of dark-eyed men in velvet and lace and women in satin gowns look down from dull gilt frames. Back of the drawingroom is the diningroom with two large windows giving a view of the garden and a Hepplewhite sideboard set with a service of Queen Anne silver. Heirlooms are these, silver and sideboard alike. The old brass locks on the doors are still in place and glow from years of polishing by hand.

In addition to the terraced garden where perennials bloom, a part of the vegetable garden at one side of the house also is given over to flowers. Here, just inside the gate, the white, star-like flowers of a sweet jessamine bloom as they did when another mistress of Lothian put on her silken sunbonnet, (still preserved in the house) and her lace mits and went out to do her weeding.

* * *

The traditional stone's throw away from Lothian stands Tudor Hall, built by an ancestor of the present occupant of Lothian. A rambling old frame building is this, smooth-sheathed on the oldest part and weatherboarded on "the new wing." A brick floored porch extends across the front and the low roof comes down to form a covering for the veranda above the porch. Across the back of the house is another veranda, half hidden by climbing roses which seem almost to pose as if aware of the decorative effect they produce. The low, gabled kitchen wing cuts off one end of this veranda and from its coign of vantage the eye travels naturally out upon the broad terrace where a tree of boxwood stands twenty feet high at the far end. Below the terrace, to the left of the kitchens, is the tracery of an old garden. There clumps of box thirty feet in circumference and dark Norway spruces assist in reconstructing in the mind's eye the garden as it used to be.

Tudor Hall makes few pretensions. It is a house of sunlight and cool breezes, an early settler's home, but its entrance door suggests that its occupants could be formal enough when the occasion presented itself. Square, simple pilasters form the en-framement which possesses genuine dignity and the sidelights display a diamond and circle pattern of good design. From the front door, if the back one is opened, too, there is a view straight through the house, over the back veranda, over the broad terrace, past the box tree to the rolling fields which give to the country just south of Annapolis a character entirely different from the sand flats north of the city.

The stairway, with two spindles to each step and a walnut handrail, rises to a landing where it divides and proceeds in two directions to the low-ceilinged bedrooms on the second floor.

The windows in the house form a study in contrasts and tell a mute story of architectural history. In the oldest part the panes are tiny, the muntins broad, producing the effect of an English cottage rather than a "hall." There are twelve panes in each sash and the same number are set in the windows of the new wing which, itself, long antedates the Civil War, but the larger size and the smaller muntins of the "new" windows spell clearly a day when glass had become comparatively plentiful and easy to obtain and prosperity was in the air.

The Hall family of Tudor has been in Maryland since 1698

[231]

when the Rev. Henry Hall, son of Robert Hall, gentleman, a graduate of St. Peter's, Cambridge, came to this country and, in May of that year, was formally inducted as rector of St. James' parish, Anne Arundel county. He had not long been in America before he married Mary DuVal, daughter of Mareen DuVal, a French Huguenot. Both the Rev. Henry Hall and his father-in-law became large landholders in Anne Arundel, Prince George's and Baltimore counties.

The Rev. Henry Hall died in 1722 and about a year and a half after his death his son, Edward, married and became the builder of Tudor. The house always was filled with visitors attracted, in the words of one of their neighbors, by "the cultivated minds and the social ease" of the hosts. In recent years Tudor Hall was considered too large for the needs of its occupants and one wing was moved bodily to the neighboring village of Owensville where it serves as a complete house.

Descendants of Edward Hall and his wife have intermarried with the gentry of the immediate neighborhood and maintain in "the West River country" a manner of living which approaches more nearly that of their forebears who transplanted there the customs and habits of the England of their day than is to be found elsewhere in Maryland on anything like so extensive a scale.

There membership in the Protestant Episcopal Church is still pre-requisite to social eligibility, and there, until the World War overturned many of the one-time standards, "the dress was made for the lady by an artist in that line and the lady was then made to fit the dress so that, when it became *a tout ensemble,* it was a thing of beauty and she was admired and modesty was predominant."

CHAPTER FOURTEEN

Of candle light on panelled walls, of bright red coats and the stake of a life on a wager, of punch in silver bowls and snuff-boxes crusted with jewels is the tale that is told by The Abbey, silent and untenanted, on a quiet street in Chestertown on the Eastern Shore.

A few hundred feet distant stands the old Custom House, built by the British for the colonial government, and, beyond that, Widehall, where Thomas Smythe flourished before the Revolution. In the vicinity are other houses of ancient vintage, sleepy looking, fitting easily into their surroundings, but it was at The Abbey during the first years of the Eighteenth century that the wine flowed most deeply red; at The Abbey where smoke from long-stemmed pipes wreathed thickest and at The Abbey where the laughter was lightest, for here lived the young British officers of the port and here they held a long wassail. The Abbey was their club and the blood leaped in their veins.

Within the last century the village street which once terminated at the edge of The Abbey grounds has been cut through, severing the broad, deep sodded lawn which slopes to the edge of the Chester river from the house and bringing the mansion up short against a brick pavement, itself wrinkled with age. A high brick wall, backed by overgrown shrubbery, conceals what is left of the garden at the side and back of the house from gaze of passersby and the tall, ivied walls of the house have assumed an air of complete inscrutability. The picture is minus its frame.

And as if resentful of the encroachment of civilization,—even so leisurely a civilization as that of Chestertown,—the old house has succeeded in interposing between itself and the world outside a barrier which it never lets down and which it only partially removes for the most understanding visitor. It is as though some undue familiarity had been taken, some reserve attacked, which The Abbey, for all its interior intimations of former gayety, has met by wrapping itself in a cloak of determined aloofness.

A granite, Neo-Grec portico, much later in date than the house and built of the fine stone which is native to the upper part of the Eastern Shore, is approached by short flights of steps leading from opposite directions and provides a formal setting for the entrance. Doric columns uphold the roof of the portico, with its panelled soffit, and the heavy front door swings in a wide arc into the entrance hall lighted by a stained glass transom over the door. The Abbey transom is unique among Colonial houses in Maryland. Such glass is to be found only in this hallway and the blue and red light it emits lends a certain suitability to the name bestowed in hilarity upon the club.

The drawingroom and library, to the right and left of the entrance hall, are rooms to conjure with. No one ever would suspect from the exterior of The Abbey the presence within of rooms like these, so different and so lovely. The drawingroom is a place for laughter, a background made for light conversation and airy persiflage, but the library is a restful retreat. The drawingroom door opening from the hall is placed almost in the exact center of one side of the room, with two windows breaking the opposite wall and two in the wall next to the street, but it is to the fireplace instead of to the pictures framed by the windows that the eye immediately travels. Upon the wide breast of the chimney is carving of such quality that it has been declared to be the work of Grinling Gibbons himself, done in England and sent over to America for installation in this house. Whether it is or not no one, probably, is destined to know, for it is unlikely

[234]

THE ABBEY: DETAIL OF CARVING ON
OVERMANTEL IN DRAWINGROOM

THE ABBEY: INTERIOR WOODWORK

THE ABBEY

Photo by W. C. Brown

that anyone ever will be brash enough to remove it from the wall in search of the signature which Gibbons invariably placed on his work.

One misses at The Abbey much more acutely than in most Colonial houses the portrait from the frame with rosettes in its ears above the fireplace. Here, one feels, the need is great for some pictured beauty in powdered hair and patches, some Gainsborough lass to look down in complete understanding upon a gay scene about the fire. Above the frame is an entablature surmounted by a broken pediment but the *piece de resistance* is the sculptured representation of a tree spreading its branches protectingly over the cottage in which the white man is said to have made a treaty of peace with the Indians. On each side of the chimney piece bows of ribbon are carved in high relief, with pendant flowers and fruits.

The frieze over the drawingroom door is carved with scrollwork and shells and the door itself is mahogany. The walls of the drawingroom are panelled, too, but in such a manner as to provide an absorbing puzzle to the person who would examine them, all the evidence tending to show that they actually are sheathed, with the moulding outlining the panels tacked on afterwards. So many coats of paint cover the panelling, however, that it is impossible to be certain of this.

A mahogany door also provides entrance to the library where the decorations are much more subdued than in the drawingroom, but no less well thought out. A built-in shell cupboard is inserted into the wall at the left of the fireplace and is provided with wide doors, found in the cellar when the house was renovated a number of years ago.

After running the length of the drawingroom and library, which it separates, the entrance hall widens out into a great stair hall at the head of the back wing and which is fully two-thirds as wide as the entire front facade. At the left a double stairway, known as the antler type from the resemblance of its design to the antlers of a deer, mounts to the second floor, the space between the two flights being taken up by a wide fireplace. The spindles of the balustrade are delicately carved and a mahogany handrail and half-handrail complete a stairway which has few equals and no superiors in Maryland houses. On the opposite side of the stair hall a door opens on to a long porch which runs the length of the back wing and faces the garden. The old wing also has a secret stairway, reached through a trap door, which probably was useful at times of Indian raids—or visits from the tax collector.

Upstairs the bedrooms have the same generous proportions as the rooms on the first floor, each being provided with its own fireplace, where pronged flames gasped and sputtered at their reflection in polished mahogany highboys. Over the drawing-room the walls of the master chamber are covered with panels four and a-half feet wide, alternating with others much narrower.

In the days when The Abbey was the home of a coterie of light-hearted young Englishmen who took their duties at the port anything but seriously, this old house was one of the gayest places in Maryland but after the Revolution it seemed, somehow, not to fit into the new scheme of things. It was owned by the Murrays, the Smyths, the Pearces and the Barrolls, all old Eastern Shore families. Charles Willson Peale occupied it at one time. Many splendid parties took place there after the Revolution, for the hall was a perfect setting for the saraband and the varsouvienne, but the spirit was gone. To none of its successive owners, apparently, was the old house completely vital. There is something about the place today which seems to admit that between it and the men and women who came and went there were no ties which it was heartbreak to sever, as there were in so many Colonial houses of the South where the bonds between men and their homes were as strong as the bonds of kindred.

After innumerable changes of ownership the house came into the possession of Senator James Alfred Pearce whose identity was impressed on it much more strongly than that of any of his predecessors after the Revolution, so much so that the house became known as the Pearce House and is generally called by that name in Chestertown today. After Senator Pearce's death the place descended to his daughter, Minnie, who married Joseph Ringgold from whom it was purchased a number of years ago by Mr. and Mrs. Henry Whaland Catlin, of New York. Mr. and Mrs. Catlin occupied it for a time, but they no longer make it their home.

* * *

Down the same street, and across the way, there is a break in the hedge, and a flight of stone steps leading between square brick gate posts, surmounted by huge stone balls, to a flagged terrace where violets push up between the stones. Beyond is another flight of wide marble steps, cracked and stained with age, the approach to a mid-Eighteenth century Georgian mansion which fully justifies on close acquaintance the air of elegance it presents.

Widehall is the home of Mr. and Mrs. Wilbur Ross Hubbard. Searching investigations which have been conducted by its owners and by architects interested in the place indicate that it was built between 1732 and 1762. Closer than that it is impossible to approximate. The property on which the house stands was sold for the traditional song in 1732 and in 1762 it changed hands to the tune of eighteen hundred pounds, a considerable sum for that period and which seems to show that, during the interval, a house of no little importance had been built on the land. Across the street, and also belonging to Mr. and Mrs. Hubbard, is the old Custom House, for Chestertown is one of the oldest ports of entry in Maryland. The Custom House is now used as an apartment house. At the end of the garden the Chester river is exceedingly busy, even though the craft which navigate its waters are predominantly on pleasure bent and the commerce of the world has passed by Chestertown on the other side.

The white doorway, constructed of wood and painted, is generous in its outlines, with an intangible something about it more frequently encountered in the colonies to the North than in Maryland, a reserve which in no way implies a lack of warmth or hospitality.

Widely spaced, engaged columns, fluted by hand, stand on each side of the eared door frame, supporting an entablature carved with Greek triglyphs. A plain, triangular pediment completes the picture. A heavy panelled door with a brass knocker opens into the hall which gives the place its name. Broad, triple arches, resting on square pillars, step the line of what would be the conventional central hall of a Georgian interior, but this hall is not to be compressed in any such fashion and proceeds to occupy an entire half of the left side of the house, with a hanging mahogany stairway sweeping up at one side to the second floor.

There is something almost human about that stairway. Wainscoted next the wall with wide, flat boards, topped by a half-handrail, it displays that costly balustrade, with its scroll step and capacious landing, like a countess showing off the family pearls. Each of the low, easy steps is made of a solid block of wood and the spindles are so like those of the stairway of Independence Hall in Philadelphia that students of Colonial manners, putting their similarity together with other points of kinship to Independence Hall which are to be found in the house, have hazarded the belief that the architect of the two buildings was one and the same person.

WIDEHALL: INTERIOR

Photo by W. Coulbourn Brown

ENTRANCE TO WIDEHALL

Photo by W. Coulbourn Brown

DININGROOM FIREPLACE AT WIDEHALL

Which is as it may be. To the right of the hall, doorways with classic cornices lead into the drawingroom and livingroom. On the left side of the house, and beyond the arch which carries out the Georgian tradition by placing itself midway between the doors of the street and river fronts, another classic doorway opens into the diningroom, which is the most distinguished apartment on the lower floor and which commands a fine view of the river, with its white bridge in the foreground.

The woodwork in the diningroom shows the best workmanship in the house. The light wooden cornice is decorated with the continued Wall of Troy design, cut on the slant, with the design meeting in the center of the overmantel and above the windows. The overmantel is adorned with a particularly fine broken pediment above an eared panel made to frame an oil painting. Upon the mantel shelf rests a Terry clock. At the sides of the fireplaces deep cupboards are built into the wall, with panelled doors and built-in drawers for silver and linen.

All of the rooms adhere strictly to the classic *motif* in decoration, but in each of them the detail is varied. The cornices display both the broken and continued Greek key design, dentils and the egg and dart, with ears on the window frames at the top and lateral consoles resting upon the chair rails above the dado. Between the livingroom and the drawingroom the door jambs are panelled in broad rectangles. In the drawingroom the overmantel also displays a broken triangular pediment, with the panelled space for a picture, but the proportions are a bit less spirited than those which distinguish the diningroom mantel. The original lock of wrought silver still fastens the door of the library and there is a legend that the original lock on the front door was silver, plated with gold.

Mahogany was used prodigally in the construction of Widehall. In addition to the mahogany of the stairway, the chair rail in the livingroom and all the window sills are of this wood. Silver knobs also appear on the inside panelled shutters in the livingroom, as well as on the doors, the richness of its detail giving rise to the conjecture that in the early days of Widehall this room probably served as the drawingroom.

On the second floor the stair hall also makes use of the decorative arch, and nearly duplicates in its proportions the size of the large hall below. While it affords a splendid upstairs sitting room it encroaches disconcertingly upon the space available for bedrooms. Only four sleeping apartments of the kind referred to in the Twentieth century as "master bedrooms" are to be had in Widehall. In one of them, however, there is a mantel rescued a few years ago from the cellar into which it had been cast a generation before, showing on the under side of the shelf the "nails of the Parthenon" and decorated across the frieze with hand carved triglyphs.

Nothing whatever can be discovered of the beginnings of Widehall, but in its existence it has endured most of the exaltations and dejections which are possible to an old house. The first family known to have lived there bore the name of Wilmer. Later, it came into the possession of Col. Thomas Smythe, first merchant of Chestertown, a justice of the Kent county court from 1759-69, and who also was a member of the Council of Safety. Later Widehall was acquired by one Bedingfield Hands. Subsequently it was the home of Robert Wright, a member of the United States Senate, and then of Ezekial Chambers, also a member of the Senate.

Washington was a guest there when he went to Chestertown on the occasion of the founding of Washington College, the only educational institution in the country which had his personal sanction for the use of his name, and he stayed there again when the Board of Visitors, of which he was president, met to discuss the affairs of the college.

Not long after the Civil War, Widehall was bought by a Colonel Crawford, of the Federal army, who had seen the place while he was campaigning in Maryland and who determined then to own it if it were possible to secure it. Colonel Crawford's ownership, unfortunately, corresponded with what one recent writer on architecture calls "that curious era of bad taste," and innumerable atrocities were wreaked on the house.

In place of the old hip room, with its dormer windows looking mildly out from every side, a Mansard abomination covered the walls. Slate mantels replaced the hand-carved wooden mantels and fireplaces were sealed up to permit the installation of stoves. Hideous chandeliers made their appearance. In short, the house conformed to the most rigid demands of the Seventies.

The next stage of Widehall's debasement saw it pressed into service as a boarding house. For more than thirty years aromas of boiled cabbage and weak gravies sifted through the aristocratic, high-ceilinged rooms which had, somehow, "to grin and bear it." Then, in 1909, it became the property of Mr. and Mrs. Hubbard, who, with the assistance of the late Howard Sill of Baltimore as their architect, undertook its restoration. With the exception of the staircase leading from the second floor reception hall to the attic, the architect and the owners of the house adhered strictly to the idea of simplicity in renovation and decoration. This staircase, unfortunately, was "dressed up" by the application of a more or less elaborate scroll design to the ends of the steps, but only a hypercritical eye would be disposed to cavil at the deviation from what, otherwise, constitutes a genuine resurrection.

On the river front a two-story columned porch has been added, running the full length of the house and terminating at one end close to an ancient Paradise tree with branches that unite and then divide, only to repeat the performance which has amazed horticulturists who have seen it.

Inside and out, Widehall possesses strong individuality. There is an easy tolerance about the ivy hung walls, with the white keystoned panels over the windows peeping through the green, and a certain independence in the course of the chimneys which lift their heads parallel to the lateral axis of the house instead of crossing it in the usual way. The floor boards of the hall betray the same independence but the spaciousness of the broad arches and the height of the ceiling present a feeling of formality and approval of accepted conventions.

Widehall is furnished with antiques of its period which have been picked up by Mr. and Mrs. Hubbard in all parts of the world and which have been assembled to conform to the character of the house. Six Duncan Phyfe chairs of the period stand in the livingroom and in the upstairs hall is an Eighteenth century camisole recently brought from Russia. In the diningroom a Hepplewhite sideboard stands against a wall which is neither deep blue nor green and yet is both, its dark mahogany contrasting with the color of the upper walls and the white, panelled dado below.

Stretching in front of the columned porch a modern addition to the river front of the house, is a broad terrace crossed by a flagged walk leading between two stone lions which sleep in the sun, half blanketed with ivy. From the terrace a step or two leads down to the driveway which cuts into the lawn between the house and the river and to one side is a box garden, with a flagged path and old-fashioned perennials in a succession of bloom. At the end of the garden, at the edge of the water, stands a pergola covered with roses and wistaria, the rendezvous of hummingbirds and Baltimore orioles.

*   *   *

The village of Queenstown, named in honor of "good Queen Anne," has grown up, in a manner of speaking, right on the front doorstep of Bowlingly, a tract of land bestowed by Lord Baltimore in 1662 upon James Boulen (or Bowling) of whom nothing further is known. In the course of time the original two hundred and fifty acres were augmented by other tracts so that, at one time, it is said that the lane into the mansion was eight miles long from the point at which it departed from the public road.

James Bowling could have held the land only for a short time, for old records show that between the years 1670 and 1675 Bowlingly was the home of one Henry Hawkins, who paid Lord Baltimore a rent of five shilling sterling "at the two most usual feasts of the year," or, as they say even now on the Eastern Shore, "at Spring Fair and Fall Fair." All "rights, profitts and benefits" belonging to the land were the property of the owner, "Royall Mines escepted." It seems unlikely, from all the evidence at hand, that the house in which Henry Hawkins lived at Bowlingly persists, even in part, in the present mansion which has all the appearance of having been built a short time before the Revolution, with later additions.

A long, attenuated house, stretching over a great amount of space, Bowlingly stands on a bluff which slopes sharply down to Queenstown creek, and is so placed that it catches all the breezes which blow from the water in summer. Its builder, however, was obviously not a light-minded individual, for while providing his family with a maximum of comfort in summer, he also took care to build warmly for the winter. Not a window appears in the end of the house nearest the water, except two tiny apertures cut high up near the roof. The same forethought is evident in the cellar, where the double walls have an airchamber between, making the place dry and comfortable at all seasons for the women who worked on the looms which were set up in the brick-partitioned rooms for the weaving of the vast quantities of linen and cloth required for the family and slaves. The house servants had their living quarters in the basement, too, but the quarters for the field hands stood at some distance from the house.

Bowlingly is essentially a country house. There is lacking about the brickwork of its walls that meticulousness of craftsmanship which is to be found in the pre-Revolutionary houses at Annapolis, but the walls are strong and staunch, and the modillioned cornice contrives to give it an air of seemliness. The impression received by the person who sees the house for the first time is one of a succession of rooms toeing a mark and strung out half the length of a city block. Nor is the impression altogether exaggerated but there is, as usual, a reason.

The original builder of Bowlingly apparently contented himself with a snug structure containing rooms which were large but few in number,—sufficient for the needs of himself and his family with little space to spare. Then he added a servants' wing and bided his time until circumstances would permit him to enlarge his home to more comfortable proportions. From the arrangement of the house it seems as if the tradition that the builder intended to double its depth is correct, but before anything could be done toward carrying out such plans the house was partly destroyed by fire and the tax upon foundations was so heavy that the new wing was built upon the foundations of the old servants' wing. Still later, the wing which now fills the need for kitchens and servants quarters was built as an "L" to the main structure and connects, by a venerable old wall, which looks years older than the present Bowlingly house, with a group of farm buildings. In all the building and remodelling the house lost an old squirrel tail oven, and an enormous fire-

STAIRWAY AT BOWLINGLY

BOWLINGLY

Photo from Collection of James Donnell Tilghman

SIDE PORCH, BLOOMINGDALE

BLOOMINGDALE: SIDE

place, where once hung a huge copper kettle always full of boiling water for whatever demands might be made upon it, was sealed up.

The main entrance, for each wing as it was added was provided with a front door of its own, opens into a wide hallway with a double stair rising at each side and meeting at a landing above a deep arch. From the landing the stairs proceed in a single flight to the second floor. This stairway, evidently, was the apple of the builder's eye, for upon it he lavished more attention than upon all the rest of the house put together. At the extreme depth of the arch which divides the two flights, panelled double doors open to give a glimpse of the water lapping the edge of the bluff. In the panelled sides of the arch are doors opening into deep cupboards, said to have been the hiding places of "slackers" during the Revolution. The sides of the stairway are wainscoted elaborately and a black walnut rail and half-handrail complete a real architectural achievement.

In the drawingroom the original mantel, with its fluted frieze and columns turned by hand, decorates the chimneypiece and the deeply set windows have three rows of small panes in the upper sash and but two rows in the sash below, a type of window to be found on many pre-Revolutionary houses on the Eastern Shore. The square upstairs hall once was used as a chapel, with family prayers every morning—the family and guests occupying the central space and the slaves forming an ebony background against the wall—for at this time Bowlingly belonged to devout Catholics who never omitted their daily devotions and who gave the most beautiful daughter of the family to the order of the Sisters of Charity.

Sixteen acres were included in the lawn which surrounded the house during its halcyon years. On the side next the present site of the village the lawn was graded and deeply sodded, but on the side next the creek it was disposed in wide terraces, planted with flowers and old-fashioned shrubs down to the wharf where the water was deep enough to permit ocean-going vessels to anchor and where frequently such big craft came, with a cargo of goods from England, to tie up long enough to permit the citizenry for miles around to visit the ship and purchase what they needed. At such times there would be a procession of quaint and curious vehicles through the estate the day long, vehicles ranging from the ox-cart to the great coach of the neighborhood beauty, for the small farmer was as welcome as the rich landholder to come and buy.

From Henry Hawkins Bowlingly passed into the possession of Richard Bennett, son of that Richard Bennett, who was one of the commissioners of Parliament appointed after the execution of Charles I to reduce the American colonists to submission, and who came to Maryland after he had been driven out, with other Puritans from Virginia. With William Claiborne the elder Bennett succeeded in stirring up a rebellion in Maryland against the proprietary government and in setting up a Cromwellian government at Providence (now Annapolis) in opposition to the government of Lord Baltimore at St. Mary's. Later the two came to terms and Bennett retired to private life and the acquisition of vast estates. The list of his son's holdings as recorded among the archives of the Land Office at Annapolis is longer than that of any other individual of his day and his wealth is said to have been greater than that of any man in Maryland. From Richard Bennett the estate descended to his daughter who married Edward Neale and from them it was devised to their daughter, Martha Neale Hall, whose portrait hung over the mantelpiece in the drawingroom when Bowlingly was bombarded by the British in 1812 while His Majesty's fleet was on its way up the Chesapeake Bay to attack Baltimore at Fort

McHenry. After the bombardment a landing party came ashore and swarmed into the house where one of the British officers saw fit to slash the portrait of Mrs. Hall with his sabre. The landing party was restrained by Admiral Cockburn, the British commander, from committing further depredations, but for more than three-quarters of a century afterward traces of the British bombardment could be discovered at Bowlingly in the form of bullets embedded in the walls.

Martha Neale Hall's life seems to have been crowded with incident and there is still current in Queen Anne's county a story that, as a child of ten or twelve, she was standing on the colonial porch of the house when three canoes of Indians approached from the shores of Kent. They landed at the wharf and, after friendly salutations, went to the grave of their former chief under a majestic walnut tree (opposite the present site of Queenstown Methodist Episcopal Church) where they performed a war dance, buried gifts and peaceably left. A young scion of the old tree is pointed out as marking the place where the last known visit of the red men to Bowlingly was made.

When Mrs. Hall died Bowlingly was sold to Captain Benjamin Massey, who was one of the American officers in the engagement of August 2, 1814, against the British under Captain Robertson at Slippery Hill, the famous old duelling ground three miles south of Queenstown. A number of years later it was purchased by Thomas Hall Rozier, a relative of the Hall family, and, still later, it became the property of Charles Mitchell, a descendant of Richard Bennett. Mr. Mitchell, in his turn, sold the place to the Queen Anne Railroad Company in 1893 and for thirty years it was used as an hotel. During the tenure of the railroad company the Colonial porches were removed and the present veranda, almost completely surrounding the house, was added for the rocking chairs of summer boarders. From the railroad company it was bought by Mr. and Mrs. Samuel Edward Whiting Friel, its present owners.

Ten acres still are set apart for use as a lawn, but of the plantation only a hundred and twenty acres are left. Between the house and the river are remains of the old graveyard, with worn flat tombstones upon which picnickers of a few years ago spread out their luncheons. On one of the stones is an inscription which never fails to arouse discussion. It reads:

Sacred to the memory of
Clarinda Underhill
Wife of Anthony Underhill, Esq.,
Of the city of New York,
Who departed this life
On the 6th of June, 1835,
At Queen's Town
Aged 66 years.
This tomb is erected by those who most valued her while
living and lament her when lost forever.

War has had its way with Bowlingly. First it was the reputed refuge of Tories during the Revolution and then it was in the line of fire during the War of 1812-14. During the Civil War the gray-clad troops of the Confederacy drilled on the lawn while the Union forces were encamped only about a mile away. During the Spanish-American War the Fifth Maryland regiment encamped for a short period near the manor house, and while the World War was in progress its drawingroom became a meeting place for members of the Queenstown chapter of the Red Cross. An old story insists that somewhere on the land there is buried treasure, hidden during one of the wars in which Bowlingly has figured, but though earnest seekers have dug the lawn over and over again, no trace of it has come to light.

* * *

A short distance from Bowlingly, at the head of a little stream known as the Back Wye, stands Bloomingdale in Queen Anne's, so known by its formal appellation in legal documents and for the benefit of strangers, but referred to invariably in Queen Anne's county as "the old Sallie Harris place."

No other woman of Maryland, not even Mistress Margaret Brent who came out strongly for woman's rights before the colonists fairly had time to catch their collective breaths, seems to have left such an impress upon the land on which she lived. No other woman, it may be, ever was such a belle as this amazing bit of femininity who is said to have numbered her "suitors" by the score, flirted with them, encouraged them and laughed at them and to have ended her devastating career by flouting them all and shutting herself up with her less volatile sister, Mary, in "the old wing" at Bloomingdale where the two of them lived in two or three rooms and where the once lovely Sallie became a "character."

Bloomingdale was known by the name of Mount Mill when it was patented June 7, 1665, by one Captain Robert Morris, who held it for nineteen years and then sold it, in 1684, to Jacob Seth, who added more land, making the tract two miles square. When Jacob Seth, who seems to have been a methodical and far-sighted man, died in 1698 he left his Mount Mill to his son John, providing that in case John died childless, the property should descend to his other son, Charles.

John did inherit the place, but he did not live to be quite twenty-one, as his father seems to have foreseen, and the place passed into the hands of Charles Seth. Two generations later it was owned by his grandson, Thomas Johnings Seth, who died without descendants and Mount Mill, as it still was called, was sold to settle the estate. The name was unchanged when it was purchased by Edward Harris in 1820, but when the gay

Sallie and her sister Mary inherited it they changed the name to Bloomingdale as more suited to the taste of a Godey's Lady's Book era.

The different building episodes which have taken place at Bloomingdale, culminating in the erection by Thomas Johnings Seth of the big brick mansion during the Seventeen-nineties, are clearly visible. Oldest of all is the primitive little building used for a kitchen when the family fortunes had grown with the growing country sufficiently to permit the erection of the portion now known as "the old wing." This part of the house is constructed of clumsy-looking brick laid in English bond, with a triple window in the second story. No attempt was made to decorate the rooms, low of ceiling and sparing of windows, which were plastered directly on the bricks of the outer walls and partitions. The fireplaces, too, were built strictly for use, their low openings giving an almost monastic asceticism to the rooms and making them the natural refuge of a woman who fled to them when the pomps and vanities failed of allure.

The main wing of Bloomingdale, the part built by Thomas Seth, for no records have been found to identify his ancestor who built either the first little cabin or the "old wing," is a commanding structure standing at the head of a driveway which leads without circumlocution from the public road between Queenstown and Wye Mills and is swallowed up in the lawn.

First sight of the two-story hexagonal portico, which stands before the front door, serves to emphasize the individuality of Bloomingdale, for this is the only Colonial house in Maryland where this geometric figure furnished inspiration for an entrance porch and not for an integral part of the house. Certain details of its finish indicate that it is of a later date than the house, but replaces a previous one of similar design. The brick walls are laid up in Flemish bond, with cornered mortar, and are finished

STAIRWAY AT BLOOMINGDALE

Photo from Collection of James Donnell Tilghman

BLOOMINGDALE: DETAIL OF INTERIOR
WOODWORK

BLOOMINGDALE: DRAWINGROOM MANTEL

Photo by W. F. Parrott

WALNUT GROVE

This house was built in 1683 by Solomon Wright of England, who was sent here by the Crown to collect taxes. The house is built of logs and bricks and has paneled walls. It is on the farm known as Walnut Grove and adjoins "Reed's Creek Farm." The farm is owned by Mr. Dorsey.

by a cornice provided with modillions and dentils, the over-hanging eaves diminishing the appearance of height. The hip roof is pitched exceedingly low, with a single dormer looking out at either side, the comb of their triangular caps being on a line with the peak of the roof. The two chimneys which serve this portion of the house are very wide and stretch up above the dormers, parallel with the axis of the house, as they do at Widehall in Chestertown. This arrangement, while it seems a bit extraordinary, perhaps, from an architectural point of view, adds considerably to the comfort and decorative possibilities of the interior, for the fireplaces, instead of being placed between end windows, are in the center of long, interior walls and all of the heat of the chimneys was conserved inside the house in days when there was no such thing as a radiator.

At the extreme end of the left wall a little portico has been built, roofed in like a miniature house, with a hooded arch over the steps, and at the back of the house a small, one-story portico stands at the top of a steep flight of steps leading up from the one-time garden, gone these many years for lack of some one to care for it.

Joining the main wing with the old wing is a low, flat-topped structure with a curious doorway covered by a peaked hood which is supported on ornamental iron brackets and ornamented in front with wrought iron scrollwork. Above, the wall is broken by arched recesses, simulating windows.

The hallway at Bloomingdale is elaborate, for at the time this house was built the owners of Maryland plantations lavished much attention on these corridors which almost always took up at least one-fourth of all the space on the lower floor and which frequently became the family sitting room in warm weather. With the well of the stairway leading to the top of the house and a door open at each end to catch any breeze that eddied

[251]

no place in the house was as well ventilated or as cool. Thomas Seth built his hall twelve feet wide and forty feet long, and provided it with three entrances, one at the front and one at the back and one at the end of the wide "L" in which the stairway is placed. The front door is set in a round arch, the pattern of its transom and sidelights being outlined by a spider-web tracery of leading.

A broad, rather flat arch divides the main hall from its "L," with a beaded oval in the center of the soffit to frame the hook from which the old candle lamp which lighted the hall at night was hung by a chain. The stairway mounts with low, wide steps at the right of the "L" hall, its flight to the second floor being broken by two landings. Its sides are panelled and the ends of the steps carved in a scroll design in high relief. Square spindles, very slender and placed two to a step, with a mahogany handrail above, form the balustrade which makes a sweeping curve on the lowest step, considerably wider than the others, and a half-handrail is inserted into the wall, stopping short at the recessed and panelled window near the foot of the stairs.

Carving done with an evident sureness of touch appears on the panelled window frames of library and drawingroom, and on the five-foot mantelpieces where small, fluted columns appear, two on each side of the fireplace, and the frieze is carved with oval medallions outlined with beading. Arched recesses flank the mantelpiece in the library and form a most unusual feature of the house, in that the reveals are formed by doors which open on shelves.

An old mill, where corn and wheat grown on the Bloomingdale acres were ground by water power into flour, was operated during the time of the Seths for the benefit not only of their own plantation, but for their neighbors as well, with a quaint old miller's house which easily might have "stood on the river

Dee." After the tenure of the Seths had passed and Edward Harris had come and gone his way, the old mill, like the old place, merged its identity with that of Sallie Harris and became known as "the Sallie Harris mill." Not far from the dwelling is a long, stark brick building with sixteen windows—the old slave quarter. This building accommodated sixteen negro families, one to a window.

"The paintings at Bloomingdale," says John Martin Hammond in his Colonial Mansions of Maryland and Delaware, "which were imported from the Old World in the stately Colonial days attracted great attention from distinguished visitors and guests and one was given additional celebrity by being the subject of an animated controversy between the venerable Bishop Whittingham and a Catholic prelate. In one room, a little winter parlor and a dreamer's paradise, were hung most of the family portraits and here were the pictures of the maiden sisters, made in the heyday of their youth and dressed alike in black velvet and pearls, but with only the outline of a family resemblance between them. The name of the artist is not known, but he gave to posterity the fair patrician faces of two of the rarest beauties of the day. The one looked down in the blue-eyed serenity of a household divinity; the other with a shade of deeper thought, or a trace of hauteur."

Sallie Harris, as one might have expected of so dominant a personality, outlived her sister and when she died willed Bloomingdale to her cousin, Severn Teackle Wallis, a Maryland lawyer whose brilliance won for him membership in the Royal Academy of History of Madrid, and made him a Fellow in the Royal Society of Northern Antiquaries of Copenhagen. Severn Teackle Wallis had been graduated from college at sixteen, had completed his law course at nineteen and had been permitted to practice although, of course, he could not be admitted to the bar until he was of age. He had sought in every way possible to prevent the Civil War, being one of the members of a committee who protested to President Lincoln against the passage of troops through Baltimore and later was arrested with other members of the Legislature to prevent the secession of the State from the union. For months he had languished in prison, refusing to take all oaths which were submitted to him as the price of his freedom and losing his health in consequence, but finally the jail doors opened and he was released unconditionally.

Such a man, it would seem, would leave his impress indelibly on the place where he lived for some time and which he retained in his possession until his death. Posterity generally is quick to point with pride to the dwelling places of the great, but not even the personality of the man who was mentally as much at home in Europe as in America and who had much to do with his country's history could serve to obliterate, or even to overshadow the association of Bloomingdale with the name of Sallie Harris.

When Teackle Wallis died—he had dropped the Severn in favor of his middle name long before—he willed Bloomingdale to his nephew who later sold it to Hiram G. Dudley, father of Frank S. Dudley, of Baltimore, the present owner.

It is inevitable that a place such as Bloomingdale should have its ghost, though there is only one recorded account of its appearance. This event, according to old newspaper accounts, took place in 1879 when Miss Sallie Harris was entertaining a guest, a Mrs. Nancy De Courcy. The two had retired for the night, their nightcaps tied under their chins, when a knock at the front door startled them both. Mrs. De Courcy, thoroughly frightened, but unwilling to stay behind while Miss Harris went to investigate, accompanied the servant to the front door and there came face to face with the wraith-like figure of William

Sterrett, Miss Harris' nephew, who had been drowned in the old mill race.

The figure moved past them, the story goes, beckoning the two to follow, and down the hall to the stairway which it mounted, and then proceeded to the door of the room William Sterrett had occupied in life. Straight through the door, which had been kept locked, it went without a pause. By this time, Mrs. De Courcy and the servant were frantic wtih fear. Miss Harris, who had joined them, produced the key to the room and when the door finally was unlocked everything was in place except the bed, which was rumpled as if someone had slept in it.

No explanation of this eerie visit ever was made. The house was searched the next day but nothing was discovered which would throw any light on the occurrence and the apparition never returned.

*　*　*

Less than a quarter of a century after the Ark and the Dove had landed in Maryland, there came to that part of Lord Baltimore's province then known as Kent county, on the Eastern Shore, a family which bore the ancient and honorable English name of Hemsley and took up land which lies now partly in Queen Anne's county and partly in Talbot. At that time neither Queen Anne's nor Talbot had been created.

The Hemsley family traces its origin to the manor of Elmeslac on the River Rye, in England, listed in the Domesday survey of 1086 and afterwards confiscated by the Conqueror. The Hemsley lands in America were the most fertile in all the rolling and picturesque peninsula which is washed by the Chesapeake and Delaware Bays. For many generations that part of their holdings known as Cloverfields was thought to have been the ancestral seat of the family in Maryland, but recent research has disclosed evidence which makes this seem improbable and which seems to show that Cloverfields was acquired by purchase from the original patentees and added to the already extensive Hemsley holdings. It is, however, more completely identified with the name than any other estate.

The earliest known proprietor of the part of Cloverfields then known as Hopewell was one Captain John Sergeant, said to have been the first man ever to tie up a ship at the Cloverfields wharf and who died a score of years and more before the land became Hemsley property. His grave was made in a field which then formed part of the estate and later became known as Pegg's Field Farm, with a stone bearing the date, May 5, 1676, to mark his final earthly abode. The stone served for more than two hundred years to recall to succeeding generations the existence of this Maryland pioneer, but finally was diverted from its purpose to become a doorstep for the tenant of Pegg's Field Farm. Since then it has been broken and lost and today there is no trace either of grave or tombstone.

It was not long after Queen Anne's county had become a separate political entity, however, that a patent was given by Lord Baltimore, the Proprietary of Maryland, bearing the signature of "our dear brother, Benedict Leonard Calvert, Esq'r, Governor and Commander in Chief in and over our said Province of Maryland, Chancellor and Keeper of the Great Seal thereof," to William Hemsley for 1622 acres known as Cloverfields.

The patent, which is dated June 16, 1730, obviously was a regrant to confirm the title to land William Hemsley already held and which had been resurveyed for him on July 16, 1726. In it were included tracts bearing the names of Triangle, Young's Fortune, part of Young's Chance, part of Mill Mount and part of Trustram Wells, all of which lay between the arms of the Wye river known as Williams' and Thomas' branches and which was to be held "as of our manour of Baltimore in Queen Anne's county."

In return for his grant William Hemsley was to yield and pay "unto us and our heirs at our receipt at the City of St. Mary's, at the two most usual feasts of the year, viz: The Feast of the Annunciation of the Blessed Virgin Mary and St. Michael of the Arch Angel, by even and equal portions the rent of two pounds, fifteen shillings and five pence, half penny sterling, in silver or gold and for a fine upon every alienation of the said land or any part or parcel thereof in such commodities as we and our heirs or such officer or officers as shall be appointed by us and our heirs . . . to collect and receive the same."

Little of the land was cleared at the time it came into the possession of William Hemsley and years of hard labor with crude and primitive instruments, which were the only kind available, had to be put in before Cloverfields yielded its owner much more than enough to maintain the manor and pay his quit rent, small as it was. Buildings had to be erected,—a house for himself and his family, quarters for the slaves, shelter for the stock, blacksmith and wheelwright shops, and, most important of all, great barns for the storage of tobacco, for tobacco was legal tender of the province and part of each crop always was maintained at Cloverfields as a bank reserve fund. A tremendous undertaking was the establishment of a great Colonial estate but William Hemsley, fortunately, was spared the complications of the labor problem, for at one time he had at Cloverfields a hundred and forty-five slaves to carry out his orders.

William Hemsley became one of the great tobacco magnates of the Eastern Shore. Enormous quantities of "the weed" were shipped from Cloverfields to the seaport towns of the colonies and to England, but often he had to wait several months for a ship to sail in for a cargo. In order to meet this condition he had built a huge tobacco warehouse on the shores of the Wye river and erected a new and substantial wharf to which, for two centuries afterwards, sailing vessels came for cargoes of tobacco and grain. Ultimately this wharf became public property and the authorities of Queen Anne's county had a road built to reach it from the Queenstown-Wye Mills road. Like many other Colonial enterprises, however, its usefulness passed. Great vessels no longer tied up beside it and only the oldest of the old-timers among the river fishermen recall the importance it once had.

The house built by William Hemsley is said to have incorporated in its being an older house which stood on the Cloverfields tract as early as 1650 and which sheltered the previously mentioned Captain Sergeant and his family. Whether or not this is true there is no way of knowing, but it seems probable that the frugal spirit of an early Eighteenth century builder would have been more likely to make use of an existing building, were it in anything like good condition, than to rebuild entirely.

With the present manor house, which came into being about 1730, (though the exact date is nowhere on record) the years have not dealt kindly as far as outward appearance is concerned, though the interior is but little altered. Almost square, with a pitched roof pierced by triangular dormers and a modillioned cornice, its inherent dignity is betrayed by a modern porch constructed when the craze for gew-gaws strewed the country with such appurtenances and tricked out houses of classic intent with "Queen Anne fronts." The porch is said to have replaced at Cloverfields a two-story, colonnaded structure which ran the length of the house and gave it pronounced distinction.

Slat shutters conceal the entrance door which has two large panes of glass, rounded at the top, in place of the wooden panels which once occupied its upper half. This change, of course, permits more light to enter the hall, but it takes another toll from the Colonial appearance of the house.

The hall at Cloverfields lacks the spaciousness of some of the other Maryland houses of the period, for Cloverfields is not large, but in the treatment of the archway which conceals the stair hall from the front part of the house there is to be found a form of decoration not duplicated in the State. The framework of the arch is extremely simple, with a keystone at the top, but within it is suspended a *tour de force* of carving in the form of a large, open fan, made of slatwork. At the center the fan is overlaid, for a radius of about fifteen inches, with goldleaf, and the ends of the fan rest on the framework of the arch. The opening below is filled by slat doors.

Just belond the arch rises a stairway of solid black walnut, simple and useful, the antithesis of frivolity. Except for the fineness of the wood, there is not even a suggestion of ornamentation about the stairway, an architectural feature which William Hemsley evidently regarded as a necessity rather than as a source of potential beauty.

In the drawingroom, to the left of the hall, the decorations take up the note of elaboration struck by the fan archway. The room is panelled from floor to ceiling with white pine, permitting the center of interest to focus on the eleven-feet-wide fireplace which projects well out into the room. Over the fireplace, now sealed up in deference to a modern steam heating plant, the chimney breast is panelled smoothly and provided with moulding in the form of a portrait frame. On either side of the center panel and completely overlaid with gold leaf, clusters of roses, sunflowers and trailing vines stand out fully two inches from their base and immediately over the fireplace, to one side is carved the representation of a wild boar hunt in high relief. The huntsman is shown just as he is about to plunge his knife into the throat of his quarry which he holds by the tail, with his hunting dog assisting in the kill by holding the boar by the ear. On the other side of the fireplace is the carved representation of an old English castle, the entire decoration being enclosed by hand-carved Ionic pilasters and lighted by candles placed in Eighteenth century sconces.

Years must have been necessary for the execution of this elaborate piece of carving, done by some unknown worker with only a crude instrument to bring out the seeds in the sunflowers, the veins in the leaves and the band around the huntsman's hat. For many years the logs in the chimney crackled against a massive fireback which bears the coat-of-arms of the British crown. When the fireplace was sealed the old fireback, which weighs two hundred pounds, was removed, still in fairly good condition, and it is preserved on the place even now as a memento of the first William Hemsley of Cloverfields.

The other rooms in the house are less elaborate than the drawingroom, though the sitting room is panelled around the fireplace and vertically above it to the low ceiling. In the attic are two "dungeon rooms" in which slaves are said to have been imprisoned when the occasion warranted. In neither of them is there a sign of light and the doors are fastened with chains.

William Hemsley lived to be only thirty-three years old, but his accomplishments were many for so short a life. In 1724, when he was only twenty-one, he was made high sheriff of Queen Anne's county. In 1728 he was chosen a member of the House of Delegates and continued to serve in that body until his death. In 1729 he was one of the county justices. He seems also to have been an interested member of the established (or Anglican) church and old parish records preserve the information that "Mr. William Hemsley agreed with the Vestry to build a gallery in the west end of St. Paul's Church (Old Chester Church near

Centreville, now demolished) opposite to the other gallery and of the same length and breadth."

In the old graveyard on the place, at the head of a well-worn slab, is carved the hooded figure of the Angel of Death, holding in one outstretched hand a trumpet and in the other a palm. Below is the inscription:

"Here lieth the body of William Hemsley who departed this life the 2nd day of October, A. D. 1736, aged 33 years."

William Hemsley's widow, who had been Anna Maria Tilghman, daughter of Col. Richard Tilghman of The Hermitage, later married Robert Lloyd, son of Robert Lloyd and Ann Grundy, who was thrown from his carriage in a runaway accident and killed on July 16, 1770. One of the Hemsley family traditions maintains that during her widowhood Mrs. Hemsley received Mr. Lloyd's attentions with the utmost coldness, but that she was led to seek his protection in the role of husband after he had succeeded in frightening her by causing a masked or distorted face to appear suddenly before the window by which she was seated, impressing her by his ruse with the need of a strong masculine presence.

The fright she received must have been extreme, for Mrs. Lloyd seems to have been anything but a clinging vine. There is a room at Cloverfields from the window of which she is said to have shot a wolf. On her tombstone are two trumpets crossed within a wreath of laurel, and, at the foot, a skull and cross bones. The inscription declares that she was "much lamented." She had lived "deservedly loved and respected." Philemon Hemsley, son and heir of William Hemsley, was admitted to the Middle Temple, London, June 29, 1750, after his father's death. It was not he, however, but another William, posthumous son of William Hemsley and the subsequent Mrs. Lloyd, who is the most prominent figure in the family history. In 1773, at the age of twenty-six, this William Hemsley was provincial treasurer for the Eastern Shore and at the declaration of hostilities with Great Britain became a purchasing agent for the Continental army, a capacity in which he was associated with Robert Morris, "financier of the Revolution." In March 1777, he was commissioned colonel of the militia he previously had served as major. Upon the organization of the State government in that year he was appointed one of the justices for Queen Anne's county. A few months later he became a member of the Special Commission of "Oyer and Terminer" and "Gaol Delivery" for the county. In 1782 he became a member of the Continental Congress and was re-elected the following year.

Col. William Hemsley was married three times and left many descendants, who married into the Tilghman, Lloyd, Emory, Foreman and Troup families. A number of them are buried at Cloverfields. One of the most remarkable tombs received the body of Thomas Hemsley, who was drowned in a mill pond and who is said to have had a horror of being buried under ground. In deference to this idiosyncracy his corpse was placed in a tomb three feet high and covered by a marble slab, but, in the course of time, the supports to the tomb gave way and the skeleton was exposed to public view, the skull serving on one occasion to drive a dinner party into hysterics when it was carried into the dining room on the end of a stick by a child at play.

About thirty years ago Cloverfields, which had dwindled to about 600 acres, was sold by the Hemsley family and became the property of Mr. and Mrs. Thomas H. Callahan of Baltimore, who have brought to Cloverfields some antique furniture which is as old as the house itself and which has been in Mrs. Callahan's family for many generations, the finest pieces being in the diningroom, where stand a handsome Sheraton sideboard with matching tables.

Cloverfields and other Colonial estates of Queen Anne's, Talbot and Cecil counties figure in a correspondence retailing particularly interesting Eighteenth century gossip of life in Maryland. The letters were written by Molly and Hetty Tilghman of Chestertown, the sisters of the distinguished Col. Tench Tilghman, to their cousin, Mary Pearce of Poplar Neck, Cecil county, edited by Dr. J. Hall Pleasants, and published in 1926 in the Maryland Historical Magazine. They were written, their editor noted, either from Chestertown, or from Bayside, where Hetty resided after her marriage in 1785, to her first cousin, Lloyd Tilghman.

The first of the series describes the marriage of Mary Hemsley, known as Polly, the daughter of William Hemsley, Jr., and Colonel Joseph Foreman, at one time consul at Amsterdam. The wedding took place at Cloverfields on April 30, 1782, the bride's trousseau, which had been made in Philadelphia, including "a white Mantua Robe, trimmed with silver and a pink striped satin Habbit, and Petticoat trimmed with Gause." The writer, Hetty Tilghman (baptised Henrietta Maria) "sent the Bride an Elegant White Sattin Pincushion and garters of the same, with white Ribbon strings."

Another epistle mentions a mysterious Baron, who, the editor of the letters suggests, may have been Baron Jean-Christophe-Louis Frederic-Ignace de Closen, born in 1752, a captain in the regiment of the Royal Deux Points, who came to America as an aide to Rochambeau. His journal, which has been published in the Maryland Historical Magazine, shows that he was on intimate terms with Captain Richard Bennett Lloyd, son of Col. Edward Lloyd of Wye, and the latter's beautiful wife who had been Joanna Leigh, daughter of John Leigh of Northcourt, Isle of Wight, and whose portrait, painted by Sir Joshua Reynolds, was for years in the Rothschild collection. The Baron, says a letter from Bayside apparently written in April, 1785, finally found in this country a wife "so that your opinion of his being born odd is without foundation."

The Mrs. Lloyd who was the subject of the Baron's admiration apparently created something of a furor on her arrival in this country. "Old ladies," says one of the letters, "who have not ventured into public gaze these thirty years have drawn forth their broadbacked robes and crowded to the Assembly (in Philadelphia) to gaze at the divinity." The first night that she appeared in public her dress was "a white sattin habit and coat covered with crepe. A gauze apron spangled with gold, and black velvet stars and looped up with wreaths of flowers. A small cap ornamented with white feathers." But the beauty, apparently, was as the same letter presciently remarks, a "fading flower." A subsequent letter protests "she is not even pretty, but it is no wonder, such an abominable husband is enough to break any Woman. . . . Tonight there is another Concert and Ball I shall just go and hear the Music. Of the Races I say nothing. They are a burlesque upon that diversion."

A Christmas "Ball," described by Molly Tilghman, which took place at Chestertown, was attended by "16 Couple, and spent a very agreeable Evening. The play came next night, which afforded a few unexpected incidents. Some Bucks of true spirit, which was increased by good Liquor, broke open one of the Windows, to the great dismay of the Ladies. As to the play, it exceeded no one's expectations. However, the Eyes of the Audience were obliged by a vast display of fine cloaths, and Jewels, which more than made up for any faults in the acting. . . . Last night it was again represented with the addition of the Irish Widow. The Ball gave such a spring to the Spirit of our

Beaux that they have made up a subscription for Assemblies, and the first, is to be held tomorrow night.

"I must not forget to tell you that poor Ferguson's fears were realized. In spite of all his animating lessons, Arnold was as cold as a Cucumber."

The Ferguson referred to, the editor of the letters believes, was the Rev. Colin Ferguson, said to have been the first Episcopal clergyman ordained in the United States, and the Arnold is unquestionably Benedict Arnold. He had married, April 8, 1779, a first cousin of the writer, Margaret, the daughter of Chief Justice Edward Shippen of Pennsylvania, and his wife, Margaret Francis.

And so the letters run on, airy details of balls and concerts and at times gravely sorrowful when the illnesses and deaths of members of the family and intimate friends are reported. Molly and Hetty Tilghman were the daughters of James Tilghman who was born at The Hermitage and, says Dr. Pleasants, "so numerous and so scattered are the prominent relations and friends referred to in the letters that we seem to have before us a veritable social register for the period of Maryland, Delaware and Pennsylvania."

CHAPTER FIFTEEN

It was a dismal day in 1929 which brought to Queen Anne's county the representative of a man of great wealth who was combing the countryside in search of panelling. Once there it was inevitable that his steps turned to Walnut Grove, the oldest house in the county, which was built in 1683 and which was lined with woodwork almost beyond compare in Maryland.

For Walnut Grove, until that moment, had remained intact from the day when Solomon Wright, who had been sent from England to collect the king's taxes, set up his household gods under its quaintly pitched roof and took possession with his bride, Ann Hynson, the daughter of Thomas Hynson to whom land, for miles around, had been granted by the Proprietary. Here was not merely a glimpse of other days, but a veritable little Koh-i-noor of Seventeenth century building, a gem of Colonial folkways.

In spite of its spoliation, however, Walnut Grove still is a place at which to linger. The engaging lines of its steeply pitched roof, coming down sharply from the comb to the lintels of the low doors and windows in front and pierced by a single dormer window, like a great eye, scanning the countryside; the dominant chimney rearing up at one end, with an ornamental cap giving it an air of pomposity; the curious old brick of the end walls and the handriven shingles which still cover the logs of the front and rear walls, all are so unusual in Maryland that it is a strong-minded person who can tear himself away from Walnut Grove in less than half a day. The temptation is to linger much longer than that.

Small as it is, Walnut Grove compared favorably in size with any house in Maryland in the day it was built. Two rooms down stairs and two up are all that the original building had, though the indications are that, at some time, there must have stood nearby an old kitchen which no longer exists. From its appearance no provision for cooking seems to have been made in the present structure, with its little office extending clear across the front of the house and the "greate" room occupying the space beyond. A steep and narrow little boxed-in stairway leads up beside the chimney from the "greate" room to the second floor.

The panelling which was taken from the "greate" room and sold was as firm as on the day it was placed in position more than two centuries ago. Carved by hand and put together with wooden pins, it was taken down only with the greatest difficulty. And when the old shell cupboard, which was the crowning beauty of the room, was removed it was found to have been carved out of one piece from a sycamore tree. Not a bit of dust appeared, not a wormhole was in evidence in any of the woodwork, even under the most minute scrutiny. The timber of which it had been constructed had been cut at the right time of the year (a method well known to Colonials and ignored in recent times), and seasoned to exactly the right degree. Doors, window frames, panelling and cupboard, all are gone from the house they had known so long and instead of a quaint little Eastern Shore farm house their setting now is the country mansion of an American Croesus.

Fortunately, however, the little office remains intact. A curious little place is this, quite long and narrow, with a fireplace set diagonally across one corner. The chimney breast is panelled, with tiny cupboards set in above the mantel shelf, a handy repository for Solomon Wright's personal flask and his powder for the trusty musket. The roof of this room slopes sharply down on the side opposite the fireplace, intensifying the air of primitiveness, and the little window set into the end wall is guiltless of a frame except for the lintel above. The original old batten shutter still does protective duty for this window.

The rear wall of the house is much higher than the one in front, cutting off the roof several feet above the first story windows. The old poplar shingles, about twice the size of the shingles used today, still show the marks of the axe which split them and the coruscations on their surface have never been planed away.

A generation or more ago a wing was added to Walnut Grove in the shape of another complete house, connected with the original by a door from the office but otherwise entirely independent. This house contains the present-day kitchen and pantries and has its own stairway so that, in order to get from a bedroom in the original house into one of the sleeping rooms in the "new," it is necessary to come downstairs, across the house, and up again. The "new" house has a wide central chimney and a gambrel roof of the type early used in Maryland, not a bad house at all, but its juxtaposition to the original would seem to indicate that, at the time it was built, the desire for space was stronger in the Wright family than the feeling for architectural harmony.

The traveller who first sees Walnut Grove in the afternoon is apt to think for an instant, if he chances to approach the house from the west, that the place is on fire, so brilliant is the reflection of the sun on the end wall. A closer view immediately dispels the illusion, of course, and a first hand inspection of the brick in the end wall will account for it. Almost every header is glazed to a depth of almost an inch, a result of some peculiar composition of the soil from which the bricks were made.

Solomon Wright, the builder of Walnut Grove, was one of the most active men of the Eastern Shore in public affairs. He came to America with his brother Nathaniel, in 1673, and took up some 2,500 acres of land in Queen Anne's county which he had surveyed in 1685 under the name of Worplesdon. In 1694 he was deputy surveyor for Talbot and Kent counties. In 1700 he was deputy commissioner for Talbot county and in that same year he became a member of the county court, a position which earned him the title of "Judge," and a member of the Provincial Assembly at Annapolis.

Walnut Grove descended, upon the death of the emigrant, to his eldest son, Thomas Hynson Wright, who was born in 1688 and held numerous public offices. Under his regime the family lands increased to four thousand acres and his family has established itself as one of the great land holders of the State.

*　　*　　*

Like the Hammonds and the Carrolls and the Tilghmans of Maryland, the Wrights were a race of builders. The year of the Revolution saw the completion by Colonel Thomas Wright of the mansion on Reed's Creek Farm, much more pretentious than Walnut Grove, from which it is not far distant. The family fortunes had waxed fat during the seventy-five years which had intervened between the building of the two places and Colonel Wright was one of the leaders of Colonial agitation which culminated in the Revolution. He was a delegate to the provincial conventions of 1774-7 and a member of the Committee of Correspondence in 1774. He signed the declarations of the Association of Freemen in Maryland in 1775 and when the Revolution actually was inaugurated he commanded a regiment of Queen Anne's county men which served, with many casualties, through the war.

Colonel Wright's house, in its day, was a rendezvous for the young people of three counties, for the Wright family connection was large and pleasure-loving. Crowds of young people gathered there to go on sleighing parties in winter or to dance in the big rooms which look almost barnlike today with the one-time merrymakers long turned to dust in their coffins and a family of tenant farmers in possession of the house which still belongs to a member of the Wright family.

Great dinners of canvasback ducks and diamondback terrapin were served at the three-section tables which once stood in the diningroom at Reed's Creek Farm, for it was a common thing for a sportsman to bag a hundred ducks when he went shooting on the flats close by and when the old ducking gun was not actually in use it stood ready and suggestive in a corner.

"It was a common occurrence," says one old account of life at Reed's Creek, "to shoot a hundred ducks in a few hours. Every point was an oyster bar, every mat of weeds alive with crabs. Foxes started on the place were pursued into Delaware, often swimming rivers and creeks, compelling the huntsmen to go around for miles." When the huntsmen were ready to start on a foray steaming hot coffee was served and the dogs were shut up to give the fox a start after he had been let out of the bag. Then, when the coffee had been drunk and everyone was in the saddle, "Uncle Peregrine Tilghman would rise in his stirrups and blow the bugle" and the chase was on. Invariably, when the hunt was over and the party had returned there was a big celebration at Reed's Creek and corn bread and mush for the hounds.

The Reed's Creek house consists of a big, square, central mass, firmly built, with a modillioned cornice and huge chimneys at each end standing up like ears above the roof line. A moulded water course finishes the foundation and belt courses add interest to the front and rear facades. A modern porch detracts unpleasantly from the beauty of the door which has an enframement of pilasters and a round transom; and a coat of whitewash about the foundation, added within recent years, looks incon-

Photo by W. F. Parrott

REED'S CREEK

This house is located on a farm called "Reed's Creek Farm," getting its name from a creek running about a quarter of a mile from the house. The house was built in 1776 and has paneled walls and hand-hewn floors. It was built by ancestors of the present Wright family of Queen Anne's County. At present it is owned by Mrs. Clayton Wright of Centreville.

Photo from Collection of James Donnell Tilghman

OLD KITCHEN FIREPLACE, REED'S CREEK

REED'S CREEK: DRAWINGROOM

REED'S CREEK: DOORWAY

gruous on such a house. A single wing prolongs the line of the facade to one side, with a chimney at its gable end.

Straight through the house the entrance hall makes its way, with another hall branching from it at right angles at the back to provide for the massive stairway with its curious balustrade. The newel post stands flush with the second step, while the lowest step extends a considerable distance beyond and is rounded at the end.

All of the ceilings are enormously high, with the huge fireplaces seeming to wait for the great logs which once they consumed so avidly; and in the kitchen the fireplace still holds the great crane and the iron contrivances upon which generations of Erebuses cooked for the Wrights. One of the rooms at Reed's Creek was known as the weaving room and there, before the Civil War, a huge spinning wheel whirred day after day making linsey woolsey to be sewed into garments for the slaves.

* * *

At Peace and Plenty, named, it is said by a bride who came there from a home called Hungry Hill, resemblance to the house at Reed's Creek is strong. The general plan of the house is similar but the ceilings are not quite so high and the walnut stairway mounts directly from the central hall.

The drawingroom at Peace and Plenty is quite large, with six large windows through which the light pours cheerfully the day long—a quality which commends the place enormously to modern minds but which must have been exceedingly hard on the nerves of some mid-Victorian mistress of the house who sought to keep her carpets bright. Particularly fine workmanship is evident in the trim of this room. The eared window frames have carved cornices and the mantel is a typical Eighteenth century affair, with fluted columns at the sides, a line of

[271]

triglyphs across the frieze and a row of dentils under the shelf. The wainscoting in this room is carved with recessed squares and the chair rail and cornice, like the mantel, are ornamented with dentils.

Walnut Grove, Reed's Creek and Peace and Plenty, are all owned now by members of the Wright family as they were in Colonial times, although the two former estates passed out of the family for a number of years. The former now belongs to Mr. Dorsey Wright and Reed's Creek to Mr. Clayton Wright, who also owns Peace and Plenty.

* * *

The oldest garden in America, people say, is the one which lends to Poplar Grove, the stronghold of the Emorys in Queen Anne's county, the air of belonging to some remote English countryside, an air which is intensified by the old house which sprawls over the ground, disdaining architectural classification.

Laid out on broad terraces, in the form of a cross, the garden stretches from the house the length of two long city blocks or more down to Emory creek on an arm of the Corsica river, a little, secret waterway which gives to the old garden that completeness of charm which only a glimpse of water can do.

For many years the garden has been permitted to go its way, with the result that the hedges of American box have grown to billowing proportions and the English box trees have grown like the natives of the forest which stand about, but the present garden is only half of the size of the one which the first Emorys who lived at Poplar Grove laid out between their house and the river. The beds of columbine and hollyhocks and zinnias which had the depth of color given only to flowers which grow near the water, were outlined by borders of dwarf cedar and box and holly and extended over several acres, but these have gone long ago. Enough remains, however, to give the feeling of otherwhereness and in the stillness of a moonlit summer night Poplar Grove takes on a look of enchantment.

Close by is the old burying ground, with its crumbling brick wall, overgrown with myrtle and trailing briars, so that it is difficult to locate some of the graves where the ancestors of the present owners of Poplar Grove lie. One of the oldest tombs contains the body of that Colonel Thomas Emory who went to England to sell the bonds of the Baltimore and Ohio railroad when American capital for the venture was not forthcoming.

The oldest part of the house was built about 1700. Low and rambling, it has porches front and back, with an enormous bay window of later vintage which is provided with an octagonal roof. A huge hydrangea, planted at the end of the office, looks in at the second story window.

Brick made in the old English mould is laid in a bond unlike any other on the Eastern Shore, with two stretchers to every header, giving the walls a distinction and individuality of their own. Originally the tract on which house and garden stood was known as Brampton and was granted by Lord Baltimore to Arthur Emory who arrived in this country in 1660. This Arthur Emory had also grants of land on the Choptank, Wye, and Chester rivers, making him one of the powerful landholders of the upper Eastern Shore.

His son, John Emory, who built Poplar Grove and laid out the gardens, was born in 1699 and in old records of 1726 is mentioned as deputy surveyor and receiver of quit rents. John Emory was one of the surveyors who represented Maryland in the survey of the boundary between Maryland and Pennsylvania, the line which afterwards was prolonged by Mason and Dixon.

Brampton, after the death of John Emory, descended to John Emory, Junior, who was born about 1710 and who died intestate. The place then became the property of John Register Emory, who was a first lieutenant of Maryland militia in 1776 and a member of Queen Anne's county board of justices. At this time the estates known as Conquest, Corsica, and Cintra also were included in the Brampton tract and other estates in various branches of the Emory family at this time were Ingleside, Warrington, Coursey-on-Wye, and St. Paul. During the Revolution, the feeling of the Emorys on the subject of the treatment accorded the colonies by the mother country became so strong that all ties and all that savored of ties with England were cut without ceremony and the name of Brampton which had been bestowed in commemoration of the Emory holdings in England was changed to Poplar Grove.

From John Register Emory, Poplar Grove descended to "Gen." Thomas Emory whose son, William Hemsley Emory, graduated from West Point, served during the Civil War in the Union army, a circumstance productive of much grief to the other members of the Emory clan who were staunch in their adherence to the Confederate cause. But William Hemsley Emory had married a descendant of Benjamin Franklin and the spirit of that strong-minded Pennsylvanian in his great-granddaughter prevailed over the desire of William Hemsley Emory to resign from the United States army. The course of this Union officer, though it galled did not alienate him entirely from his family, however, and after the war the breach was healed. The old estate, which had been divided and subdivided a number of times since the tenure of the first owner, passed on to his descendants. There are now only about three hundred acres in Poplar Grove which belongs to Mr. and Mrs. Lloyd Tilghman Emory, who live in England, but who are restoring the place, even with an ocean between, to a semblance of its Colonial appearance.

[274]

It has been said, with much truth, that the secret ambition of every Englishman is to own a piece of land and then to build a wall around it. Certainly the loveliness of English gardens is attributable in no small degree to the mellow old enclosures which form the background of their bloom, and there is little doubt that this deeply rooted predilection for walls was carried across the sea by Englishmen who sought to establish a new England on a new continent. It accounts, unquestionably, for the crumbling old line of brick which stretches from the wing of the old Hollyday mansion known as Readbourne, across two broad terraces and down to the Corsica river.

This wall, by all the seeming, is much older than the house, which was completed about 1734, and serves, as it mellows in the sunlight, to stir up all manner of imaginings and vain speculations. Nothing is known of its origin or of the men and women who once walked in the vanished garden which was laid out, precise and intricate with box, under its protection. Tall althea bushes lift white and purple cups above the wall today, but the thyme and the fever-few are gone with the rosemary and Judas-tree. There is a sadness about the old structure which cannot be exorcised.

Readbourne is always spoken of in Maryland as a "Hollyday place" but the Hollydays were not the first to live there. The estate including more than a thousand acres was granted in 1659 to one George Read and probably owes its name to this grantee who died without heirs. Several owners then held successive title to the place and in 1732 it was surveyed for James Hollyday, who purchased it soon afterwards and built the mansion which was one of the finest of its day in Queen Anne's.

The capital letter "E" (minus the central bar) forms the outline of the main wing of the house which faces the river. Its roof is steeply pitched and the ornamental caps of the chimneys which rise at each end provide a distinct architectural feature. A moulded water course, mark of a wealthy man's home in the Seventeen-thirties, finishes the top of the foundation and a projecting belt course appears between the first story and the one above. Heavy modillions look out from under the wide eaves and dormer windows, with six small panes and triangular caps, providing light for the sloping attic rooms. The front door is cut into a recessed panel and opens into a square panelled hall with three arches across the end wall. From under one of them the stairway rises in an "L" designed to receive it. The center one frames a niche built into the wall for a piece of sculpture and the third opens into the office.

At the left of the hall the drawingroom is entered through a heavy door. This room once was panelled elaborately from floor to ceiling, but it, like Walnut Grove, has been divested of its beauty to enrich the home of a millionaire. When the panelling was in place the Readbourne drawingroom was both a thing of beauty and a mute evidence of the high degree of culture which existed, even at that early date, among men and women of wealth in the remote countryside of Maryland. The fireplace was the focus of interest in the room, with a mantel of considerably later date placed between fluted and reeded pilasters which rested upon panelled bases the height of the chair rail. The mantel itself was well carved, an excellent thing in its way, but the room must have been more satisfying before it was installed.

On each side of the fireplace deep, set-in cupboards had panelled doors rounded at the top and swung on H-hinges and the walls were lined with rectangular panels, with the fields raised and bevelled. Deep seats were provided below the windows, two of which faced the river and the other the wide farmlands back of the house. All this woodwork has been sold, but in the stair hall and in some of the bedrooms the panelling remains to show how delightful the house must have been when James Hollyday went there to live. One of the upstairs rooms in particular is interesting for the diversity of woodwork to be found in it, some of the panels having the field bevelled and raised, and others showing the field recessed.

The eldest son of James Hollyday was James Hollyday, barrister, who was admitted to the Middle Temple December 3, 1754, and who entered public life in America only as the result of the persuasions of men who were able, from personal knowledge, to appreciate his abilities. Almost immediately upon his return from London, where he had spent four years, he was elected to the Lower House of Assembly and during the acrimonious controversies over the "Vestry Acts" (which, it will be remembered, empowered the clergy of the Church of England in Maryland to be provided for by a tax on tobacco) Hollyday and Daniel Dulany, the younger, sustained the validity of the Acts against the opposition of William Paca and Samuel Chase.

Upon the recommendation of Governor Sharpe, James Hollyday was offered a position on the Council in 1765, but he declined the honor. He accepted, however, membership in the Eastern Shore branch of the Council of Safety in Maryland in 1775 and again in July, 1776. And with Charles Carroll of Carrollton and Gustavus Scott he was appointed in January of 1776 to revise the journal and proceedings of the Maryland convention. After the Revolution he was a member of the General Assembly of Maryland as a State and of the Assembly of 1788 which ratified the Constitution of the United States. He died that same year, unmarried.

His death, however, did not end the regime of the Hollydays at Readbourne. Through one of his brothers the estate passed from father to son for seven generations to the late Richard

Hollyday, last of the name to occupy it. The first sale of the place in more than one hundred and fifty years took place in 1903, but since then it has changed hands a number of times. Traces still may be discovered, by dint of painstaking search, of the foundations of the old brick kitchen, dairy and other farm buildings which were connected with the main house by covered ways and only a few years ago the ruins were removed of the old "store," supposed to have been the repository of supplies used on the plantation and which had to be acquired in large quantities because of the difficulty of securing goods from England and the infrequency of their arrival.

Readbourne is forlorn and forsaken now. Its panelling, which was its greatest beauty, has been taken away and its garden is only a memory. But one of the great charms of an old house lies in the fact that it never grows really old. The walls of Readbourne are ready as ever to respond to the sound of music and dancing feet, were anyone disposed to put it to the test. And it has a secret laughter if anyone stops to hear, laughter which cherishes the memory of "good company, good wine, good name."

*   *   *

Of great antiquity is the family of Tilden, its spelling changed by the mutations of language from Tylden some time after the emigration to America of Nathaniel Tylden who left Kent, in England and came to Cape Cod in 1628. The first of the name to come to Maryland was Marmaduke Tylden of Great Oak Manor, Kent county, who was descended from Sir Robert Tylden who was living in the reign of Henry II and Richard I.

Marmaduke Tilden, son of Marmaduke Tylden, is said to have been the largest landholder in Kent county, which then included Queen Anne's as well, and whose holdings extended well into Talbot. It was on this Queen Anne's county land that he built, about the year 1740, the house on the large farm now known as Handy Point and which recently has come into the possession of Mrs. Isaac Dixon of Baltimore who has restored it to a condition of habitation after it had been neglected for decades, and has added to the front of the house a *porte cochere* reminiscent of the porch at Mount Vernon.

Handy Point farm house must have taken years to build, so painstaking was the workmanship which was revealed when its renovation was undertaken. All of the wood, most of which was black walnut and white pine, was cut from native forests, seasoned for months and then shaped by hand to the purpose for which it was to be used. The bricks were made on the place and the hinges beaten out by the smith employed for the purpose. So strong and elaborate are the walls of the basement, which was divided into a number of rooms for the occupancy of slaves, that it must have taken as long to erect this part of the house alone as the construction of an entire city block of small two-story houses would require today.

The house is built in the shape of a capital "T," the tail of the letter being years older than the wing which crosses it at the top. On this wing one ancient, panelled shutter swung on a broad strap hinge still imprinted with blows from the blacksmith's hammer, covers an absurd little window and remains to show what its companions must have been like. The others vanished long ago.

The walls which form the head of the "T" are laid up in Flemish bond, covered on one of the gable ends by a heavy tapestry of ivy, while those of the older portion of the house are in English bond. All of the door and window frames are made of black walnut, fastened together at each corner with a wooden pin and remaining as firmly knit as the day they were placed in position. The entrance to the house is unostentatious to a degree. A short flight of brick steps leads to a door framed by fluted pilasters upholding a triangular pediment which is well proportioned but severely plain. A round transom appears over the two-ply door, panelled on the side it presents to the world, battened on the inside.

Within, the house completely contradicts the impression presented by the exterior. Here is a house built not merely for shelter and constructed of good materials because they were easily available, but a well-considered home built for gentlefolk and finished in a manner which brings instantly before the eye a picture of rooms filled with damask-covered chairs and inlaid tables, Sandwich glass and books from London. The central space is occupied by the hall, with a stairway built of woods which have not warped nor cracked in a century and three-quarters. The steps and the square spindles of the balustrade are of ash, but the rail is mahogany and so are the newel posts and the finials which look like drops of water on the posts at the turns of the stair. The hall is wainscoted with rectangular panels of yellow pine, the wainscoting continuing up the side of the stairway. Fluted posts and a half-handrail set into the wall complete the effect. All of the wainscoting is put together with wooden pins and so is the stairway itself.

The two landings between the first and second floors break the stairway into three flights and over the central flight a square window is placed to illuminate the hall which otherwise would be exceedingly dark, for very little light can enter through the transom over the door. The drawingroom opens from the hall at the left of the entrance, a large, well-lighted room with an elaborate chimneypiece panelled with native pine. An eared moulding waits for a family portrait and fluted pilasters support the triangular pediment which repeats the decorative *motif* of the entrance to the house.

The mantel is carved with the Wall-of-Troy design and the low fireplace has an eared architrave. Low, panelled window seats add to the finish of the room and the window frames have ears. The diningroom, on the opposite side of the hall, has a simple mantelpiece, but it possesses a built-in china cupboard with scrolled shelves which is glory enough for a Colonial diningroom.

In the bedroom over the drawingroom the chimney end is panelled in a most charming fashion. A large rectangle appears to one side of the center of the chimney, with smaller rectangles occupying the space to the left, and the room has built-in powder closets with ears on the door frames. Panelled recesses with ears add to the beauty of the windows and a heavy wooden cornice appears at the ceiling, completing a bedroom where once a high four-poster bed stood in a corner and a low slipper chair was drawn up close beside the fireplace.

Only a few of the wrought-iron H-hinges are left in the house, but the front door still fastens with its original lock which measures seven inches by twelve.

The estate probably received the name Handy Point during the occupancy by the great-grandchildren of the first Marmaduke Tylden in Maryland, Mary Tilden, daughter of the fourth Marmaduke, having married George D. S. Handy.

CHAPTER SIXTEEN

Three of the oldest estates in Maryland, places that go back to the days when the forests were terrible with Indians and settlers dared not venture far from the water's edge, are to be found on the Eastern Shore. One of these is The Hermitage, in Queen Anne's county, and the other two are located in Talbot, where Gross' Coate lies a few miles to the north of Easton, the county seat, and Crosiadore a short distance from the little hamlet known as Trappe.

Both The Hermitage and Gross' Coate are associated indelibly with the name of Tilghman and at Crosiadore Dickinsons have lived ever since the Lord Proprietary of Maryland dipped his quill in ink—or directed his secretary to do it for him—and made out a grant for the land in the Seventeenth century. At each of these places part of the original house remains, only a small part, it is true, and so altered that no semblance whatever can be discovered of the original contours. At The Hermitage and Gross' Coate bits of wall can be seen which, it is certain from the size and shape of the bricks, belong to the era when the houses were built and, within, the rooms in these parts of the house show the proportions which mark them as Colonial. At Crosiadore the original house exists only in a small upstairs room which was taken out carefully when the old house was torn down a number of years ago and incorporated into the late Nineteenth century house which took its place.

These estates, however, maintain an importance which new wings and extensive rebuilding cannot diminish, for on them lived men who played in the development and independence of the nation parts as vital as those which have enveloped with a permanent lustre the names of Randolph and Revere, Harvard and Endicott in other parts of the country. In the case of the Marylanders, however, their achievements scarcely have been hymned at all beyond the borders of their own State, and even there comparatively few persons seem to know of them.

Of the Tilghman family the invididual whose exploits most vividly catch the imagination was Col. Tench Tilghman, aide-de-camp to Washington. Colonel Tilghman was born December 25, 1744, and he it was who galloped by night and day to carry to the Continental Congress then sitting in Independence Hall, in Philadelphia, the news of the surrender of Lord Cornwallis' army at Yorktown.

Col. Tench Tilghman seems to have been one of Washington's most cherished associates, the General retaining for him an affection which endured until his young aide's death in 1786. So close was the tie which bound them together that the letter written by General Washington to Colonel Tilghman to congratulate him upon his marriage to a cousin, Miss Anna Maria Tilghman, in June, 1783, is couched in terms of friendliest intimacy:

> Why have you been so niggardly in communicating your change of condition to us, or to the world? By dint of enquiries we have heard of your marriage; but have scarcely got a confirmation of it yet. On the presumption, however, that it is so, I offer you my warmest congratulations and best wishes for the enjoyment of many happy years; in both of which Mrs. Washington joins me very cordially.

Later, when Colonel Tilghman engaged in business in Baltimore, he became General Washington's agent for the transaction

of almost every conceivable form of business, making contracts
with workmen for building, hiring servants from emigrant ships,
selecting and making terms with the man who went to Mount
Vernon to tutor Mrs. Washington's children, even purchasing
the china for her tea table. And when he died, on the eighteenth
of April in 1786, Washington grieved:

> He was in every action in which the main army was
> concerned. A great part of the time he refused to receive
> his pay. While living no man could be more lamented. No
> one had imbibed sentiments of greater friendship for him
> that I had done. He left as fair a reputation as ever be-
> longed to a human character.

But if the life of Colonel Tilghman was the more spectacular
it was only slightly more adventurous than that of his great-
grandfather, Dr. Richard Tilghman, first of the name in Maryland, who built The Hermitage on the Chester river and who,
in making his will, referred to himself as a "chirurgeon." Dr.
Tilghman was born in London, a descendant of the Tilghmans
of Holloway Court, a noble English family of Kent, and made
the nerve-wracking crossing to Maryland in the ship, "Elizabeth
and Mary" which came to anchor in 1657. With him came his
wife and eighteen persons, a service for which he demanded of
the Proprietary a special warrant of one thousand acres of land.
Upon this warrant a certificate was issued a number of years
afterwards on the strength of which four hundred acres were
surveyed, according to the Rent Rolls for Queen Anne's county,
on the tenth of October, 1666, "for Richard Tilghman." This is
the land which he called "Tilghman's Hermitage," the name
being shortened later to The Hermitage.

This land originally belonged to John Coursey, who called
it Cedar Branch, but it had been permitted to escheat to the

Proprietary, much to the satisfaction of the good "chirurgeon" who was so enamored of it and its water view that he selected it as part of his thousand acres and built his home upon it.

Not far away Solomon Wright lived on Reed's Creek, and William Coursey's place, an estate now called Blakeford, on Coursey's Neck, was not far away. Henry Hawkins lived at Bowlingly, on the edge of "Queen's Town," several miles to the South. All of them were friends as well as patients to whom Dr. Tilghman ministered, making his calls in a little "batteau" with a "leg o'mutton" sail and taking along a crew of slaves to row when the wind failed. It took no little courage to be a "chirurgeon" in Maryland during the Seventeenth century, for journeys were beset with danger, even at the best of times.

Dr. Tilghman died in 1675, and was buried at The Hermitage, within sight of the house. An elaborate stone covers his grave in a plot now shaded by weeping willows and made fragrant with boxwood and lilacs. The inscription is partly in Latin and reads in full:

Always Remember
The 5th of November,
But doe not forgett
Death will have no lett
Consider thy end
And thy time well spend
& soe shall thou have
A crown in thy grave
"Vale".
Ita Dixit
Richardus Tilghmanus, B.M.
In artique chirurgi Magister
qui sub hoc tumulo sepultus
est
Obiit, Janu. 7 mo. Anno 1675.

The "5th of November" was the day on which Dr. Tilghman was married.

Dr. Tilghman's grandson, Matthew Tilghman, when little more than a boy, was made commander of a troop of horse to protect outlying settlements from Indians. Then he was one of "the worshipful, the commissioners and justices of the Peace" for Talbot county, an office of distinction in the days when justices of the peace served as judges of the county court. He was wealthy and well educated and was selected deputy to the lower house of the Assembly, later being chosen president of the Maryland Provincial Council in June, 1774. For two years he presided over that body, missing only two meetings during that time. He was, also, chairman of the delegates from Maryland to the Continental Congress, his associates being Charles Carroll of Carrollton, Samuel Chase, William Paca, Thomas Johnson, the first governor elected by the people of Maryland, Thomas Stone, Robert Goldsborough, Robert Alexander, John Hall, John Rogers and Benjamin Rumsey. During the Revolution Matthew Tilghman was dubbed affectionately by his colleagues in the Provincial Convention, "the patriarch of the Colony."

The road to The Hermitage from Queenstown leads through a mile-long stretch of pines, aromatic in warm weather, a welcome show of green in winter. At the end of this avenue the road turns sharply to the left and changes its character from a public thoroughfare to a lane which passes a long row of low brick buildings, built to serve Dr. Tilghman's estate as smokehouses, dairies, spinning houses and other ways. Their one or two tiny windows apiece give them a most ingenuous appeal which is augmented by the ivy, roses and honeysuckle which climb over them.

These little buildings were saved when the main house, with

[286]

the exception of the back wing, was burned in 1832. The homestead was rebuilt in 1859 and a number of changes have been made since then. It is regarded as one of the show places of Queen Anne county.

*   *   *

Gross' Coate came into possession of the Tilghman family through William Tilghman, an uncle of the Revolutionary Col. Tench Tilghman, who acquired the place partly by gift and partly by purchase from his mother and aunts, the daughters of Henrietta Maria Lloyd, who was one of the outstanding feminine figures in the early annals of the State and is said to have been the god-daughter as well as the namesake of the English queen.

Before the Lloyds added it to their already extensive holdings, however, the place had been granted to one Roger Gross. It descended to his son, John, who, dying about 1676, willed it to a younger brother, William. In 1696 the estate passed into the hands of the Lloyds and was known as Henrietta Maria's Purchase. At some later period, in the way such things happen, the name was changed again to Grosses, an appellation by which it was known until comparatively recently when a chance perusal of the original grant revealed its pristine name, now restored to it.

The removal of two coats of paint from the walls during a post war renovation resulted in a close study of the character of the bricks and the consequent discovery that the part of the house now used as the entrance hall is the oldest portion of Gross' Coate. What is known as the "back building" also is undeniably of Eighteenth century origin, with the original cross-panel doors still swinging on their hinges and a little, low fireplace, without panelling or mantel in an upstairs room long known as the nursery.

In the drawingroom, restored to its position in the house some fourteen years ago after a sojourn which must have lasted a full century in one of the stables, is a hand-carved mantel, high and narrow of shelf, with reeded pilasters on each side of the fireplace and a virile rope carving, tambour fluting and beading across the frieze.

Gross' Coate, like almost all the other old places in Maryland which have remained in possession of the same family for generations, has its family portraits, including one of Richard Tilghman, son of William, painted by Charles Willson Peale in 1796, one of his wife and two children in a family group and one of Richard Tilghman's sister, Mary Tilghman Roberts, considered by some critics Charles Willson Peale's finest portrait.

About the portrait of Mary Tilghman Roberts there is an interesting romance for while the artist was painting it he fell desperately in love with the dark haired girl who sat for him, although Mary Tilghman was then little more than a child and Peale was a widower with grown children. Their disparity in age, however, seemed to make no difference to either of them and before he had been very long at Gross' Coate, Charles Willson Peale asked permission of Richard Tilghman to marry his sister.

The request was summarily refused. Richard Tilghman was furious at the idea of a man so much older than the girl whose portrait he was painting, and a man whom he regarded as far beneath her in the social scale, having the audacity to propose such a thing. With brotherly highandedness he locked his sister in her room until her lover had finished the other portraits he had been engaged to paint and had departed. Scarcely had she been released from her isolation when Mary Tilghman retaliated against her brother by marrying the scapegrace of the county.

After a hectic married life her husband died and Mary Tilgh-

GROSS' COATE

Photo from Collection of James Donnell Tilghman

DRAWINGROOM MANTEL AT GROSS' COATE

man Roberts, bent and crippled with rheumatism, came back to
Gross' Coate to live with a nephew whom she admired deeply
but upon whom she bestowed none of the affectionate warmth
she felt for his brother, the impetuous, lovable black sheep of
the family who had left home and gone to Queen Anne's county
to live. By the time the rheumatism finally had made her helpless
and the years had added to her ills Mary Tilghman Roberts
determined that, if she could bring it about, the nephew whom
she admired and his brother whom she loved should be recon-
ciled. When she was on her deathbed she sent for the wayward
youth, telling him of her wish to see him before she died. He
came at once and when she told him of her desire to bring
peace into the family he agreed to bury his differences with his
brother and to return to the fold.

Delighted at the success of her overtures, the old lady then
sent for the upright brother, told him what had happened and
asked him, on his part, to forget the past. The upright brother,
however, flatly refused—and banged the door behind him. The
old lady did not live long after that and often at night, strange
noises are heard at Gross' Coate which, the Tilghmans say,
are the tapping of a cane as the spirited little "Aunt Molly"
travels about the house, seeking her inflexible nephew to insist
again on the restoration to family rights of that other boy whose
rebellion she understood so well.

That there was some foundation to the story of Mary Tilghman Roberts' blighted romance, which has afforded succeeding
generations of Tilghmans delightful material for family gossip,
was brought to light a inumber of years ago with the arrival of
a letter to a member of the family from a descendant of Charles
Willson Peale who was seeking to establish the identity of various
Maryland families mentioned in his ancestor's diary. A response
assured him that the Tilghmans of Gross' Coate were the ones

he sought and subsequent correspondence revealed that the artist had entered in his diary an account of his request for the hand of Mary Tilghman and the gruff refusal he received.

Gross' Coate also has another ghost manifest in the form of a phantom coach which drives up to the house in anticipation of deaths, supposedly to carry away the body of the "departed."

With its various changes and additions Gross' Coate has become not only a prototype of an English country house as closely as the original builder could have approximated such a thing, but has developed as landed estates have done in that country, with a wing added at one period, an extension at another, sun rooms at still another. Its present owner, Mrs. Charles Tilghman, has been indefatigable in preserving what has remained of the past.

* * *

At Crosiadore, several miles distant from Gross' Coate, clumps of perennials which are in constant bloom from early spring until late autumn, stand at the gateway to the estate where once lived John Dickinson whose brilliant career failed only of achieving the highest office in the country because he had refused, as a member of the Continental Congress, to sign the Declaration of Independence.

Crosiadore now is the home of Mr. and Mrs. Edward Hughlett, the latter a direct descendant of the Maryland statesman who also served at one time as governor of Pennsylvania and for whom Dickinson College is named in acknowledgment of his interest in its foundation.

The estate lies in that part of Talbot county known as Grubin Neck, a section exceedingly fertile and given over to large estates where lived, in the past, the Hughletts, the Goldsboroughs, the Thomases and the Martins, in addition to the Dickinsons. From the gateway the road makes its way between well-fenced, carefully cultivated farm lands, barns and outbuildings, always maintained at the pink of perfection, to another gateway at the edge of the lawn dotted by trees that John Dickinson knew. The sod is fine and thick, even under the trees, and at the edge of the lawn the Choptank river moves toward the Chesapeake Bay. A boathouse at the water's edge contains motorboats now instead of the sailing craft in which the owners of Crosiadore plied the rivers in Colonial days and across the river is a view of Cambridge, the county seat of Dorchester which, like almost all of the Eastern Shore towns, reveals in its name the national origin of its founders.

The present house follows in the arrangement of its interior the general fashion of an earlier day, with a hall through the center and living rooms on each side. At the head of the stairs stands a grandfather's clock which was made in London, antedating the house by at least a century, and on the walls hang family portraits, together with two extraordinary mourning tapestries, made by a Goldsborough ancestress who had been educated at the Moravian School at Lititz, Penna., and who designed them in addition to doing the needlework.

Ancient chairs and card tables, and old butler's sideboard, with built-in desk in which the butler kept the household accounts, and an old davenport which appears as part of the composition in some of the portraits, all stood in the original house at Crosiadore and in the hatrack in the hall stands a rapier cane, scarcely thicker than an umbrella rod, which belonged to a former owner of the estate.

The old house at Crosiadore in which John Dickinson was born, after having sheltered generations of this public-spirited family, was adjudged unsafe for occupancy during the latter years of the Nineteenth century and was razed. With it went a unique stairway with a free-standing rail of carved mahogany, but "the John Dickinson room" was preserved and incorporated into the present structure. In the reconstruction the old farm buildings were left untouched and the rows of little outbuildings, with the white-painted negro quarters at one end of the garden, remain just where they were, suggesting now by their arrangement rather than by any outward and visible signs of antiquity their connection with the past.

The famous John Dickinson, who proved himself no less a patriot because he had believed separation from England to be unwise, was the grandson of the Walter Dickinson who patented Crosiadore in 1669, taking up in this tract land that had been surveyed for Edward Lloyd—"four hundred acres known as Cross Dower on the North side of the Choptank river," twenty-five acres described in the Rent Roll for Talbot county as the "Cross Dower Marsh, on the North side of the Choptank river, adjoining the land of Edward Lloyd, Esq." A tract of two hundred and twenty acres, "Cross Dower Addition" also was surveyed July 29, 1695, for William Dickinson, becoming part of the entire estate now known as Crosiadore.

This name, which by its sound brings up mental pictures of crusades and conquistadores, is said to have been an Anglicization of the French, Croix d'Or, Cross of Gold. What its application may be to the home of the Dickinsons in Maryland it is impossible to guess, but when it is recalled that many of the fantastic occurrences which are said to have taken place along the shores of the Chesapeake Bay and its tributaries between "the voyages of the discoverers" and the Seventeenth century actually were rooted in fact, the name may not be so far-fetched after all.

CHAPTER SEVENTEEN

Passengers who have crossed the Chesapeake Bay on the ferry from Annapolis, landed on the Eastern Shore at the little hamlet of Claiborne and whirled away in a burst of nervous energy down the road leading towards Easton seldom suspect that they are leaving behind not only one of the oldest estates on the Eastern Shore, but one which occupied a position of great importance for almost a century before the Revolution.

For not a quarter of a mile from the ferry landing and in plain sight of it, if one looks closely through the trees, is Rich Neck, the present home of Colonel and Mrs. Wilford Judson Hawkins, but which first appears in the annals of Maryland in 1651 when Captain William Mitchell took possession of his grant of one thousand acres of some of the most productive land to be found in the present Talbot county.

Intimations of the age of the place come almost as soon as one has turned away from the main road and entered the lane which curves comfortably up to the house, for its course carries past a large, gray-walled burying ground where the headstones crumble and vines obliterate the outlines of graves which have been there for more than two centuries. Within this silent enclosure is the last resting place of Capt. James Murphy, who bought the Rich Neck in 1684, from Philip Land, high sheriff of St. Mary's county, who had acquired it from its first owner. The date, 1692, is carved on the stone which marks the grave of the captain, and below it appear a skull and cross bones, bringing up unfathomable conjectures concerning the swash-buckling Colonial officer.

Was he a pirate, perhaps? For pirates flourished in the early days of Maryland. Or did his widow merely follow to the end her conviction that life led but to the grave and have this gruesome symbol engraved upon her husband's tomb in melancholy testimony of her belief? It is impossible to say. All that is known for certain of Captain Murphy is that he had married the beautiful Mabel Dawson, daughter of Captain Ralph Dawson, whom tradition sets apart as the fairest girl in the Maryland of her day. But pirate or mere dragoon, Captain Murphy must have loved her wholly, for in his will he left her all of his property to do with as she pleased.

Mabel Dawson Murphy apparently was not born to mourn. At least not for any great length of time. Soon after her husband's death she took another spouse, Matthew Tilghman Ward. Their marriage was brief, and Mabel lived only a few years after the ceremony took place. Matthew Tilghman Ward also seems not to have been inconsolable. A short time after the death of his first wife he married Margaret Lloyd, a daughter of Col. Philemon Lloyd, whose brother was master of Wye House. It was during his lifetime, too, that Rich Neck came first into the limelight, for Matthew Tilghman Ward was president of the Council and Lieutenant-General of the militia of the colony, both positions of high rank, and attracted to his home the leading men of the day. Matthew Tilghman Ward left no children to carry on either his political career or his name and after the death of his widow the estate passed by the terms of his will to his cousin, Matthew Tilghman, born at The Hermitage, who made Rich Neck his home and lived there the rest of his life.

Matthew Tilghman seems to have inherited his cousin's taste for public life together with the estate and during his regime the manor house was the rendezvous of many of the leaders of the Revolution. His career began as justice of the court. He then was made speaker of the Assembly and a delegate to the Continental Congress at Philadelphia. He was president of the first constitutional convention of the State and during the war with England was a member of the Committee of Safety, a post of high honor.

The manor house at Rich Neck bears evidence of two distinct building periods, the older portion being to the right of "the great wing" and placed a considerable distance back of it, though the two are connected by a passageway. While no exact year can be ascribed to the building of the old wing it is believed to have been erected between 1680 and 1700. Following the lines of the early settler type, with square little dormer windows looking out from its sloping roof, this house has a brick floor and heavy, discolored beams in the ceiling which make it appear fully as old as tradition claims it to be. The solid shutters have long strap hinges and at one end the deep throated fireplace looks capacious enough to justify the tales that young deer were roasted whole in it when Captain Murphy sat at the head of the table.

Immediately in front of the old wing stands a tiny, vine covered building, the origin and intent of which are lost in mystery. For years it popularly has been supposed to have been a dairy and it has been used as such since 1860, but the cruciform window in one end and the low vaulted ceiling never were built in any dairy in Colonial Maryland. Nor are the rounded brick the kind which would have been likely to have been used in an outbuilding. Everything about it, size, shape and its position in relation to the house, indicate that this quaint little structure was built for use as a chapel. Perhaps it was here that Capt. James Murphy knelt to ask for the remission of his sins, or perhaps not, for the Eastern Shore of Maryland has been, from the beginning, overwhelmingly Protestant in character and the little building faces neither north nor south, neither east nor west as churches do. The most diligent search through old records and old papers connected with the place has failed to offer any solution of the matter and the curious little building keeps its own counsel.

A long, screened porch has served to alter considerably the lines of the "great wing," but, except for this deviation, it conforms closely to the fashion of the latter part of the eighteenth century when it was built by Matthew Tilghman some time after he came into possession of the estate. The brick walls are surmounted by a heavy modillioned cornice, which is carried around the gable ends to form triangular pediments at the top. A round transom appears over the massive front door which is panelled in octagons and supplied with a heavy brass knocker in the form of a dolphin.

The stairway, placed at the left side of the hall, is surprisingly light for a house with so solid an exterior. Two small, square spindles to each step form the balustrade and the slender mahogany handrail curves about the spindles into a spiral on the lowest step.

Tradition has designated the large room immediately to the left of the entrance as the "bow drawingroom," the name being given because of the bow window which lights one side of the room and which was rarely used as an architectural atrribute of old Maryland houses. In Matthew Tilghman's lifetime this room is said to have been a ball room. To the right of the hall is the diningroom with a wide, built-in arch in the wall next to the hall, a device evidently intended to enhance the effect of some cherished piece of furniture, probably a sideboard, since this particular object occupied a large place in the esteem of the Colonial planter.

Upstairs the bedrooms are large, with deep-set windows which seem shorter and wider than those of the most Eighteenth century houses. Bathrooms have been installed during recent years and the old, unfinished attic has been made over into modern bedrooms.

The 1,000 acres of the original survey have shrunk to less than half of that during the two centuries and more of the history of Rich Neck. Its present owners acquired title to just 465 acres.

* * *

In a section of Maryland where almost every house of early building has a water view, the prospect at Mary's Delight, now known as Webley, yields place to none and few estates, even in Talbot county, can equal it in this respect.

Mary's Delight, the old place has been called for "time out of mind," as they still say on the Eastern Shore, but the designation given to it by its original owners was Webley and Webley it has become again in the nomenclature of its present owners, Mr. and Mrs. Harold Walker, who purchased the place a number of years ago and who have not only restored, but developed it by the addition of wings which the builder probably intended to erect when the opportunity presented itself, but which never materialized.

Standing on a low bluff—there is no such thing as a high bluff in this section of Maryland—the house overlooks the Chesapeake Bay to which its lawns slope down, the tall white pillars of its two-story portico framing constantly changing seascapes. On a clear day the outlines of the Western Shore appear on the rim of the horizon and constantly is the eye diverted by the busy traffic of the Bay. Sails of tiny skip-jacks, the dead-rise of the oystermen or of big, four-masted schooners, piled high with lumber, gleam in the sunlight, now and then yielding interest to a big six-masted fruiter coming up from the West Indies with its cargo of bananas. Or a tramp steamer, which has poked its nose against the Gold Coast and steered its course under the Southern Cross since its last appearance in these waters, trundles lazily past on its way to Baltimore. At night the lights of the boat to Norfolk shine like Gargantuan lightning bugs in the darkness and sometimes a trans-Atlantic liner (there were many of them during the World War) steams down toward the Capes with an air of importance. A splendid place is Webley to sit and dream—and let the world go by.

By land Webley is a mile or two distant from the little village of McDaniel, with its single traffic light. From the public road the driveway leading into the house makes a sharp turn to the right and proceeds between a wide file of Lombardy poplars, tall and aristocratic trees, to the entrance. The front door opens into a hallway of adequate, though not spacious proportions, and should the opposite door chance to be open at the same moment, the visitor is regaled at once with a vista through the house and across the lawn to the Bay.

In its present estate Webley strongly resembles White Hall, the home of the Colonial Governor Horatio Sharpe, which stands almost directly opposite it, twelve miles across the Chesapeake, near Annapolis. Its massive central portion dates back to Colonial days, but the gabled wings and rounded windows of the newer portion are in such accord with the original that the whose seems almost to have been built at the same time.

Three staircases afford access from the first floor to the second, the one in the central portion ascending to the right of the entrance having a light balustrade with a delicately turned newel, capped with a walnut handrail. The side of the stairway next the wall is panelled with diamond-shaped *motifs,* the spandrel being finished with a smooth sheathing. A conventional scroll

[298]

carving appears on the ends of the steps which are broken by two landings between the first and second floors and one between the second floor and the attic.

To the left of the hall is the library, and to the right, the diningroom. Both occupy the entire depth of the house. A beamed ceiling adds a strong emphasis to the library and the walls are finished with a heavy wooden cornice carved with the Greek key design. The chimney breast seems wide, even for the day in which it was built, and is panelled on each side of the fireplace with hexagons and squares to the height of the mantelpiece. The mantelpiece itself is exceedingly ornate, with fluted and reeded pillars supporting an elaborate frieze showing a square medallion of tambour fluting in the center, with sunken ovals, outlined with beading, directly over the pillars. The shelf is narrow and high—the fashion of its day.

Beyond the library is the drawingroom, occupying both the connecting wings and the end wing and presenting two levels. From the upper level, in the connecting wing, a twisted staircase goes up to the south bedrooms, its mahogany rail making a high, sweeping ramp in the ascent.

The diningroom across the hall, like the library, is supplied with an exceedingly ornate mantel. Tambour fluting in the herringbone pattern appears on the pilasters at the sides of the fireplace and across the frieze stretches an elaborate decoration of rosettes, fluting and gouged drapery, with a line of hand-cut fretwork immediately below the mantel shelf. As in the library, the ceiling shows heavy beams and a classic cornice.

The soft blue-green which appeared in so many Colonial houses in Maryland finishes the walls of the breakfast room. From this room the third stairway of the house connects with the north bedroom and is an exact duplicate of the one in the drawingroom. The end wing on this side of the house is occupied by the service quarters.

Webley was one of the earliest Eastern Shore land grants and was patented in 1659 to Edmund Webb, its first owner. Three hundred acres are included in the estate which passed before the turn of the century into the possession of the Kersey family, conspicuous in the early life of Talbot county, although now the name is almost extinct. It was during the tenure of this family that Webley became Mary's Delight, a connotation literally bestowed because of the affection lavished on her home by a daughter of the house.

Last of the Kerseys to own it was John, who is remembered still in Talbot for his accomplishments as a scholar. Four daughters inherited the estate at his death, the interest of one of them being purchased and that of another being acquired through his marriage to her by Dr. Absolom Thompson, who forthwith resided there.

Dr. Thompson established at Webley the first hospital on the Eastern Shore. Hospitals were few enough in the great cities in those days and in the country districts of Maryland they existed not at all, but Dr. Thompson waited for no one to take the lead. Possessing extraordinary skill as a surgeon, he is said to have performed in his hospital operations that lesser men would not have dreamed of attempting and to have achieved a reputation that was more than State-wide. A picturesque old character was this early physician from the reports that have come down of him, a man who deemed profanity indispensable to complete expression and who masked a nature of keen sensibility under a cloak of surliness.

Even in his will, on record in the Talbot county court house at Easton, there is evidence of this characteristic.

"I give and bequeath all my estate, real, personal and mixt,

Photo from Collection of James Donnell Tilghman

PEACE AND PLENTY

RICH NECK

RATCLIFFE MANOR

RATCLIFFE MANOR: DRAWINGROOM

of every sort and description, to my dearly beloved son, Absolom Christopher Columbus Americus Vespucius Thompson, provided he shall ever be found alive, who is now supposed to be dead, except the legacies hereinafter given."

The heartbreak of that other and earlier father whose cry "Oh, Absolom, my son," has come down through thousands of years sounds in this remarkable document. For years the gruff old physician had not seen the boy who had gone away to roam the world and who had neglected to keep his father informed concerning his movements. For years Dr. Thompson continued to treat and browbeat his patients, always mourning the son who never wrote and to whom he bequeathed, "provided he shall ever be found alive," a large estate of real and personal property.

Not long after his feather's death Absolom Christopher Columbus Americus Vespucius Thompson returned to his home and claimed the estate. For a number of years he resided at Mary's Delight, but later removed to Georgia. Soon afterwards the property was sold and its name changed again.

No old box gardens are to be found at Webley but in spite of their absence the place proclaims its hold with the past. Its pillared portico, with the semi-circular window in the triangular pediment which crowns the columns, imparts an air of stateliness to the house and recalls that the well-to-do planters of Colonial days in Maryland were aristocrats whose homes were far more the expression of themselves than are most of the houses which men build today.

*   *   *

It was neither sheer sentimentality, nor the sudden welling up in some Colonial pioneer of poetic impulses which would not be denied, that gave to the placid little tributary of the

Miles river some two miles north of Easton, in Talbot county, the name of Peach Blossom creek. On the contrary, it was the eminently practical and to epicures vitally important circumstance—if tradition speaks true—that along its banks burgeoned and bore fruit the first peach trees imported from Persia into Maryland.

Be that as it may, on the banks of the Tred Avon river, not far from the mouth of Peach Blossom creek, stands a Colonial house which has become, during its almost two centuries of existence, as much a part of the landscape as the old mulberry tree which towers above its chimney caps and has grown rotund with age. Ratcliffe Manor was built in 1747 by Colonel James Hollyday as a wedding gift to his bride, Anna Marie Robins, and it has been declared by that connoisseur of Georgian houses, Mr. N. W. Isham, of Wickford, R. I., to be the finest of its period that he has seen. Certainly there is not in Maryland a Georgian country house built before the Revolution that will surpass it in sincerity and refinement of detail.

Ratcliffe Manor house has been fortunate in many things, but in none more so than the disinclination of the three families who have owned it to "make improvements." Necessary repairs there have been, of course, a nail here and a shingle there, even a new roof when it was necessary, but none of the ruthless dissatisfaction which has expressed itself in all too many cases with new porches, slate mantels and "golden oak" paint. Nothing has had to be "restored," and in all its essentials Ratcliffe Manor appears today virtually as it looked when Colonel Hollyday carried his bride over the doorstep into their new home, "just for luck."

Virtually the same, that is to say, but with the addition now of a softening blur to its contours and the contrast of color to its deeply red brick walls given by masses of lush English ivy and a prodigal growth of boxwood which has claimed an entire garden for its own instead of girdling the flowerbeds primly with its green. With these exceptions the place is unchanged from the time when it formed a link in a chain of big country houses which extended from Cecil county south to the Virginia Capes, and where a gay party of some sort almost always was in progress until the Civil War, with its disruption of slavery, put an end to an existence as idyllic as any the new world has known. Guests frequently "rode a mile and stayed a week" at Ratcliffe and on special occasions, when some visitor of distinction arrived from a distance, the entertainment took the form of a concert with musicians imported from Baltimore or Philadelphia, and "a Ball" which ended only when the dancers were too weary to take another step.

A rustic signboard, hung by chains from the limb of a tree, announces to the traveler along the Miles river road the location of Ratcliffe Manor. The road from the main highway to the house is a simple country lane, hugging a row of trees on one side and bordered by a large field of corn or wheat, as the case may be, on the other. Suddenly, a break in the hedgerow brings into view an open field with an airplane circling downward, for sons of the present owner of the estate do much of their traveling by air, finding no difficulty whatever in adjusting themselves to a pre-Revolutionary house after a flight in a Twentieth century machine.

Leaving the flying field the road skirts a group of farm buildings, some of which have been standing as long as the house, and is swallowed up in the turf into which the foot sinks deeply as it might on the lawn of some country house in a land where the proud boast of lawns is that they "have been rolled and watered for three hundred years."

Ratcliffe Manor house is not large as Georgian houses go.

[303]

It makes no open challenge for admiration as some of the other pre-Revolutionary houses in Maryland do. Before the door stands a plain little canopied portico with square, white painted posts and wooden benches, obviously not the work of a craftsman who followed carefully the design in a book, but who achieved an entrance perfectly suited to the house and its surroundings.

In everything, as in the doorway, the house is an expression of simplicity and felicity of proportion. The relations of length to depth, the slope of the roof, the height of the chimneys and the lines of the foliated dormer windows which make the attic a romance in itself draw the eye again and again.

The house is rectangular and follows the Georgian law, honored as often in the breach as in the observance, of two windows on each side of the door in the first story and five windows in the second—one over the door and the others exactly in line with those below. The windows at Ratcliffe are, in themselves, objects of interest with their twelve small panes to each sash on the lower floor—producing an effect which is the object of much striving by the builders of "modern" Colonial houses who can't seem to make them look quite the same, no matter how carefully the measurements are followed. In the second story the windows have twelve panes, also, in their upper sashes, but in the lower there are only eight. The small sash was quite enough for the Colonial sleeper, however inadequate it may appear to Twentieth century eyes, for the night air was "bad" when Ratcilffe was built—and chills and fevers never were invited to enter by way of windows flung high at bedtime.

All of the brick was moulded and baked on the place, with special care to have the "bats" for the belt course and the watercourse, which shows an ovolo curve, particularly fine. The foundation as well as the walls is made of the brick, with a first course of headers and the rest in a Flemish bond so painstakingly laid up that, in the words of one observer, "modern guns might shoot holes through them but they would remain standing." The pointing is perfect after almost two centuries.

Two inside chimneys are placed at each side of the house, forming gable ends of the kind seen more often on a house with a pitched roof than on one with a roof of the type at Ratcliffe which shows the jerkin tendency. The dormers— three on each side—have but six small panes to the lower sash,— another certain indication of the age of the mansion. A wide wooden cornice comes down almost to the lintels of the second story windows, with the heavy modillions at the roof arranged in pairs, completing an exterior which, though it embodies the details which are to be found in Georgian houses from Massachusetts to Carolina, is distinctively of Maryland. At one end of the house are low, one-story wings, given over to servants' quarters and kitchens, indicating by their general appearance that they probably were standing before Colonel Hollyday built the "big house."

The framework about the entrance is formed of substantial, hand-cut moulding, and the front door opens into a small, square hall which seems larger than it really is. At the right is the stairway, which has a balustrade of turned spindles, and a mahogany rail, its small, square newel post being flush with the line of the steps. The soffit, or underside of the stairway, is panelled and beneath one of the landings is an arch with a carved keystone, so low that a tall man would have to stoop to pass beneath it, marking the entrance to the servants' quarters.

The door at the left of the hall opens into the office, a room provided with its own exit doorway so that it was possible for the overseer to enter and leave the room without appearing in the rest of the house. Beyond the office is the drawingroom, panelled from floor to ceiling with white pine and as much a work of art as a cup by Cellini. This room is rectangular and so designed that the end wall is on a line with the far edge of the front door. This method of construction affords a vista through the house and out the garden door, placed directly opposite the front door, without devoting unnecessary space to the hall.

The chimney end of the drawingroom has an elaborate treatment, with a high opening to the fireplace outlined by eared moulding and wide, rectangular panels above, the one next to the ceiling being much wider than the one below, and both enclosed by fluted and reeded pilasters broken a third of their length by an astragal moulding. At the left of the fireplace is a shell cupboard, with a fluted keystone crowning its arch, and at the right another arch frames a window, with bookshelves built in at the side. In the days of Colonel Holly-day the woodwork, now painted an ivory white, was brown and red, touched with gold.

Beside the garden door hangs a mirror which is said to have been made in London by the firm of Thomas Chippendale especially to fit this place, the proportions being secured by measurements sent over from Maryland, and beneath stands a Chippendale chair from the work rooms of the same craftsman and imported directly to Ratcliffe. All of the interior doors have the original brass locks and the door to the garden entrance is fitted with a curious old iron lock, with the key doing duty for a door knob.

The diningroom, like the drawingroom, overlooks tthe garden and the water, a room less interesting than the drawingroom. Its fireplace, however, is provided with a notable mantel, reeded to form a double herringbone pattern on each side of the fireplace opening, with beaded ovals across the frieze and dentils supporting the shelf. Hand-carved mantels also appear in the bedrooms upstairs.

So much of the time was spent by Maryland Colonials out-of-doors that the gardens on their estates came in for quite as much attention as their houses. Frequently they were laid out by English experts, or, if no expert were available, the master and mistress of the plantation (frequently the latter) adapted designs from books just as they did for the houses they built. The garden at Ratcliffe is celebrated and is, within a year or two, as old as the house. Serried flowerbeds, bordered by box-wood and shaded by wide-spreading trees, stretched between the house and the river until the box grew to such enormous size that it had become a veritable maze and it was impossible to utilize it longer in the guise of borders.

Even without the flowers, which grow in profusion else-where on the estate, the garden at Ratcliffe is a fascinating spot, full of hidden paths leading to places so sheltered by the thick rows of box, now grown about twelve feet high, that they serve as a solarium on bright days, even in the coldest weather. From every angle of the garden the little white portico in front of the house always is in sight, sometimes so reduced by the perspective that it appears almost in miniature. A turn of the head will bring the two-branched Tred Avon river into view, making a prospect full of variety, yet always the same.

Ratcliffe Manor was granted to the Hollydays in accordance with Lord Baltimore's custom of giving two thousand acres to all settlers who would completely equip twenty men with arms. Only half that number secured the allotment of one thousand acres which formed the original extent of Ratcliffe. When Colonel Hollyday died he divided his estate among his three sons, giving to each three hundred and thirty-three and a third acres equally well cultivated and wooded.

For the last twenty-five years Ratcliffe Manor has belonged to Mr. A. A. Hathaway who came to Maryland from the West and who maintains his Colonial home in every detail exactly as its first owner might have done.

* * *

Back to the days of Charles, third Lord Baltimore, weaves the history of The Anchorage which rims the shores of the Miles river about five miles north of Easton and is the home of Mr. and Mrs. Milton Campbell who have lived there for two decades and who are descended, through different lines, from the families which owned it a century and more ago.

On one of those ponderous sheets of parchment, inscribed with the flourishing penmanship of some accomplished fellow who delighted in the embellishment rather than the legibility of his handiwork, Lord Baltimore patented the land on March 30, 1677, to one Daniel Walker who makes his brief appearance in this fashion on the sensitive plate of time and disappears forever. From his ownership the place passed to the possession of Richard Bennett, and then became the property, on June 24, 1720, of Richard Bruff.

In the will of Richard Bruff, who bequeathed the plantation to his son, Thomas, appears the first mention in any of the archives of Maryland of a dwelling on the land and, in the absence of either tradition or evidence to the contrary, it may fairly be taken for granted that the little log house which he built on the riverside was the core of the present mansion of late Georgian architecture which includes in its being another which has all the earmarks of antedating it by at least a hundred years.

To the cleverness of a woman who lived in the days when the accomplishments of a lady were limited by social consent to nods, becks and a well-tempered tune on the clavichord, the felicities of this house owe their existence. This woman, Sally Scott Lloyd Lowndes, the daughter of Colonel Lloyd of Wye House, received The Anchorage as a wedding gift from her father when she became the wife of Commodore Charles Lowndes, U.S.N., in 1831, and while living in the stuffy little house built by Richard Bruff drew the plans by which it was enlarged and developed.

Using Wye House, her childhood home, as a model Sally Scott Lowndes evolved a house which represents as nearly, probably, as any in Maryland the popular conception of the home of a Southern gentleman of the "ante-bellum period." Tall white columns uphold its two-story portico and broad low steps which lead from the portico down to the driveway pierce into a lawn of thick, springy turf. In the exact center of the driveway a kingfisher builds its nest, confident of protection. Low, rambling lines follow the course of the wings which bear exactly the right relationship to the central wing. Clumps of boxwood cleave close to the house and down near the river, to one side, a formal garden displays old fashioned flowers.

The Anchorage shows none of the architectural shortcomings of Wye House, an indication that Mrs. Lowndes combined with her devotion to her girlhood home a clear and discerning eye. Its masses invite no criticism, even of kindly intent, and the three arches of its entrance hall are achievements which any architect might be glad to have fathered. In every room in the house faithful adherence to the late period of Georgian building is evident in detail, except in the little room where Richard Bruff may have dined on "oisters and corn pone," or sat in front of the fireplace and toasted his shins on the fender. In this room doors and woodwork are of the simplest and most primitive character, an indication that Richard Bruff was not a man of wealth in an era which saw the erection of some lordly mansions in Maryland.

A number of years after the death of Richard Bruff his son, Thomas, sold the property to the Reverend John Gordon, rector of St. Michael's parish, and typical, apparently, of the parson who flourished in Maryland during the years immediately preceding the Revolution and made mock of religion. Parson Gordon, as he is familiarly spoken of even today in Talbot county, is said never to have wanted for a sizable congregation to listen to his dry-as-dust sermons. His church was filled to the doors every Sunday when the weather was fine and after service parson and congregation repaired as one man to the race-track back of the church where each man backed his own steed with fervor and large quantities of tobacco. Parson Gordon's giddy leadership of St. Michael's parish was of short duration, apparently, for the property was sold again on October 12, 1765, to Anthony Banning who died, leaving an only daughter, Catherine, later the wife of Benjamin Chew. In 1793 The Anchorage was sold to Jacob Lockerman and ten years later it was bought by Edward Roberts who lived in the old house until his death, devising it in his will to his son, Samuel, from whom Colonel Lloyd bought it for his daughter.

During the Civil War one of the grim coincidences which were frequent in Maryland throughout the conflict, found living at The Anchorage a commodore of the Federal navy and directly opposite, across the river, was the home of Admiral Franklin Buchanan, who staked his fortunes with the Confederacy. Admiral Buchanan's estate was known as The Rest, but the house in which he lived has burned to the ground. Succeeding Commodore Lowndes as owner of The Anchorage was his son, Dr. Charles Lowndes, who sold the place in 1894 to General Charles Chipley from whose heirs it was purchased by Mr. and Mrs. Campbell in 1909. Their connection with the earlier owners of The Anchorage comes through the descent of Mr. Campbell from the Lloyds and, on the distaff side, of Mrs. Campbell from the Banning family.

Although Mr. Campbell is the first of his name to live at The Anchorage, his family patronymic long has been held by important participants in the affairs of Talbot county. During the Revolution his great-grandfather, Zachariah Campbell, was a member of the Committee of Safety. Charles Campbell, brother of Zachariah, was a member of the first committee to establish a navy in Maryland and William Campbell, another member of the clan, in a letter to his sweetheart, who was Miss Susan Murray, informed his waiting fiancee, in 1774, of his departure on a secret mission for the Continental Congress and his consequent inability to pay her the visit they both desired.

Levin Hicks Campbell, the son of Zachariah Campbell, was one of the most erudite of the galaxy of early Maryland lawyers and owned an estate in Talbot county called Maiden Point, patented to him in 1793, and which recently has come into the possession of Milton Campbell. In his early manhood he held the post of high sheriff of the county, but his career was ended abruptly by his death at the age of forty-four.

Another member of the family was the father of Margaret Goldsborough who became the wife of Governor John Henry. As a wedding gift she received from her grandfather, Zachariah Campbell, a gift of land in Dorchester county afterwards known as Hampden, the consideration named in the deed being "love and affection and a peppercorn once a year."

The lands of The Anchorage have varied with the years. At one time they numbered about six hundred acres and, at another, approximately a thousand. Mr. Campbell's holdings include about three hundred acres and serve as a practical farm upon which modern methods produce crops of corn and wheat which would have amazed the early owners of the estate.

CHAPTER EIGHTEEN

Time seems an illusion and progress a mad charade when one comes to Myrtle Grove and finds at last a place "where it seems always afternoon." Here, where generations of Goldsboroughs have lived and loved and laughed and died for more than two hundred years there is no thought of strife. Only peace —and infinite content.

A short distance north of Easton, in Talbot county—the exact distance cannot matter when the way leads through a country where the woods are deeply green and step aside at unexpected places to give the traveler a glimpse of some serenely winding river or languid creek—this house is reached by a country road which knows not the touch of macadam and twists and turns and reverses itself until finally it stops short at the gate which is the entrance to Myrtle Grove.

The deep, pervasive hush which compasses the place about has in it none of the quality of expectancy. Instead, the phut-phut of some unseen little motor boat skimming the creek beyond the garden seems somehow to come from another world and to increase the stillness rather than to break it.

Between the gate and the house stretches an expanse of turf green with the hue that comes when there is water nearby and the driveway proceeds between an avenue of dark old cedars that were hoary with age a century ago to a mansion which is associated in every fibre with the traditions of a cavalier State. The house is large and rambling, built partly of brick and partly of frame, and bears abundant evidence of the fact that, as the Maryland phrase has it, "the place never has been out of the family."

The frame wing, it can be told at a glance, was built first, the wedding gift of Robert Goldsborough of Ashby (an older Goldsborough homestead) to his son, Robert. The brick portion, stately and dignified in contrast to the low, dormered structure it seems to take under its wing, was built in 1789 by the third Robert Goldsborough who became a judge and a man of great influence in the State, the date of its erection being fixed by a reference in the diary of Charles Willson Peale who visited Myrtle Grove to paint the portraits of Judge Goldsborough and his family and who noted that he had spent the night at Ashby as his patron's home was not yet completed.

Marylanders ascribe the term "Early Settler" to the type of architecture of which the old wing at Myrtle Grove is an expression and the name will do as well as any to attempt to put into words the whimsical appeal of a building which cannot be put into words at all. The first story walls are covered with wide clapboarding painted a faint cream color; a brick-flagged porch stretches its way across the front and dormer windows twinkle in the sloping roof. It almost seems as if some laughing girl, with a lace cap on her hair, must look out at any moment to call a tiny maiden in to cambric tea.

At Myrtle Grove there is not even a hint of the almost inevitable tradition that the bricks in the house were brought from England. On the contrary, Mr. and Mrs. Robert Goldsborough Henry to whom the place has descended from Mr. Henry's uncle, the late Charles Goldsborough, take pride in the fact that they were made on the place and that the outlines of the excavation from which the clay was dug still may be traced. Careful workmanship done under a watchful eye is evident in the accuracy of the Flemish bond in which they are laid and

THE ANCHORAGE

MYRTLE GROVE: THE OLD WING

DININGROOM, MYRTLE GROVE

the color they have taken on reveals the sorcery which wind and rain, sunshine and shadow alone can accomplish.

A moulded watercourse finishes the top of the rather high foundation to the "new" wing, and a second look at the facade will serve to show that the bricks have been laid to outline a triangle above the triangular pediment of the doorway. The doorway itself displays the characteristic treatment of the period with fluted pilasters, a panelled recess and round transom. Otherwise the facade is plain except for a modillioned cornice which extends across the gable end to form a triangle with the overhanging eaves. An oval foliated window occupies the center of the triangle.

From the front door at the extreme right of this portion of the house a wide high-ceilinged hall stretches past large double drawingrooms to the river front and opens upon a small open porch almost touched by the branches of a magnolia tree. To the right of the hall a hanging stairway ascends to the attic, true to line as the day it was built. Each step is a solid block of wood, a rare thing to see, and the square spindles and handrail of the balustrade are of walnut.

This stairway boasts a quiet fame of its own among architects who are interested in Colonial building and who have been invited to see it, for Myrtle Grove never has been permitted to assume the role of a "show place" but has been maintained from the first as the home of a gentleman, with the constant inviolability of the walls. A close study of the construction of the stairway probably would result in the discovery that certain of the spindles were made of iron, cleverly painted to assume the character of the others, and that iron rods held it firmly to the wall, for in this manner were most of the hanging stairways built.

The drawingrooms are dignified and formal. An Adam frieze

appears directly beneath the ceiling cornice and the original cornices showing the American eagle decorate the windows. So large are the drawingrooms that they occupy the entire lower floor of the brick wing, with the exception of the space taken up by the hall.

The diningroom extends the full depth of the old frame wing, with windows at each end, and has been evolved from two smaller rooms in such fashion that it has become the most interesting room in the house. A fireplace occupies the center of the long side wall and the chimney breast above it is sheathed in perfectly matched panels from the woodwork which appeared above the fireplaces in the two original rooms. The walls are the blue of an old Chinese damask, the panelling is oyster white and the sideboard and table and chairs are heirlooms of mahogany which have been waxed and rubbed for generations.

Luckily enough, the stairway of the old wing was left untouched by Judge Goldsborough when he built the brick house and seems to have come straight out of some little English cottage into this house across the sea. Just wide enough to permit one person to ascend or descend at a time (always remembering to duck the head at the proper place) it winds up by the front wall and comes out upon a tiny hall which has only one straight wall, the other sloping to follow the slope of the roof, with the dormer windows increasing the effect of antiquity. In this little passageway stand two diminutive nail-studded trunks, much like the one placed at the foot of the bed in the room where Washington died at Mount Vernon, and which are filled with yellowed letters and documents of family interest.

Equally remote from a sky-scraper world are the bedrooms of the old wing. Their funny little fireplaces seem rather to belong in the domicile of some spectacled don at Oxford or to the Inns of Court in London. Neither panelling nor mantelshelf detracts from their simplicity and to supply the lack would be to commit the unpardonable blunder. Fortunately, there is no danger!

In the brick wing the bedrooms once boasted proportions identical with the drawingroom below. In their huge fireplaces negro house servants built the fires every morning before the occupants of the rooms were out of bed and at night they robbed them of their coals to fill the gleaming brass warming pans which were passed over the linen sheets on the four-posters to take off the chill. The demands of modern life have taken toll of these rooms in the form of space enough for the bathrooms and clothes closets, but the alteration has been effected without seriously injuring the proportions of the rooms.

The land on which Myrtle Grove stands forms a peninsula washed by the waters of the river now known as the Miles, but called St. Michael's in the old deeds, and Goldsborough creek. Down near the water, slightly to the left of the house, is the box garden which is taking the place of the one which vanished many years ago and which may have occupied the self-same spot, it seems so well meant for a garden. At the far end of the parterres stands an enormous oak, large and beautifully shaped, the blue-ribbon winner of its species in a State-wide contest held a number of years ago.

All of the trees at Myrtle Grove bear an air of venerability. Close to the old cedars in front of the house stands a tiny, one-story building which historians of Talbot county declare to be the oldest law office in America. It, like the brick house, was erected by Judge Robert Goldsborough and it now, after many years of disuse, is being restored to serve the Henrys as a library. The Eighteenth century panelling above the fireplace is sound and solid. No wormholes are there to be filled in—or to be left as a badge of age—and the wooden pins which keep it together

[317]

are holding the panels as firmly in line as in the day when the smoke from Judge Goldsborough's pipe eddied about the little room as he pondered some abstruse point of the law until it swirled up the fireplace flue. To the left of the chimney a staircase as narrow as that in the old frame wing of the house goes up between the walls to the little room where slept the students who, during the day, "read law" with the judge.

Myrtle Grove has been the home of men who have been conspicuous in the service of their country. The first Robert Goldsborough who lived there was a member of the Court of Justices of Talbot county when feeling ran high in consequence of the Stamp Act and met with other members of the court at the county seat to declare that they would "detest, abhor and hold in the utmost contempt all and every person who shall meanly accept of any employment or office relating to the Stamp Act; or shall take shelter or advantage under the same; and all and every Stamp-pimp, informer or favorer of said Act; and that they will have no communication with any such person except it be to upbraid them for their business.

"And in testimony of this, their fixed and unalterable resolution, they have this day erected a gibbet twenty feet high before the Court House door and hung in chains thereon the effigy of a stamp informer there to remain *in terrore* till the Stamp Act shall be repealed."

Robert Henry Goldsborough, who has come down in tradition as "the Chesterfield of the Senate" was the son of Judge Robert Goldsborough and twice served as United States Senator from Maryland in addition to raising, equipping and leading a troop of horse in Talbot county in the second war with Great Britain, a war which, incidentally, he had opposed bitterly.

The Goldsboroughs always have entertained lavishly at Myrtle Grove. From the day when the young bride of Robert

Goldsborough, happy in her new home but somewhat apologetic concerning its lack of shrubbery, pointed to a straggling bush and cried banteringly as she greeted some unexpected guests, "Welcome to our Myrtle Grove," the estate has been the center of a gay, pleasure-loving society. The old floors have echoed night-long to the sound of dancing feet and innumerable candles have burned in the old silver candlesticks to make light for merrymakers in lace ruffles and buckled shoes who bowed before girls in powdered hair and silks which would stand alone. Few invitations were refused to a party at Myrtle Grove. House guests stayed weeks at a time, with slaves to attend to every want, for the Goldsboroughs were among the largest slaveholders in the county, forty-one being accredited to the master of Myrtle Grove at the first census.

Today the slaves are gone, but their descendants remain and some of them work on the place where their forefathers toiled. Freedom has not changed their allegiance to the Goldsboroughs.

* * *

Some six or seven miles from Easton as the crow flies—they still have crows on the Eastern Shore—encircled by a deep stretch of woodland and the curving arm of the Miles river is Fair View, one of the fine jewels of Colonial Maryland, but little known even to those who make a cult of ancient things.

Hidden completely from the public ways, undisturbed by the radio and unreached by the daily paper until afternoon, Fair View broods apart. There, things which seem elsewhere to matter greatly become vastly unimportant and life remains untroubled as on the day in 1663 when Lord Baltimore bestowed upon Andrew Skinner 300 acres of land which are designated on the records in Annapolis as Huntington, the name afterwards being changed to Fair View.

The first glimpse of the house from the gateway reveals a stately mansion of homemade yellow-painted brick with a single wing of frame, added much later, though it, too, is quite old. Green shutters frame the windows and white Ionic pillars outline the portico which stretches the full height of the building. About the house several acres are included in an enormous lawn, where trees, magnificent as any to be found in the famous Arnold Arboretum in Boston, stand about, oblivious to admiration.

From the entrance there is no hint of the old box garden, one of the most beautiful in Talbot, which is laid out back of the house. In it long lanes of boxwood, tall enough to screen completely from view a man of six feet in height, wind in and out, and there "voices" are said to have been heard in the twilight, although no human being was about. So splendid is this boxwood that Mrs. Samuel S. Wales, the present owner of Fair View has received repeated offers of $50,000 for it, offers which have been consistently refused. Two hundred years, at least, are believed to have elapsed since the garden at Fair View was laid out and the boxwood planted.

The mansion itself is an excellent specimen of Eastern Shore homes erected during the half-century immediately preceding the Revolution, the date of its construction being traditionally placed at 1729. This is the second house to have been built at Fair View, the first, which stood on another site, having been destroyed by fire and all trace of it lost.

It would be difficult for anyone who finds delight in old houses not to rejoice in Fair View. Here are strength and beauty of line, correctness of proportion, simplicity and that ineffable something called charm. The house consists of a central portion flanked by great chimneys on each side, two stories high and divided through the center by a wide hall. On each side of the hall are two rooms of graceful measurments, finished with wood-work carved by hand. None of it is ornate and there is no display in the result, the builder obviously preferring to obtain his effects through the use of fine material and painstaking work-manship. The wide, uneven boards of the original floors are in use just as they were two hundred years ago and seem in con-dition to withstand two centuries more of constant wear.

Fair View has no imposing staircase winding up from the hall to the rooms on the second floor. The first floor is the center of interest and forms a complete whole.

The same honesty of construction is to be found in the spacious wing where there is a huge kitchen with an old Dutch oven and where, today, the presiding genius is a fitting replica of the erstwhile slave who conjured into existence such beaten biscuit and fried chicken, such crab soup and terrapin as epicures always associate with Maryland.

Comparatively little is known of the first owner of Fair View. From the records at Annapolis there is obtained the information that to Andrew Skinner was granted, in addition to the three hundred acres then called Huntington, six hundred acres in what afterward was known as Queen Anne's county. Evidently, however, Fair View was the more desirable tract of the two as, except for record at Annapolis, there is no knowledge of the land in Queen Anne's. A few years after he received the grant he is mentioned as high sheriff of Talbot and in another early document the name of Andrew Skinner appears as coroner.

Andrew Skinner married Ann Sneden. His son, also Andrew Skinner, married Elizabeth Feddeman, and their son, the third Andrew Skinner, on June 12, 1759, became the husband of Ann Sutton of Charlestown, Mass., the bride being the great-great-great-granddaughter of William Brewster, leader of the Pilgrims who came to Massachusetts in 1620.

The fourth Andrew Skinner was born at Charlestown, Mass., on September 11, 1763, and married Elizabeth Harrison, of Appleby, Dorchester county, Maryland. Their last surviving child, the late Mrs. Henry Cooke Tilghman, who was born September 3, 1817, lived to be 94 years old, her death occurring September 10, 1911.

Christopher Harrison, at one time Governor of Indiana, who laid out Indianapolis in the days when circumstances made it expedient for him to keep all of his money under a plank in the floor, was a cousin of the family, and one of the family treasures is a snuff box which he used in those hectic times.

After the death of Andrew Skinner in 1843 Fair View was bought by his son-in-law, Thomas P. Williams, who sold it to Thomas Harrison Oliver shortly before the Civil War. Mr. Oliver was a relative of Mrs. Andrew Skinner through the Gale family, Mrs. Skinner's grandmother having been a Gale, so that from 1663 until 1914, when it was bought by Mr. and Mrs. Wales, the ownership remained within one family.

Mention of Mr. Oliver's name in Talbot county never fails to elicit an expression of interest. He had inherited a large estate and used it not only to maintain Fair View as its history deserved, but to enhance its beauty. Trees were one of his great passions and old residents of the county to this day tell how "Harry" Oliver moved large specimens from one end of the county to his place at the other until he had there a collection of more than one hundred and fifty varieties, all of them superb.

Big game hunting, at which he spent more than twenty-five years in Africa, sending trophies of his prowess back to Fair View until the attic was filled with them—and moths—was another of his hobbies, but it was his trees which proved the talisman resulting in the sale of Fair View to Mrs. Wales, since no one who had sought to buy before her seemed to him to be filled with what he considered sufficient appreciation of their beauty.

By comparison with other estates in Talbot county, Fair View was quite small, as the first census shows Andrew Skinner to have had but 18 slaves. Within recent years part of the land has been sold to Glenn Stewart, of New York, who has built upon it a Spanish castle and who calls his tract Cape Centaur.

During the time that the mansion remained unoccupied by the Oliver family neglect resulted in direful damage to house and garden, especially the garden, so that when Mr. and Mrs. Wales took possession it was necessary literally to chop away cartloads of honeysuckle and other creeping vines before the plan of the garden could be traced. Then it was found that one entire row of boxwood had been cut away to provide decorations for a wedding which had taken place in the mansion during a brief season the place had been occupied by renters. The boxwood has been replaced, however, and is growing as rapidly as this slow-growing shrub ever seems to do. Mrs. Wales, in addition to maintaining and restoring the garden, is developing a new one. When it has been completed the combined gardens will stretch almost down to the river.

In addition to the "voices" in the garden, Fair View is said to have four accredited ghosts. A member of a house party of young people who were being entertained in the house upon one occasion, had a delirious story to tell when the hostess returned from a brief absence, of a little old lady, quaintly gowned, who came and sat by the fireplace. The youth was much shaken by the circumstance, but regained his calm after a day or two.

Another ghostly visitor to Fair View is described as a beautiful girl, dressed in a ruffled, hoopskirted gown, who is said to have been recognized as the wraith of Alicia Lloyd, once the toast of Talbot county and who lies buried in the graveyard at Fair View.

On the beach, at the hour when spirits walk the earth, there is said to wander a wraith of a headless sailor, but though several persons are said to have seen him no one ever has been found who will hazard a conjecture concerning the original of this fearsome apparition. Up and down the figure moves, perhaps searching vainly for its head, and then disappears until such other night arrives as best befits its spectral purposes.

More frequent in its appearance is the man on horseback who haunts the lane by the woods and has been known to charge madly straight through guests arriving by automobile. Whether or not this is the spirit of the cavalier age, outraged at the encroachments of latter day methods of travel, or whether it is the actual shade of some frustrated horseman no one will venture to say.

But what is an ancient manor without its shades? The "voices" in the garden, the little old lady, the hoopskirted girl, the galloping horseman—all seem to belong, somehow, to the equally intangible spirit that is Fair View.

CHAPTER NINETEEN

The waters of the Wye river ruffled in the breeze which blew from the shores of Talbot county one early summer morning more than a century and a-quarter ago. At the end of a jutting green peninsula a pleasure barge was tied to the wharf. Twelve blacks with velvet caps on their heads ranged themselves, six on each side, within the barge and grasped the oars, plying them slowly, just enough to counteract the current.

Six other negroes, similarly garbed, stood rigidly at attention, holding six shining brass blunderbusses. In wooden dugouts other negroes were storing away a marquise of sufficient size to hold a dozen people, beds and bedding, chairs, provisions, and all manner of equipment. A slight stir on the bank announced the arrival of still another retinue of negroes and into the dugout went the final consignment of supplies—china, glassware, boxes of clothing, chickens making a great to-do with their clucking, dozens of "crabbes" and last, and perhaps the most important of them all, a cask of finest Madeira.

When everything had been placed on board a young slave, tense with excitement, ran to the bank.

"Massa's comin'!"

Instantly an overseer snapped out quick commands as a group of women wearing flowered satin morning gowns, with cobwebby lace caps, lace on their petticoats and outlining the necks of their bodices, with shoes colored to match their gowns, approached on the arms of men wearing equally elaborate plumage. In the gay party were Mistress Mary Tayloe Lloyd, a beauty, and young Francis Scott Key, later to become renowned as the author of a great American song of battle. The center of the group was Edward Lloyd, master of Wye, arrayed, according to the chronicle which has come down to tell the story of the party, in fine cloth breeches lined with silk and finished with gold buttons; a buff lapeled waistcoat; white silk hose and black shoes, buckled with silver. The master of Wye House and his guests were departing on a pleasure jaunt.

Beside Edward Lloyd walked a page in blue coat and breeches, holding his master's snuff box and a volume just arrived from a London print shop. Gingerly the revellers stepped into the barge and sank back against satin cushions stuffed with down. When Edward the Magnificent, as his friends referred to him, had been seated a signal was given. Brass blunderbusses were lifted to black shoulders and six shots volleyed across the water. The party was off, with the ensign of fifteen stripes, full size, in the red, white and blue of a free Colonial empire flying at the masthead.

Wye House, at the time of this ceremonious "picnic" already was one of the show places in America. Ever since 1668 there have been Lloyds at Wye, with seven Edwards succeeding one another to the great ancestral estates which, at the time of their greatest extent, numbered thousands of acres and were tilled by negro slaves, many of whom were unknown, even by sight, to the master of the house.

The estate is considerably smaller now, but it still is an extensive domain. Enormous wrought iron gates, imported from Italy, stand at the entrance on a country road about eight miles from Easton and open into a park where sheep graze in apparent realization of their decorative effect. At the end of the park the road crosses a "Ha-Ha," which looks like a moat on a miniature scale and is said to be one of the two of its particular type in America. Its brick bridges, covered with turf, are the same age

FAIR VIEW: FRONT ELEVATION

Photo from Collection of James Donnell Tilghman

WYE HOUSE

Photo from Collection of James Donnell Tilghman

WYE HOUSE: ORANGERY

Photo from Collection of James Donnell Tilghman

WYE HOUSE: GRAVEYARD

as the "Ha-Ha" and, beyond, other Italian gates open on the lawn where the driveway circles about an old sundial.

The present house, built of frame, replaces one of the Early Settler type which was burned by the British during the Revolution. The one which is standing today is of late Eighteenth century architecture and has been visited by devotees of Colonial history from all parts of the United States. The picture it presents is a blend of Georgian and Colonial ideas, with wings a trifle low in proportion to the central building. A small, closed-in portico with arched, window-like apertures cut into the sides to admit light and air, stands before a front door which is several inches thick and heavy enough to withstand a small force of armed men. A brass lock, six inches by fourteen, secures the door and shows plainly its origin in London.

At the right a door with a brass handle opens into the office which is panelled over the chimney and fitted with inset cupboards provided with silver keyholes. A landscape painting appears in the panel over the fireplace. The high mantel is carved with the Greek key design and the old call bell is there even now to summon a negro servant who replaces the slave delegated to answer its summons in the era of Edward the Magnificent. This room, in addition to its use as an office, serves as a repository for the sporting equipment of guns and fishing tackle which form part and parcel of existence on the Eastern Shore.

Opposite the office is the sitting room. The panelling across the chimney is similar to that of the office, with the little built-in cupboard to the right of the fireplace and to the left of it a horizontal panelling of flat sheathing. An eared moulding, designed to frame a portrait, outlines the space directly above the fireplace.

At the end of the entrance hall corridors connect the main building with two-story wings, one of which is used as the library said to have been the great pride of the builder of Wye who filled it with rare and costly books in which he took the keenest sort of delight. The other wing is given over to the pantries and kitchen where descendants of the old slave cooks still perform. At the right of the hall, from a carved archway, the staircase ascends at the right to the top of the house, its light balustrade with tiny, square spindles contrasting with the black walnut woodwork of the stairs themselves.

The walls of the hall are lined with Shakesperean prints, the work of Boydell, ordered by Edward Lloyd IV from London, with the specification that they be "framed handsomely in glass," and prints of other historic and subject value which represent the work of Bartolozzi and Ryland after Cipriani, Angelica Kaufman, and other artists of the Colonial period.

Across the corridors leading from the main hall to the wings, doors showing the Wall-of-Troy design on carved cornices, open into the diningroom and drawingroom, both large and high of ceiling. Light cornices finish the walls of both rooms and high carved mantels are surmounted by panelling and eared moulding. These rooms present today a picture almost identical with their appearance during the period just after the Revolution and are furnished with rare pieces of Chippendale, Hepplewhite and Sheraton, not only in excellent condition but in a true setting.

In the upper hallway an arch corresponds exactly in position to the one in the lower hallway at the approach to the stairs. From this pasageway glimpses may be had into bedchambers the size of the rooms on the first floor and filled with carved chests of drawers, easy chairs and wide four-poster beds once provided with heavy curtains to keep out the draughts.

Terminating the lawn back of the house is the orangery, the only one of its period in America and one of the most celebrated appurtenances of this feudal-like estate. The orangery either was overlooked by the British when they swarmed over the place and burned Wye House in 1776, or they considered it of insufficient importance to merit destruction. In either event, it stands today as it stood then, French rather than English in feeling, with great, blinking windows, a hipped roof and walls hung with ivy, a compelling reminder of what life really was like on a great Maryland estate before the Revolution.

Beyond the orangery are gardens, acres in extent, of boxwood and flowers, gardens which grow only to increase in beauty and a quiet mystery. All of the winding walks are outlined by borders of thick growing box, which, it is said, would reach ten miles if placed in line.

To the left of the orangery an ancient brick arch said to be as old as the first Wye House, is known at Wye as the "graveyard gate" and affords entrance to one of the most interesting private burying grounds in the country. There seven Edward Lloyds rest in line, but the oldest of the gravestones is the one which marks the last abode of Henrietta Maria Lloyd, that wealthy and mysterious personage who was the wife of Philemon Lloyd, son of Edward the First. Eulogistically it is engraved:

Henrietta Maria Lloyd,
Shee who now takes her Rest within this Tomb
Had Rachel's Face and Leah's fruitful womb,
Abigail's Wisdom, Lydia's faithful heart,
With Martha's care and Mary's better part.
Who died the 21st day of May
(Anno) Dom. 1697, aged 50 years.
——months, 23 days.

To whose memory Richard Bennett dedicates this tomb.

Lavish the tribute, but lavish also was nature to Henrietta Maria Lloyd. Born of a notable family, it is said that Queen Henrietta Maria of England stood sponsor for her when she was baptized and when she came to the home of the Lloyds as the bride of Philemon Lloyd she won the admiration and the affection of the countryside. One enthusiast has declared: "The name of this beautiful, gracious lady stands for whatever is gentle in birth and in breeding, for whatsoever is excellent in character and conduct, for whatsoever is of good report of the honorable men and women of old Maryland."

That Henrietta Maria Lloyd epitomized the woman of position and fashion of her day is evident from all that remains to give account of her. An inventory of her estate, made according to law after her death, mentioned specifically, "1 satin gown and petticoat, 1 silk gown and petticoat, 1 old silk gown and coat, 1 mourning gown and quilted petticoat, 1 silk mantel, 2 silk petticoats and scarf, a good warm gown, 2 smock coats and 2 waistcoats, a parcel of laces, a pair of bodices, a gauze coat, 1 flowered satin party coat, 4 party coats, 4 pairs of shoes and 1 pair of galoches, silk and worsted stockings, 2 head dresses, a box of handkerchiefs, 3 pictures, a parcel of neck lace, 1 diamond ring, 1 mourning ring, 4 stone rings, 3 rings and a pair of earrings, 2 pictures, a little box of cash, a flowered 'satting' morning gowne, a long scarf lyned with velvet, a parcel of silver lace and footings, 2 pair stays, 1 black scarfe, 1 parcel of beads and silver cross and snuff-box, 1 gowne and party coat, 1 silk petticoat with silver fringe, 1 silk morning gowne, 1 riding gowne, 1 sable tippet and strings, 2 short aprons, girdle and mark," and so on and so on.

A "great" wrought silver dish, was one of the many treasures which Henrietta Maria Lloyd disposed of in her will, leaving this emblem of luxury to her three daughters. To all of her children she left an inheritance of good looks and charm and to at least two of them a capacity for high romance which equals any amorous idyll of early America. Edward Lloyd, the second, and

Philemon they were, both rivals for the beautiful Sarah Covington whose questing eyes peeped from beneath a dun-gray bonnet as, mounted on a pillion behind her sombrely garbed father, she rode from Somerset county to Talbot to attend that famous Tred Avon yearly meeting which also was attended by William Penn, Lord and Lady Baltimore and other Colonials of note.

Both of the young cavaliers from Wye were there, too, for diversions were scarce enough though they had scant sympathy with Quaker doings, and both fell madly in love with Sarah of the roseleaf complexion. When the meeting had ended, neither of them said a word to the other, but, booted and spurred, they rode away by different routes into Somerset and met, face to face, at the gate of the Covington home.

Something had to be done. Each guessed at the other's secret, though neither mentioned it. After beating about the bush at some length they agreed that the one who first had seen Sarah should have the first opportunity of offering her his heart. Philemon declared that the moment he had entered the stark little meeting house his eyes had rested upon her; but Edward insisted that before the meeting house had been reached at all he had encountered the Quaker and his daughter upon the road and, at the Quaker's request, had pointed out the way to the meeting house.

Crestfallen, Philemon acknowledged his defeat and rode away. Edward watched his brother until he had become a mere speck in the distance, for the two were devoted each to the other and life suddenly had become a serious thing. Then, when he no longer could see the retreating figure, Edward knocked at the Covington door and in his efforts to win the girl he desired forgot completely his brother's heartbreak. Before long he won the promise of the comely Quakeress to marry him and Sarah came to Wye House to preside over the mansion where the important Henrietta Maria had preceded her. Sarah outlived her husband and later married James Hollyday who became master of Wye during the minority of Sarah's oldest son, Edward, and who built the mansion at Readbourne for her, when they went to Queen Anne's county to live after Edward became of age.

Two brothers were the first of the Lloyd name to come to America, Edward and Cornelius, who emigrated to Virginia about 1635 and took up land along the Elizabeth river which they received in grants from Captain John West. Edward Lloyd had been educated for the law and practiced his profession in Norfolk in 1645, serving also as a member of the Virginia House of Burgesses from 1644 until 1649 when, for reasons best known to himself and which have not come down to posterity, he came to Maryland. When Anne Arundel was formed into a county in 1650 Edward Lloyd was named by Governor Stone to be its commander, but when Talbot was organized in 1750 he determined to look more closely after the lands he had acquired on the Eastern Shore and built his home on the banks of the Wye river, calling it Wye House.

Another momentous incident occurred in the life of Edward Lloyd (already known as "Colonel") in the year of his removal to Wye when Cecilius Calvert, second Lord Baltimore, commissioned him, together with several others, to be deputy governors of Maryland in the event of the death of Governor Philip Calvert. Colonel Lloyd's son, Philemon, died while his father still lived so that when the colonel, in the fullness of time, sickened and died, the estate descended to his grandson, Edward Lloyd, the second.

A fragment of the original house which was, from all indications, larger than most of the homes erected by the early settlers, remained after the British had completed their work of destruction, and appears as the brick house near the stable.

This, almost certainly, was the old north wing, and in dry weather the outlines of the main house can be traced. The old smokehouse, with narrow slits for windows, bears a striking reminder of an old fortress.

No house built in Maryland before the Revolution was more richly filled with luxurious appointments than Wye. Such a treasure-trove could not but appeal to the rapacious instincts of an invading army and, in addition to burning it, the British looted it of its fine paintings and costly plate. Worse still, in the eyes of the present generation, all the family records which had been kept carefully up to that time perished with the house. Several years after the war a number of pieces of plate bearing the family arms were returned to Maryland by the crown and are treasured by the family at Wye today.

Before the smoke of the Revolution had vanished Edward Lloyd, the fourth, had begun the erection of the present Wye House. Nine generations of Lloyds have lived there in direct descent, loving and mating and dying finally to be buried in the old graveyard which, with its central grassy aisle bordered by over-arching trees, forms a natural cathedral.

Edward Lloyd, the fourth, was one of the most conspicuous men of Talbot during the Revolutionary period, serving as a member of various committees, and aiding in the reconstruction which presented many and bitter problems after the peace had been signed. In 1780 he became a member of the House of Delegates and in 1781-1786 and 1791 he was elected to the State senate. During 1783 and 1784 he was delegate from Maryland to the Continental Congress and in 1788 was a member of the State convention to ratify the Federal constitution.

The fifth Edward Lloyd followed his father to Congress, being a member of the Federal body from 1796 until 1809, giving up his seat to become governor of Maryland. In 1812 he was a presidential elector, casting his ballot for Madison, and four years afterwards he again entered national affairs as a member of the United States Senate.

With the sixth Edward Lloyd interest in public life was secondary to his career as a country gentleman. He preferred to attend closely to the affairs of his estate and gloried in the size of his crops. He imported cattle from the Channel Islands and built up a herd of stock impressive to behold.

During the period of the Civil War a strange character appeared in the land, the like of whom had not been seen before, and whose name was connected with Wye House. Petted and made much of by the abolitionists and reformers, Fred Douglass, a well-educated and traveled mulatto, excited a furor throughout the country, finally becoming Minister to Hayti and later Marshal of the District of Columbia. But years before that he had been a little pickaninny at Wye, the son of a white man of considerable learning and a negro woman who was owned by a sailing master employed by Governor Lloyd. During his childhood he played constantly at Wye, sometimes with the other negro children, and sometimes with the governor's son, Daniel. When he was about nine years of age, the story goes, Colonel Lloyd took the boy, who had been given his freedom, with him as valet on a trip to Saratoga Springs. The boy took advantage of the opportunity to disappear and the Lloyds heard nothing of him until he challenged attention as a man of wide experience and good education. Douglass, as an old man, revisited Wye in 1881, making a sentimental journey to the haunts of his childhood, dropping at times into negro dialect as he pointed out by name little points and bayous where he had frolicked with "Mars Dan."

Edward Lloyd, seventh, proved himself in the part of a country gentleman as excellent a personage as did that other Ed-

Photo from Collection of James Donnell Tilghman
WYE HOUSE: DRAWINGROOM MANTEL
The "North Parlor"

Photo from Collection of James Donnell Tilghman
FRONT PORCH, WYE HOUSE

OTWELL

Photo from Collection of James Donnell Tilghman

ward, Seventh, who comes inevitably to mind, on a far more ambitious scale on the throne of England. Widely separated as were their destinies they had much in common, not the least of which were kindliness of heart and courtliness of manner. The present owners of Wye House are the heirs of the late Charles Howard Lloyd who maintained there during his lifetime the traditions of his ancestors.

*　　*　　*

On the other side of Easton from Wye House going south, smiling like some old English manse which refuses to take too seriously the foibles of men, Otwell, on Trippe's creek, has been the home of a line of Goldsboroughs for two hundred years and is associated entirely with the name of this family rather than with that of William Taylor to whom it was patented in 1659, or Foster Turbutt, who was its next owner, and who, for many years, was clerk of Talbot County.

There is something intangible about the house at Otwell, straggling over the ground it occupies and half swallowed by ivy, some subtle understanding which seems to make it the peculiar "find" of everyone who sees it for the first time. Just when the place, sometimes spelled Ottwell in old records, came into possession of the Goldsboroughs is somewhat foggy, but it is said to have changed hands through the marriage of Foster Turbutt's daughter, Ann, to John Goldsborough. All that can be proved are the facts set forth in an old document showing that in 1721 a survey was made of the land as a Goldsborough holding. From this date its history is easily traceable, for Otwell descended directly in the male line from father to son until it came into the possession of the late Matthew Tilghman Goldsborough who died in 1928.

Otwell is gambrel-roofed in part, with additions of an archi-

[335]

tecture impossible to ascribe to any of the conventional categories, and so low to the ground that it seems almost a part of it. The oldest portion, which is believed to have been built between 1721 and 1725, is in the shape of a "T," with thick walls of brick showing, where they can be seen, every conceivable color a brick can be, all burned on the place.

The foundation walls are stone, gathered up on the place and many of them still encrusted with the oyster shells which had adhered to them. The entrance door in the long side of the "T" head is almost on a level with the ground and is plain to the point of severity. Tiny windows huddled close to the eaves have many rows of small panes but no shutters and the little peaked dormers above give the exterior the effect of an illustration for a book of fairy tales. Copious chimneys, with ornamental caps, rise at each end of the "T" head and the shingles of the roof are so overgrown with moss that they look almost as if they might have been put there when the house was built instead of a comparatively few years ago.

When it was built Otwell consisted of an office and "greate room," now the drawingroom, and a hall with wide, uneven boards and a black walnut stairway, carved on the ends of each step with tulips in relief. No plaster covered the brick partition walls, which first were whitewashed and later painted. The sloping walls of the gambrel roof encroached considerably upon the space of the tiny bedrooms above which are exactly the same now as they were two hundred years ago. No bathrooms have been introduced to alter their proportions and a negro servant still heats the water for baths in the kitchen at the far end of the house and carries it upstairs by hand. Nor have electric lights ever been installed to furnish an incongruous if convenient illumination. Oil lamps are lighted every night at nightfall and sometimes candles serve instead, flicker-

[336]

ing with every breeze that blows and castings grotesque shadows on the walls of the low ceilinged rooms. In every sense Otwell has kept to the old ways, not scorning the new, it seems to imply, but satisfied with things as they are.

The door which leads from the hall into the diningroom was cut from a tree so large that a single board, smoothly planed on both sides, with two bevelled panels, sufficed to make it. This door has a large brass lock and H-and-L hinges, too. Over the chimney, at the opposite end of the room, a tiny cupboard appears near the ceiling where powder was stored for use in the old musket which always stood conveniently at hand, the heat of the chimney assisting materially in "keeping the powder dry." In the diningroom is the old sideboard which stood there before the Revolution, only to be thrown away during the reign of terror which cast out all such treasures and replaced them with atrocities. The old sideboard evidently had been bestowed upon a negro servant and forgotten until the revival of interest in antiques started the descendants of the open-handed but misguided ancestor upon a voyage of recovery and led to its discovery in the cabin of a servant.

Back of the diningroom are the store rooms and the kitchen, the latter a genuine bit of folklore. The cavernous fireplace occupies almost one entire side of the room into which light comes uncertainly only through two windows, one at each end. So small are these windows that they are really little more than loopholes and a batten door has a heavy wooden lock which, more than once, was bolted against the lurking Indian. Everything about this old kitchen wing contrives to make it appear to have been built before the rest of the house but the Goldsborough tradition is strong that the "T" end came first and the kitchen later. Perhaps tradition is right, but the feeling persists.

Each addition to the house as it was built was provided with its own chimney and its own doorway, reached by low wooden steps. Within recent years a porch has been added on the land side and it, too, is overhung with vines. Roses climb over the door which faces the river in the "T" wing, but in other days the wind was sweet with the odor of grape blossoms on the vine which swung near the south door. The old well and sweep have vanished, too, and the house seems to miss their companionship. The slavequarters, some distance away, have become stables for horses and cows and are much altered in appearance.

The old sunken garden at Otwell was the pride of generation after generation of Goldsborough women who dug daintily in it and pulled the weeds with due regard for "lily hands," leaving the heavier work to slaves. With the passing of slavery and consequent readjustments of labor and fortune the old garden ceased to be, but its ghost reappears every year in a sweep of daffodils between the house and the water. The grandfather of the last Goldsborough owner of Otwell could not remember when the daffodils had not come up on the same spot in the spring.

Trees more than twice the height of the house stand protectingly at each end of the old homestead making a picture that Corot would have ached to paint could he have seen it. And a hedge of mock orange, at least a quarter of a mile long, screens the place from the view of the public road which stops short at the gate. Otwell is in fact, as in seeming, a journey's end.

Judged by Colonial standards Otwell was a small estate. One thousand acres and no less constituted a manor, while the patent to William Taylor embraced only five hundred. But there were compensations in water for what the place may have lacked in land. The shore line breaks constantly into curves and little inlets, providing beauty as well as opportunities for companionship with the owner of the land across the creek. Men had to stand together against many enemies in the days when William Taylor took up his grant—three years before Talbot county became a political entity on its own account. In the water was to be found, too, an abundance of food which made the immediate production of crops a secondary considera- tion. Oysters and ducks, fish and terrapin abounded here as everywhere on the Eastern Shore in such quantities that laws ultimately were passed, prohibiting the feeding of diamondback terrapin to slaves more than three times a week.

Otwell makes no pretensions, but builders of the present era would stand aghast at the idea of putting door and window frames of black walnut into a simple farmhouse such as this. Or of building a blacksmith shop and hammering out the nails they used, one by one, with only the crudest tools to do the work. The number of nails which went into the construction of Otwell were few and far between, wooden pins being used whenever possible. In the attic at Otwell the joists were crossed as well as pinned, making the house literally as solid as a rock.

*　*　*

To the voyage of a forthright New England sea captain who sailed up the Chesapeake Bay one day and made his way into the pleasant Choptank river, the old, rambling house still known as Potter's Mansion owes its existence. Captain Potter was beguiled exceedingly by the land he saw, so friendly and so easy-going it seemed after the "stern and rockbound coast" where existence was hard and life a constant warfare against natural odds, and he made arrangements to return there and settle as soon as the requisite preliminaries could be made.

Captain Potter settled in the vicinity of Conquerious Creek which then was a busy little watercourse and which has dis- appeared completely except as a name on old maps. The small brick house he built on a little knoll overlooking the water was known as Potter's Landing. It remained in use for generations. To the wharf which the enterprising captain built sea-going vessels came constantly to load tobacco for English seaports and Captain Potter himself commanded one of the vessels, building up an already substantial fortune. Returning, the ships brought supplies to the colonists of the vicinity.

Possessed of the prescience which many sea-faring men have, Captain Potter seemed to know before he began it that a certain voyage was to be his last and in preparation for his departure, he made his will which was probated in 1761. Two sons survived, Dr. Zabdiel Potter and Nathaniel Potter. The latter inherited the place and became one of the active patriots of the State during the Revolutionary period, serving in the Maryland conventions of 1774 and 1776 and then as first major of the militia. An even greater responsibility devolved upon him in the post of purchasing agent for the Continental army in Caroline county. At his death the property passed to his brother, Dr. Potter, who had resigned his commission as captain of the Flying Camp to serve as a surgeon, a post in which his skill was desperately needed.

Both these men were born in the old log wing which was used as a kitchen after the building of the large mansion by William Potter, son of Zabdiel Potter, about the year 1808. This house gives the impression of being extremely high and the cupola, which came after the house had begun to be known as "the old Potter mansion," adds to the effect. Big end chimneys, two on one side and one on the other, contribute a certain formality to the exterior and in the wing, which is much lower, the windows follow the custom which arrogated to the upper sash more panes than the lower.

The house faces the water with a broad, sloping lawn be-

Photo from Collection of James Donnell Tilghman

STAIRWAY AT OTWELL

Photo by William H. Fisher

DININGROOM DOOR AT OTWELL

THE POTTER MANSION

tween. Fluted pilasters flank the front door on each side and the moulding which frames the round transom of the prefanlight era has a keystone in the center. The stairs ascend in a flight of broad, easy steps and light balustrade at the right of the hall and on the other side doors open into a drawingroom which occupies almost two-thirds of the space on this side of the house, with a small office beyond.

The drawingroom forms an appropriate setting for the entertainments which county tradition ascribes to the house. The fireplace at the end of the room is provided with a mantel carved with a stout rope design and the tambour fluting, which is so much in evidence in the woodwork of houses on the Eastern Shore. The fluting is used straight and in herringbone pattern on the mantel, and appears again on the chair rail.

Inset cupboards add to the interest of the office and use is made in this room, too, of the tambour carving. Upstairs the same motif appears in the form of square inlays in the chair rail in the bedrooms which duplicate in size the rooms below.

The diningroom and pantries are in the low wing. From the diningroom there is a restful view of the lawns and the river, but there is very little wood carving. For many years long, two-story verandas stood before both the river and the land fronts of the house, but these recently have been removed and replaced by small porticoes which are replicas of the ones which stood there when the house was built. The pillars which once adorned these porticos now are in use on a house in the village, a short distance away.

A brother of the William Potter who built the main wing and son of the Revolutionary Dr. Potter became Dr. Nathaniel Potter who founded the School of Medicine at the University of Maryland and was a practitioner of wide repute as well as a teacher who attracted students from distant States. William

Potter carried on the military tradition of the family and became brigadier-general of the Maryland militia. His son, Zabdiel Webb Potter, inherited the mansion but sold it soon afterwards to Colonel Arthur John Willis who, as the first Zabdiel Potter had done, kept a line of sailing vessels in the Baltimore trade until the closing years of the Nineteenth century. During his tenure the little village of Williston came into being in connection with the shipping business, but when that came to an end, the village languished.

Several owners followed Colonel Willis and finally, in February, 1928, the Potter mansion was purchased by Mrs. Katherine Clark, of Philadelphia, who has restored it to its original mien, except for the cupola, which remains.

CHAPTER TWENTY

A veritable ghost of a house, surviving like some aged and decrepit lady of the court in a world changed beyond the telling, its beauty gone, its power forgotten, its jewels sold, My Lady Sewall Manor House stands aloof from its neighbors and broods over its memories.

But what memories they must be, if the tales that are told of this little old house on the banks of a nondescript little stream in Dorchester county be true! For in its day, the story goes, My Lady Sewall Manor House was the finest mansion in Maryland, built to receive a very great lady, and so elegant in its appointments that it was the talk of smart circles in London. There men who wore their hair in queues picked their way gingerly out into a muddy street to ask of a woman in a sedan chair if she had heard the latest news concerning the needlepoint which was being made specially to cover the chairs upon which Lady Sewall was to sit in Maryland and girls in farthingales put their heads together in the Queen's palace envying the lucky Jane Lowe while they considered whether the finest house was worth what Lord Sewall's young wife would have to pay for it in her journey across the Atlantic and the rigors of pioneer life.

To eyes blinded by the dust of Newport palaces and Adirondack camps with a hundred rooms it will seem that all this was a tremendous pother about nothing, for the tiny structure on the banks of Secretary creek is but a story and a-half high and contained, when it was built, but two rooms downstairs and two above. All of it, at least all of the original brick wing, easily could be put into the livingroom of a present-day shooting lodge!

But the story goes deeper than that. A brick house was, in itself, a badge of superiority in the days when this house was built, for the colonists had little time to spare from clearing the wilderness and planting corn and tobacco to devote to making brick, a slow and discouraging process, when moulds had to be imported from England. Nor had standards of size become overgrown in the day when My Lady Sewall came to America as the chatelaine of her Manor House. One room was all that most houses in the colonies could boast at that time, with a loft upstairs.

Local traditions concerning the age of Colonial houses are prone to exaggerate, but in the case of My Lady Sewall Manor House the records bear out the story. Lord Sewall was a person of position in England and his comings and goings were made the subject of chronicle. In 1661 Lord Baltimore bestowed upon him a warrant for two thousand acres of land, describing him in the grant as his "secretary." Lord Sewall lost no time in taking up his grant and brought with him to Maryland his wife, who was the daughter of Vincent Lowe and Ann Cavendish, and their children.

The land which Lord Baltimore bestowed upon his "secretary" was not particularly well situated as far as the beauty of the tract was concerned, nor was it as fertile as much of the other land which he bestowed with prodigal hand. Throughout, it displayed the characteristic flatness of the coastal plain, with little to break the monotony, "its only accidents being in the clouds." Even its streams had not that quality of unexpectedness to be found in other parts of the Eastern Shore.

But Lord Sewall made up in the elegance of his house what his patron's gift lacked in other ways. Discovering, after what must have been a long search, a low elevation on the banks of a deep creek, he built his home which is one of the few of its era remaining in Maryland and which now is neglected entirely by the community whose history it helped to form.

The old square brick of the walls has a grisly hue, but the brick work is interesting nevertheless for the Flemish bond in which it was laid with an accuracy remarkable considering how few were the skilled artisans in the colony. The mortar clearly shows the oystershell and sand composition indigenous to the Eastern Shore, with the native silica in the soil glazing the heads of some of the bricks.

Completely rectangular in shape, the solid entrance door is exactly in the center of the long side, with a narrow, two-paned transom above, placed there for use and not for ornament, but invested by the passing of centuries with a certain quaintness. The narrow cornice of heavy oak beams comes down almost to the top of the transom and from the steeply pitched roof three peaked dormer windows, with panes missing here and there, look out like sightless eyes. Finishing the sides and caps of these dormers evidently proved a difficult problem for the builder who solved it by sheathing them smoothly.

Handriven shingles cover the roof, not the original covering, of course, but still a product of the pre-millwork age. At one end a deep chimney with an ornamental cap rises above the roofline and in each of the gable ends there is a single window, one of them surmounted by a rounded arch of brick, a device which evidently was forgotten when the other window was put in, for over the latter the arch is flat. Some of the original, iridescent and slightly cloudy glass remains in the windows and their dividing muntins are surprisingly thin for a period in which workmen seemed afraid to trust anything so costly and so perishable as glass to anything but a stout framework.

It was in the interior of Lord Sewall's house rather than on the exterior, however, that the greatest attention was lavished. For its adornment he had made a panelling of beautifully carved wood and a rosewood and mahogany stairway. The panels and the stairway were ripped entirely out of the house in 1929, however, and taken to the Brooklyn Museum of Art where they were set up in their entirety.

On one of the ends of the house the marks still can be seen of the low, one-story wing which was used as a kitchen, but which was built some time after the original house was completed. At the back of the house, forming a "T," with the brick structure, is the frame wing, also the product of a different period, but bearing all the marks of being very old. In the cellar where the stout white oak beams of the framework of the house have acquired the hardness of iron, are the remains of the old jail into which offenders against Lord Sewall's authority were thrust, a space so low that a man could scarcely have stood upright in it, and so restricted that it offered little space in which to move about. There was no softness in the dealings of Maryland lords of the manor with obstreperous underlings.

At the chimney end stands a very old Chinese mulberry tree and an ailanthus tree which looks as if it might be a contemporary of the original house. A formal garden is said once to have been the pride of Lady Sewall's home, but there is no trace of it to be found anywhere.

Lord Sewall served during his short stay in Maryland as secretary of the Colony, but he did not live long to enjoy the benefits bestowed upon him by Lord Baltimore to whom he is said to have been closely related. He died in 1665 and Lady Sewall returned with his body to England. In 1666 Governor Charles Calvert, who became the Lord Baltimore, was coming out to Maryland on the ship on which Lady Sewall was returning to take up the responsibility of her family and the estate and met the attractive widow. The acquaintance soon became a wooing in the long days aboard the little sailing vessel and soon after their arrival Lady Sewall became the wife of Charles Calvert. Afterwards, of course, she was Lady Baltimore, and lived with her husband at Mattapany, in St. Mary's county.

* * *

On the outskirts of the somnolent little village of New Market, its chimney caps just visible among the trees, is Friendship Hall, a place which has an extraordinary air of knowing much more than it has any intention of disclosing even to the most insistent and sympathetic scalpel. Looking at it from every side, however, lingering to study the brickwork and to muse over the broad, strap hinges and the curious tympana of the garden door, it comes as no surprise to learn that the Colonial owners of Friendship Hall were named O'Sullivane and that in their veins ran the blood of Irish kings.

Historians and antiquarians, men who like to go back to the beginnings of things, are fond of pointing out the tendency of the American colonists to reproduce in the new world, with what success they might in view of the resources of a primitive land, the homes they left in the old. It was a natural thing to do, of course, but few houses in Maryland present today so much of the spirit which envelops an old-world house as Friendship Hall.

Here, amazingly, in a flat, tidewater countryside, is a place which seems to be not so much of a reproduction of a bit of Ireland, as a bit of Ireland itself. In the lines of the roof, in the proportions of the house, in the blending of its walls with the earth upon which it stands, in the "feel" of it all, the illusion is complete.

O'Sullivane was the name of the two brothers who, for reasons now lost in the fog of the past, came to Maryland in 1690 and took up land in Dorchester county. Sullivane the name became after they arrived in Maryland and Friendship Hall first comes to notice in the annals of the family as the home of James Sullivane built on a tract of land inherited from his father, Daniel Sullivane. Across the road from Friendship Hall a similar tract descended to James Sullivane's brother, Daniel, and he, too, built a house which burned to the ground before the Revolution.

A lane half a mile long leads from the "stone road," as modern concrete highways are called on the lower Eastern Shore, through wide fields of grain which turns gold in June and up to the lawn where dappled shadows cast by trees of ample girth make arabesques on the grass. Set well back among the trees, the house is large and square with a one-story wing so low that it looks as if it were bobbing a curtsy—and that's the Irish of it. The wing presents its gable end to the front, with a single tiny window close under the eaves enhancing its story-book appearance. Connecting the wing with the main house is another wing with a pointed roof that comes steeply down like a huge eyebrow over the two small windows set close beneath it.

The brick of the walls bears a peculiar hue, not quite the color of salmon and yet verging upon it, and is laid up in great elaboration. A moulded course, following the line of an ogee curve, defines the watershed and a projecting belt course, three bricks wide, separates the lower from the upper story. At each end of the main wing a brick pilaster, with a brick base and brick capital, is placed in relief between the watershed and the belt course. The walls themselves are a melange of Flemish and English bonds.

Low brick arches curve above the doors and windows of the lower floor, the windows themselves being set in narrow, moulded frames, with rounded, projecting sills. The part that windows always play in determining the character of a house is brought out strikingly at Friendship Hall, where some of them show the eight-paned lower sash, with the twelve-paned sash above, in contrast to others of much later date which have replaced some of the originals and seem as much out of place in this setting as a black-eyed Susan in a bed of valley lilies.

In common with many other houses which had become landmarks before the Revolution, Friendship Hall has two front facades, one overlooking the garden and the other commanding a view over the broad lawn. Before the entrance door stands a square, open porch, railed solidly at the sides, while the garden door is supplied with a portico. The pitched roof has an easy angle to its slope and overhangs the walls to form wide, comfortable-looking eaves. The cornice continues around the gable end, the triangle formed in this manner with the roof being decorated with heavy modillions. Two well designed bull's-eye windows also appear in the triangle where one might be expected.

Within the house displays individuality as marked as that of the exterior. The pretentious, panelled stairway rises immediately to the left of the doorway, facing the road, with two landings to break each flight. Across the center of the hall stretches an arch with a fluted keystone and panelled spandrils; none of your light airy structures is this arch, but solemn as a superstition. The arch once was painted to simulate marble, but now is "golden oak." At the end of the hall the garden door appears in perspective, swung on hand made strap hinges, almost as wide as the door itself. The door, like the arch, is ponderous and substantial, its six panels and crude transom just as they were when the house was built, but the old lock is gone.

* * *

One of the most tantalizing, as well as one of the most securely locked secrets of Colonial days, often is the story concealed behind the name of a tract of land bearing the seal of some early grant. Two such stories, and possibly three, are bound up with Brentwood Farm, the present name of the Somerset county estate belonging to Dr. and Mrs. George W. Jarman, formerly of New York, who have owned it for the last twenty years and lived there the greater part of that time.

The first recorded name of Brentwood Farm was Adam's Adventure. Who "Adam" was and what was the character of the land which made its acquisition an "adventure" no one, probably, will ever know. The logical supposition, of course, is that when it became the property of this nebulous "Adam," Indians still lurked menacingly in the forests and this theory is probably the true one, but proof there is not.

No one knows, either, when the name was changed to The End of Strife, or why, but again the probable solution may be ascribed to the red men who either capitulated to superior brains —coupled with powder and shot—or chose the better part of valor and left the neighborhood entirely. At any rate, the name of this tract of land which lies along the State road running south from Salisbury to Princess Anne and borders on an arm of the Wicomico river, was known first by one of these names and then by the other and then by both, being referred to in old documents still extant as Adam's Adventure or The End of Strife. In 1806 the place was called by the simpler but less diverting name of Brentwood Farm, the name it has continued to hold ever since.

The house stands on the bank of the river, a combination of the original, rather small, square brick structure and a modern addition which has been built to one side in harmony with the old, but which is in the gambrel roof manner. A driveway, about a quarter of a mile long, passes through wide fields and skirts a clump of woodland between the State road and the lawn in front of the house, forming a circle under the trees. A short flagged walk, flanked at the end by two clumps of boxwood, leads from the driveway to the hooded portico over the entrance door.

There is an old, even trite, observation to the effect that the doorway to a house proclaims the spirit within, but the saying takes on real significance at sight of such a doorway as the one at Brentwood Farm. Simplicity and a certain ease inhere in the lines of the portico, and in the carved shell which takes the place of the usual transom over the door there is the quality of a folksong. The house apparently was built about 1737 or 1738. Except for the doorway and the plain wooden panels over the windows the exterior is entirely without ornament, though Colonial enthusiasts will find absorption in the size of the brick, in the low second story windows with broad muntins dividing the panes, in the wide wooden cornice and the lines of the pitched roof, guiltless of dormers.

Only a few Maryland houses of the first half of the Eighteenth century have the hallway parallel with the long facade of the house, but Brentwood Farm is one of them. Originally a circular staircase stood at the end of the hall, but the steps were so narrow and the opening above so small that it was impossible to carry furniture, or even a large trunk up or down them, so the old stairway was removed when the house was enlarged. In its place an arch was cut to connect the old hall with the new wing which has a wide, almost square hall of its own, with a mahogany stair-way of the Eighteenth century type.

Immediately opposite the entrance door, on the far side of the hall, another door, panelled with the double cross and swung on H-and-L hinges, opens into the livingroom with a panelled fireplace and built-in shell cupboard which saved the entire house from being razed when the Jarmans acquired the property, for Brentwood Farm twenty years ago was in a complete state of "innocuous desuetude" and its restoration was a much greater undertaking than the erection of a new house would have been.

The fireplace cuts diagonally across the end of the room, its arched opening low and deep-throated, with the panelling cut out slightly above the brick facing to correspond. A moulding at each corner of the diagonal wall turns at about the height of five feet from the floor apparently to stretch across the chimney breast, but breaks instead to form a base for fluted pilasters at each side of the vertical panels above the fireplace. Glass doors, rounded at the top, enclose the shell cupboard which occupies the corner opposite the fireplace and all of the door and window frames in this room, as elsewhere in the old wing, are provided with ears at the top and at the chair rail.

At the left of the hall is the library, the union of two smaller rooms of equal size, with a fireplace occupying the center of the outer wall. Upstairs the bedrooms are simple and well propor-tioned, without ornament. From the upstairs hall a primitive stairway formed of logs, squared off and boxed in, led to the attic until the house was remodeled and the building require-ments necessitated its removal. On the end of one of the steps initials, presumably those of a workman, had been carved, with the date which is taken to establish the age of the house. Old plank floors put together with wooden pins, which had been in the house since the first days of Adam's Adventure were in such bad condition that it was useless to attempt to preserve them and so they, too, were removed and replaced by hardwood floors, a real loss but one which could not be avoided.

Deep as the mystery which hangs over the name of Brentwood Farm is another enigma, the clue to which probably is bound up with the names by which the place first was known. This mystery existed until the new wing covered it, in the form of a cave about fifteen feet deep and ten feet wide, which had been dug at a distance of about twenty feet from the house. A smuggler's cave it may have been, of course, as a perfervid imagination might suggest, for the arm of the Wicomico river upon which the Brentwood Farm house is built has three feet of tide at this point. But more likely the old cave was a fort, built to repel "the Red Man or Indian." So perfect was the protection which the old cave provided that one man inside could cope with a large number of enemies outside and what could be more plausible than the supposition that it was this primitive bulwark which brought Adam's Adventure to The End of Strife?

*　　*　　*

One of the oldest houses in the section in which it stands is the house built in 1795 and which blocks the end of a tree-lined street in Salisbury. The street, which terminates abruptly at the foot of the brief lawn in front of the house, is called Poplar Hill avenue and the old house itself is known as Poplar Hill Mansion.

Big and square, shorn of the old colonnade and kitchen which formerly added picturesquely to its appearance, the old house once commanded a vast tract of land known as Pemberton's Good Will. The estate was purchased by one Major Lewin Handy who came to Maryland from Rhode Island just as the Eighteenth century was hurrying to its close and who married the daughter of Captain John Winder, then owner of the land.

[353]

A small, square portico which makes no claim whatever to classic inspiration, stands in front of the house and is surmounted by a Palladian window which conforms exactly to the proportions laid down by the Italian architect. At the roof line the walls are finished by a wide cornice provided with modillions and dentils.

Of New Jersey heart pine is Poplar Hill Mansion built. The heavy front door, panelled with a cross above the center stile, opens into a long hall, twelve feet wide and divided through the center by an arch resting on fluted pilasters and finished to represent marble by a process which was familiar enough to painters in the Eighteenth century but which later was so completely lost to the knowledge of Maryland decorators that a few years ago, when the house was being refurbished, no one could be found who was familiar with it. The edges of the arch show a heavy rope carving and the soffit is panelled.

Back of the hall the stairway rises in a single flight to the second floor. The ends of the steps are decorated with a scroll carving and a light balustrade winds to a spiral on the lowest step without benefit of a newel post to terminate its convolutions. The wainscoting of the wall beside the stairway originally was marbleized to harmonize with the finish of the arch, but when the house was redecorated the wainscoting was painted a plain color.

The drawingroom measures eighteen by twenty-eight feet and was large enough for a ballroom in the days when the population of the country was small. It is a pleasant place, too, with the six and eight-inch boards of the original flooring showing no evidence of their century and more of wear. The room is wainscoted and derives individuality from the treatment of its chair rail and cornice which are reeded in groups of eight ridges, all of the carving, despite the several coats of paint which cover it, still showing the slight irregularities of hand work. The high mantel, adorned with fluting and the Greek key *motif,* which rises above the fireplace, like the wainscoting was marbleized by the original decorator.

In the library deep cupboards have been set into the walls on each side of the fireplace and provided with shelves for books. Each cupboard also is fitted with a writing table which pulls out by means of a small brass ring and can be pushed back into place when it is of no further use. All of the rooms on the lower floor are provided with huge brass locks, equipped with the old pull bell handles, and the house also boasts a back stairway, in itself a mark of aristocracy during the Eighteenth century.

Upstairs, over the drawingroom, the master bedroom reproduces the proportions of the room below and has five windows and a high mantel which also displays the marble work of the arch. In the attic, which never has been finished, the rafters show the mark of the adz which shaped them and in the cellar, once occupied by slaves, the rooms are divided by brick partitions and provided with doors which open and close on wooden hinges. So thick are the walls and so well finished are these basement rooms that they form an excellent retreat in summer for the present owner of the house, Mr. George Waller, who has a sitting room and office there.

The old colonnade which apparently antedated the house, was twenty-four feet long and connected at the far end with the kitchen where a portly negress, her head done up in a red bandanna, ruled with a rod of iron before the Civil War. Within recent years the old colonnade and kitchen fell into such disrepute that to repair them was inadvisable and the problem they presented was solved by their removal at the direction of Mr. Waller.

After the death of Major Handy, who built the mansion,

Poplar Hill was owned by Peter Dashiell, a member of a large and aristocratic Eastern Shore family. Later it became the property of Dr. John Huston, his brother-in-law.

The Captain John Winder from whom Major Handy purchased Pemberton's Good Will was the progenitor of a line of Marylanders some of whom have, in the past, attained no little distinction in public life. One of them, Levin Winder, was governor of the State and another became Major-General William H. Winder.

Dr. Huston, the predecessor of the Wallers as occupants of the place, was one of the type of fast vanishing family physicians. Early and late he drove his horse and phaeton over the trails which passed for roads on the lower Eastern Shore before the Civil War, traveling on horseback when the roads were in such condition that no four-wheeled vehicle could get through, and never refusing a call for help. His pay he took, when he received it at all, in the form of a bushel of apples or a spotted pup as often as in actual cash, and there was never a birth or a death in the county for miles around without this kindly physician present to hear the first cry of life or to close the lids of sightless eyes.

Dr. Huston kept a large staff of family servants at the old house. There were slaves to polish the old brass locks and slaves to carry the wood; slaves to attend to the stables and slaves to till the land; slaves whose dispersion by the Civil War ended the great days of Poplar Hill Mansion. One of Dr. Huston's daughters married Thomas Robertson, whose family occupied the place until it was purchased by Mr. Waller some thirty-five years ago.

Originally Pemberton's Good Will covered three hundred acres of land. The city of Salisbury is built, for the most part, on this old estate, and the old house stands on a little handkerchief-like plot of a single acre.

* * *

One of the few survivors of pre-Revolutionary brick houses on the lower Eastern Shore is Pemberton Hall, so generally forgotten that many of its immediate neighbors do not know of its existence and now so far removed from the dignified estate which gave it the appellation of "Hall" that it is occupied by a family of negroes with innumerable pickaninnies, cats of all sizes and descriptions and "houn' dawgs" running at will through the rooms.

Yet it is easy to discover, even in its present condition, the important house that Pemberton Hall has been. From the massive brick arches in the cellar which strengthen the foundation to the huge beams of the attic the Hall is as sound today as any house extant and it has a mien which neither time nor change of fortune can wholly obliterate.

Purely American Colonial in type, with a gambrel roof and dormer windows, it stands well back from the public road about three miles from Salisbury, the largest city on the Eastern Shore, so lost behind a thick clump of intervening trees that if it is noticed at all by passersby, it might easily be supposed to be one of the outbuildings on the farm on which it stands. The lane leading to it from the public road drives straight past the side of the big modern farmhouse itself, a circumstance which contributes to the seclusion of the historic old structure, for Pemberton Hall really is historic in addition to being Early Colonial.

The brickwork of its walls, which are laid up in the decorative Flemish bond, derives additional merit from the quality of the bricks which are deeply red, with here and there a black "header," scintillating in the light as the result of the admixture of sand particles in the clay. The sidewalls of the first story and the high, narrow end walls are of brick, with the gambrel roof shingled after the familiar manner. Originally three dormers cut the roof line on each side of the house but when repairs were made a number of years ago two were sealed up and only one was left to show the pattern.

Front and back, the eaves overhang widely and the chimneys which rise at each end, with elaborate caps at the top, seem to exaggerate the narrowness of the house which really is not narrow at all. The double panelled front door still fastens with a primitive wooden button at the top. The back door has been replaced by one of modern millwork, but over it the three tiny and absurdly narrow panes of the original transom remain.

The plans of Pemberton Hall are simplicity itself. To one side of the doorways runs a panelled partition which formerly divided the lower floors into two parts, one the "greate room" and the other the diningroom. The two rooms connect by a round-topped panelled door, still swinging on its H-hinges.

The one-time "greate room" was worthy of its name. Of excellent proportions, the panelling of the partition was balanced at the chimney end by panelling which, a number of years ago, so excited the cupidity of a collector that he succeeded in purchasing some of it together with the fine old shell cupboard and its round-topped glass door. The rest of the panelling remains, however, to show how the room originally must have looked. Fluted pilasters rise on each side of a fireplace (so wide that it has been fed by fence rails chopped in half) and wide bevelled panels, with raised fields complete the wall. No mantel ever was there and the bricks of the hearth are square. Behind the chimney a boxed-in stairway rises to the second floor.

In the diningroom the chimney breast is panelled, too, only

a shade less elaborately than the "greate room," with set-in cupboards at one side. In each room there is one window, front and back, windows which have nine small panes and wide muntins in the upper sash and six in the lower, and which were protected by solid shutters with the original iron holdbacks still set into the walls. A short flight of steps leads from diningroom into the old kitchen where the fireplace, the negroes on the place recall, "took three pots of 'lahd' in hawg-killin' time."

One of the traditions of Pemberton Hall has to do with a secret passage which led from the house to the river a short distance away, a tradition which has been given some semblance of truth by the discovery on the lawn of a deep pit with scattered brick near the top. The underground tunnel, if it did exist, is said to have been used for the transportation of slaves between the river and the cellar where they were kept in pens ready to be sold. Pieces of heavy iron chains by which negroes are said to have been shackled remain in the walls.

The verifiable history of Pemberton Hall goes back to the year 1707 when, on October 10, Lord Baltimore, then governor of the province of Maryland, granted a tract of land known as "Pemberton" to Thomas Pemberton of Sussex county, Delaware. In 1722 Thomas Pemberton conveyed the tract to his brother, Joseph T. Pemberton, an English colonel living in Delaware.

Four years later Colonel Pemberton deeded the land to Colonel Isaac Handy, "Planter and Merchant of Somerset County in the Province of Maryland." In 1741 Colonel Handy built himself the brick house which he called "Pemberton Hall," and to which he referred in his will, which was made in the same year, as his "Mansion House." Colonel Handy lived to enjoy his home until 1763 and after his death the house passed into the possession of his son, Henry Handy.

During the War of the Revolution that part of Maryland

which forms the lower part of the Eastern Shore peninsula was a hotbed of Toryism. The country was remote from civilization and was not dependent, as was most of the State, on tobacco for its wealth. Consequently, the encroachments of the royal government upon the colonies affected it but little. There were ardent patriots there, however, and in sufficient numbers to make it advisable for the Tories to walk warily, so that Pemberton Hall in its isolation, with a master ultra loyal to the British crown, was an ideal place in which to hold loyalist meetings.

Henry Handy lived through the war and died in 1804, intestate and without children. The estate became the property of his heirs-at-law and was purchased from the others by Dr. Thomas W. Handy, of New Castle County, Delaware, youngest brother of Henry Handy "for good and valuable consideration." In 1855 Dr. Handy sold Pemberton to John Parsons of Somerset county, Maryland.

The Handy family had been in Maryland since 1664 when Samuel Handy came to America on the barque "Assurance," arriving at Annapolis. A number of years later he emigrated to Somerset county and on March 31, 1679, married Mary Sewell. Colonel Isaac Handy, first of the name to own Pemberton Hall, was the youngest of their fourteen children, thirteen of whom were living when Samuel Handy died in 1721, or at least were mentioned in the will which was drawn for him on May 15, 1721, and probated September 13th of the same year. Many of them achieved prominence and as lawyers, merchants, and physicians, exerted a strong influence in Maryland, Delaware and Virginia.

Jehu Parsons, who became the owner of Pemberton Hall when it passed from the possession of the Handy family, was a planter and by his will devised Pemberton to his son, Captain Allison C. Parsons, who organized the local militia of Salisbury. At his death the estate was purchased jointly by James Cannon, a Salisbury merchant (father of Bishop James Cannon, jr., of the Methodist Episcopal Church South) and the then Governor Elihu E. Jackson. Mr. Cannon and Governor Jackson later divided the estate, the former obtaining the portion on which the Hall was located. In 1884 Mr. Cannon conveyed his holdings to Cadimus J. Taylor who died in 1908, willing the land and the Hall to his son, James I. Taylor, who is the present owner.

During the Civil War, while Captain Parsons was the owner of the estate, the Eastern Shore peninsula, like most of Maryland, was predominantly Southern in sympathy and Captain Parsons' heart was bound up completely with the success of the Confederate arms. He was known to have been a man of high purpose with an independence of spirit second to none and it is said that, during the early days of the war, whenever a Confederate victory was announced, Captain Parsons fired his old cannon at Pemberton, the shot being audible for miles. Union soldiers demanded that he surrender the arms and ammunition of his command, but, instead of complying, he and his brother, Milton A. Parsons, who was also a strong Confederate sympathizer and a wealthy planter to boot, together with an old slave, buried them on the estate.

They never have been found. The Union forces came in search of them that very night and ransacked the house, but were forced to return empty handed to Salisbury. Within recent years the ground near the house has been dug over assiduously, but scientific instruments of the kind necessary to locate such things were lacking and the present owners of Pemberton Hall are still convinced that the captain's guns are somewhere on the place.

CHAPTER TWENTY-ONE

Few Eastern Shore houses built before the turn of the Eighteenth century can boast the size or the splendor of Kingston Hall, on the banks of the Annemessex.

To the imaginative person the whole story of the place may be discovered in its name and in its location. A proud mansion, unquestionably, and the home of an aristocrat who brought to the new world the *cliches* of the old and established a landed estate in a wilderness where the streams were called by the names the red men had given them.

More than two generations have gone to dust since Kingston Hall began to lose something of its magnificence. Today the old house, the deep yellow of its walls worn to a saffron tint, stands in the midst of its overtowering trees like a castle in a tapestry, unreal, but still part of the picture.

In the spring, when the trees cover their branches with their lacy first leaves and the great magnolias bloom in the old gardens, when the red bud appears and the mock orange bushes distill in the moonlight, Kingston Hall seems fleetingly to renew its youth. Daffodils and narcissus run wild over the grass, let loose from formal designings. Old-fashioned roses, survivals of whole hedges of them, make game of the worldling who strives to reconstruct the lines which once they followed, and the dark billowing lines of box "make up" a bright green, all seemingly as part of a conspiracy to draw the old house away from its slumbers and back to the time when lovers walked in the gardens and slaves in livery waited to obey their wishes.

Six thousand acres are said to have been included in the grant which Major Robert King, an Irishman of good family, obtained from the Lord Proprietary in Somerset county and which he then called Kingland. The name, in the light of subsequent events, was not without its implications, for if not kings, the land has, at least, furnished to Maryland its only governor and its only United States Senator who have come from Somerset county.

From the outset Kingston Hall has been identified with the political, social and professional life of the State. Like all Irishmen, Major King was born with a flair for politics and as soon as he arrived in Maryland proceeded to indulge it. He became a member of the House of Burgesses and justice of the provincial court of the State and later received the appointment of naval officer for the Pocomoke district.

Kingston Hall is about ten miles from Princess Anne and stands at the head of King's Creek, headwater of the Annemessex. The river, like the estate, has dwindled considerably in importance, for it once formed the highway of the county and in front of the mansion a box-bordered path led to a boat landing where guests arrived in barges, often of considerable size.

The box-bordered walk is still there, and in the midst of the untrimmed hedge is the old farm bell, hung to call the slaves, but the boat landing is gone and never will be rebuilt. The approach to the house now is over a long lane which makes its way through a plowed field and then turns at right angles and drives directly for the front veranda. This old lane, or at least that part of it which proceeds from the turn to the house, also was used in the early days of Kingston Hall when journeys by land were to be made in the great painted coach with liveried outriders, but in those days the lane was bordered by a line of Lombardy poplars and cedars.

[363]

Length of days has had no effect whatever on the ponderous brick walls of the central portion of the house which appear to be fully capable of maintaining their present condition for at least two centuries more. Few windows let in the light, for windows were still a luxury when Kingston Hall was built. Some of the earliest clear glass which was used in the colonies formed their panes, a number of them, with traces of "tears" still intact. A two-story veranda bricked on the lower floor and bordered by an intricate bronze railing, stretches across the front of the house. Above, a gable pierced by a bull's eye window breaks the roof line. One wide chimney at each end is capped in the early manner and belt courses of brick break the Flemish bond of the walls.

The front door opens into a square stair hall, in size almost a perfect cube. In the stairway the ingenuity of some provincial workman comes strongly into evidence and the result is quite different from any other stairway in the State. Placed at the far side of the room from the front door, the lowest step and the one immediately above it are triangular, like those of an ordinary winding stair but usually placed several steps up in the flight. Having accomplished its turn, the stairway runs straight to the second floor where its walnut balustrade reverses its direction and borders the well string back to the outer walls. Upstairs the hall is wide and spacious, with a narrow corridor leading from it to the bedrooms overlooking the river and a front door which opens out onto the upper veranda.

Few early Maryland rooms have excited the cupidity of panel hunters to a greater extent than the drawingroom at Kingston Hall. Still in perfect condition, it is painted the color of old ivory and through the moulding of the light, graceful cornice runs a line of gilt. The drawingroom fireplace is set diagonally across the corner of the room and in the panelling a bell, which is still there, was rung in the old days for a slave to replenish the wood when the blaze showed signs of diminishing. Not long ago an ancient, white-wooled negro died in Somerset. In youth he had been a slave at Kingston Hall and he told with pride that his had been the duty of serving the drawingroom fire. He had no other task, except the daily polishing of the bronze rail on the front veranda. There are secret panels in this drawingroom, too, which open easily if one is lucky enough to touch the spring, and the woodwork below the windows is "stepped."

The connecting wing and colonnade are still standing and in fairly good condition. Beyond them is a quaint brick house, two stories high, with small windows set in frames of hand-worked moulding—the old kitchen, with slave quarters above. As at Mount Vernon, the floor of the kitchen is bricked and at one end the fireplace occupies almost the full length of the wall, being nine feet long and correspondingly deep. Its huge crane still swings on protesting hinges and the old fire irons are there, ready for use.

Upstairs, where the house servants slept, the rooms are well finished, one of them even having a fireplace to provide comfort in winter, for if the owners of Kingston Hall preferred to live on a grand scale, with slaves to anticipate desire, they believed in treating their negroes well and were famous for their kindness to their dependents. Quarters for the field hands were provided at some distance from the house, but when the days of slavery had passed the old quarters were torn down. The other old buildings are gone, too, the stables, the tool house, the weaving house, all but an octagonal ice house which stands, a dejected survivor, some distance away to the right.

Gone, too, is another wing which formerly stood on the left side of the house. It was removed some years ago, but the house still contains twenty-two rooms. Its absurd little cupboards, as well as its panelling, give it a personality of its own and in the attic, which has been half finished, it is possible to see how well those great-great-grandfathers of modern carpenters knew their business. Beams are fastened together by wooden pins and remain as firmly held as the day they were put there. Here the chimneys assume strange curves before they push through the roof at the middle of each gable, curves made necessary because the rooms across the land front of the house are shallower than those fronting on the river and the fireplaces are necessarily out of line with each other.

From the attic a narrow, devious stair mounts to the cupola at the top of the house, where there is a view of miles over the country side and down the river. Though architecturally incongruous the cupola emphasizes the impression of arrogance which its former owners always conveyed.

When Major King, the builder of Kingland, died the estate passed to his son, Colonel Robert King, and then to his son, Robert King, III. The latter had no sons and only one daughter, Elizabeth Barnes King, who inherited the estate, known by this time as Kingston Hall, and who continued to live there after her marriage to Colonel Henry James Carroll, of Susquehanna, St. Mary's county. The alliance created a tremendous furore in Somerset county, which was a stronghold of Presbyterians who were much incensed when they learned that the heiress of Kingston Hall had married a Catholic. The newlyweds paid but scant attention to the commotion, however, and as Colonel Carroll was wealthy in his own right life at Kingston Hall became more ceremonious than ever. Every summer the colonel and his lady travelled to the White Sulphur Springs, the journey being made in the family coach, with silver-mounted harness on the horses, and liveried outriders.

Kingston Hall descended from them to their eldest son, Thomas King Carroll, who was born April 29, 1793, and who, for the brief period from 1830 to 1831, was Governor of the State. A strange person, apparently, was Thomas King Carroll, whose life began when America was still in the experimental stage and who lived through the second war with England, through the devastating upheaval over the negro question and the reconstruction period without once becoming involved in the whirlpool.

Although all of his public acts were democratic in character Governor Carroll is said to have been anything else in his contacts with life. He was proud and ceremonious, even with his family, and is said to have carried himself with such dignity that deference instinctively was paid him. When he retired as governor he was offered a seat in the State Senate, but declined it. Later he was considered for the United States Senate but when he learned that his name was being mentioned in this connection he made it known that he would decline to be a candidate.

When he relinquished the office of governor, Thomas King Carroll returned to Kingston Hall, but in 1840 he removed to Dorchester county, where he had an estate, and Kingston Hall was purchased by a member of the Dennis family who furnished Somerset with its only United States Senator. From their hands it became the property of an Alabamian and now belongs, as the result of another sale, to Harry T. Phoebus, who also lives in Somerset county, but who leases the estate to tenants.

The six thousand acres which constituted the grant to Major Robert King have shrunk to several hundred. On one subdivision the little village of Kingston has become established and the nearest railroad station also is known as Kingston.

It is a difficult feat in mental gymnastics for the average person to think of a Georgian house and a bow window in the same connection, though the combination is encountered frequently enough in England. To most people the bow window is part and parcel of the so-called Queen Anne revival which swept over the country about the time of "the mauve decade," filling the suburbs with horrors, and in their estimation it has no place in a system of formal design which achieves its effects almost entirely from clever manipulations of the square and the cube.

There is much, of course, in this point of view, but because it is so universal it is particularly stimulating to discover on so faithful an adherent to the Georgian cult as the mansion on Beverly Farm, in Somerset county, an ingenious use of this architectural device which seems so completely a part of the architectural scheme that the house would lose much without it.

The bow window occupies the exact center of the front facade of the house. Before it stands a low, open porch, flanked by siderails in the Chinese Chippendale pattern. The front door is in the center of the bow window, with a semi-circular transom above, and in each of the diagonal sides of the bow is a small window, rounded at the top to correspond with the line of the transom, lighting the big hall.

Except for the bow window, which adds such a strong fillip of interest to Beverly Farm, the front and rear facades show little difference in treatment, though the entire house gives rise to a strong belief that the builder had been to Annapolis and had been so much impressed with the beauties of Chase House and the Hammond-Harwood house that he incorporated in his own home the characteristics of both which he most admired.

The mansion on Beverly Farm takes rank in every respect

BEVERLY FARM

FRONT HALL AT BEVERLY FARM

DRAWINGROOM AT BEVERLY FARM

with the great houses built by aristocratic denizens of Annapolis during the heyday of the Maryland capital, presenting in size and elaboration of treatment the characteristics of that gay little Colonial city. In addition it holds for the present generation a peculiar claim to attention as the center of a plot of international proportions and one which would, had it succeeded, probably have much to do with changing the destiny of nations.

Beverly Farm now is the home of Mr. and Mrs. Lynde Catlin and is but a short distance from the Somerset county town of Princess Anne, where still stands the old Washington Tavern, once famous for its cooking, and where the dour old pile known as the Teackle mansion completely blocks further progress at one end of the town by cutting off the end of the street.

The section of the State in which Beverly Farm was located was thoroughly Tory during the Revolution and remained so for years after the tumult and shouting had died out. The house was completed, according to an iron plate on one of the chimneys, in 1796, and stands now, six generations after the death of Nehemiah King, who built it, as a monument to the wealth and importance of an Eighteenth century planter.

There was, in the vicinity of Princess Anne during Colonial times, a county society modelled on that of England and supported by an income from great plantations, an extensive shipping trade with European countries and the natural resources of the Chesapeake Bay. Nehemiah King's neighbors were men who presided over estates as large as his own, but misfortune in one form or another has overtaken almost all of the families which maintained in Somerset county a tradition of aristocracy long after the means to support it had vanished. Few of them are left, even as names. Fires and crumbling fortunes have brought down the old homes in which they "lived like lords" and entertained with lavish hospitality, and mingled their timbers with the dust. The descendants of the ancient gentry are scattered to the ends of the earth, but the mansion at Beverly Farm somehow escaped destruction. Its battle was almost lost, however, before it came into the hands of the Catlins, who had come from New York to Maryland in search of health. Years of neglect had put their seal on the house and it has taken unremitting persistence as well as skill to resurrect it.

From ten to twenty years are said to have been occupied in the building of the thick brick walls and the finishing and decoration of the interior. A long time, but it was no easy matter in the days when brick had first to be made, the oyster shell lime burned and the timbers seasoned, when every labor had to be performed by hand, and when war intervened to complicate the process, to build a house as large as this. For Beverly Farm mansion measures forty feet by sixty, and from the deep basement to the dormered attic the result of workmanship which refused to countenance slipshod performance is evident.

All of the interior walls are of brick, with the plaster applied directly to them. The central hall runs from front door to front door and is twelve feet wide. Its floorboards are of heart pine, all selected, cut an inch-and-three-quarters thick and laid transversely.

Back of the arch, which divides it midway, the hall makes an "L" turn to the right to provide for the staircase which, though following the main lines of the stairways of the period, has a strong claim of its own to preferment. Made entirely of native black walnut, the square spindles still show the faint mark of the knife which cut them and the almost imperceptible deviation from line which proclaims the hand-made article. Instead of being solid at the turns the posts are cut out below the handrail to form four spindles growing, in a manner of speaking, on a single stem. This type of balustrade is seldom, if ever, found outside of Maryland. The side of the stairway next the wall is wainscoted and capped by a half-handrail of black walnut.

All of the ceilings on the lower floors are fourteen feet high and show the influence of the Brothers Adam in their decorations. A light carving of the classic Ionic cyma appears on the frieze over the doors and the walls under the windows are panelled with deep seats let into the embrasures.

To the right of the hall is the drawingroom with a cornice of modillions and rosettes above a frieze decorated with the urn and scrollwork. The window frames have ears and the high mantel above the fireplace carries out the classic spirit in a line of triglyphs across the frieze. In this room hangs a portrait of that canny Catlin ancestor, the second president of the Merchants' National Bank of New York who, unlike the modern Dives, lived in rooms over his banking house in Wall Street. The portrait has been placed in the space created for such a purpose in the panelling over the mantelpiece and completes the effect evidently desired by the builder of the house. Other heirlooms of the Catlin and Stuyvesant families complete the furnishing of this room and of the other rooms in the house as well, for the present master of Beverly Farms is a direct descendant of the famous Peter Stuyvesant who brought the name to America, and his family was the last to occupy the old Bouverie House in New York.

The old Stuyvesant pier mirror hangs between two windows and a rosewood Bible table is a rare piece. Rosewood sofas and chairs have their original coverings and on the mantel stand a pair of Florentine vases brought by an ancestral traveler from Italy and which not long ago, formed a part of the exhibit in the Metropolitan Museum. In this room are some unusual miniatures, too, the most interesting of them all being one of

Helen M. Kip, a kinswoman, painted by George Catlin on wood instead of in the usual way on ivory.

In the library, directly across the hall, are other mementoes of the old Bouverie House, particular interest centering in a mirror and pair of girandoles which once were used in the Stuyvesant homestead and which had descended, the mirror in one branch of the family and the girandoles in another, only to be united again on the high Adam mantel at Beverly Farm by inheritance of Mr. Catlin. The frames of pictures in this room were made from the wood of an old pear tree on the Bouverie farm and there is, too, a seascape painted in water color on the back of his visiting card by General Lew Wallace while he was stationed at the Dry Tortugas and presented by him to the Catlin who was there with him at the moment of inspiration. The portrait of that ancient Lynde Catlin who was the great-grandfather of the present holder of the name, hangs on the library wall and near the fireplace stands a light screen which once stood in the Bouverie house to shield the eyes of a Knickerbocker ancestress from the glare.

Back of the library is the office where Mr. Catlin manages his estate and which served Nehemiah King in the same capacity. The desk at which Mr. Catlin works stood in the old Custom House at New Haven in 1770 and in the book cases are ancient Stuyvesant Bibles, printed in Dutch before the Revolution.

The diningroom is in the oldest wing of the house, its diminutive windows and low ceilings making it exceedingly picturesque. At one end of the room stands a massive tilt-top mahogany table from which many a solid meal was served in the Bouverie House and kept in the built-in cupboards are hoards of ancient Stuyvesant and Catlin china, deeply colored Nanking ware and paper-thin services, one of which went through the siege of Vicksburg and is still resplendent with gaudy, decorative flowers. A heavy linen tablecloth bears the design of St. George and the Dragon and honest Dutch silver gleams with the polish of generations.

The breakfast room, with its fireplace "catacorner," contains curious old platewarming devices, one inherited from the Catlin, one from the Stuyvesant branch of the family and as different from each other as canals are from castles. In this wing, too, is the kitchen, its old fireplace sealed up, never again, probably, to know the roar of sparks that fly upward while a juicy fowl roasts on the spit.

Space which would drive a present day economist to despair is "wasted" in the hall on the second floor which virtually duplicates in size the one below. A round-topped window in the center of the bow carries out the decorative note of the front door and the hall itself is furnished to serve as an upstairs sitting room. The bedrooms are large, each with its own fireplace and high mantel. Most of the furniture upstairs as well as down was brought from the ancestral Stuyvesant home but, of it all, none is as interesting as the small, poster beds which have been made by hand from the mahogany doors taken from the Bouverie House when it was sold.

So large a plantation as Beverly Farm naturally required the labor of many slaves. The old quarters have been razed but traces of their presence still are evident in the bricked basement with grim peepholes in the partition walls which served the overseer in his task of keeping them in order and in the dark corner where troublemakers were shackled.

In violent contrast to this dark memorial is the secret chamber which was built into one of the bedrooms beside the chimney. This room was the focus of the plot by which Nehemiah King and Jerome Bonaparte, the brother of Napoleon, who had become intimate during the sojourn of the latter in Baltimore, planned to rescue the exiled emperor from St. Helena, bring him to America and secrete him in the house at Beverly Farm.

The details of this hazardous exploit had been worked out to the last possible move but just as the boat which was to sail clandestinely from Cape Charles to carry out its part in the scheme was preparing to embark, word came that the "Emperor" was dead. The secret room became an empty gesture and an undertaking which might have diverted the course of history died still-born.

CHAPTER TWENTY-TWO

One of the rarest items of Americana is an unpainted pine door in a house built before the year 1800. And there is such a door at Chanceford, the home of John W. Staton in Snow Hill, excellently preserved, in the attic!

Popular belief has held that Chanceford, formerly known as Ingleside, was built by Robert Morris, the financier of the American Revolution, but this, alack for romance, is not true. Its builder was James Rounds Morris, clerk of the court of Worcester county, who purchased the ground upon which it stands from Francis Ross, the rector of All Hallows Church, in 1790, and built at once.

Chanceford is one of the fine houses on the lower Eastern Shore, and is situated well back from the road on a slight elevation, in itself a fact well worthy of mention in so flat a country. The house is one instantly to attract attention with its architecture of another century and its white stucco exterior patterned over with ivy said to have been brought from Kenilworth Castle, its greatest beauty being apparent at the garden door. This ivy, which is said never to bloom until it reaches the century mark, flowers regularly on the walls. Unlike most old Maryland houses, Chanceford presents to the street its gable end, all of which is included in the pediment which finishes the wall. Dentils and modillions appear on the pediment and a bull's eye window, with a star pattern in the center of it and three small windows below, give the street facade of Chanceford its individuality.

Big house, little house, colonnade and kitchen! This was the accepted plan for colonial builders of the lower Eastern Shore peninsula and the rhythm of the words finds expression in the houses themselves. Chanceford is no exception. Its rambling ways and sunlit rooms were constructed for a world which could, upon occasion, take itself seriously enough, but which, for the most part, preferred its ease and lack of restraint.

Houses such as Chanceford are tangible evidence of the lives led by the men and women of their day who loved the soil from which they sprang, accepted its fullness without question and defended it with their lives. An open, moss-grown brick "stoep" stands before the front door, with a heart-and-star leaded transom overhead.

The hall transverses the end of the house. Heat was difficult enough to secure under the best of circumstances in winter and by placing this little used passageway between the outer walls and the living rooms it was possible to secure infinitely greater returns from even the deepest and most willing fireplace.

Three doors and four windows, each of the latter having twenty-four small panes, break the exterior wall space of the hall, but it is the doors which are most interesting. Each of them, the front door and the two end doors, is of two-ply thickness, the inner layer being applied diagonally, and both are fastened by stout wooden bars placed across them and resting on hand cut brackets fastened into the door jambs. Additional security is provided by means of huge wooden locks. H-and-L hinges (superstitiously said by some lower Eastern Shoremen to represent the initials of the words "Holy" and "Lord" and to possess the power to charm away witches from the houses in which they were used) support them on their frames.

A well proportioned arch divides the hall across the center and just beyond the stairway, with the slenderest of mahogany railings and a sweetheart step, leads to the second floor, its flight

Photo from Collection of James Donnell Tilghman

CHANCEFORD: DRAWINGROOM MANTEL

Photo from Collection of James Donnell Tilghman

CHANCEFORD

Photo from Collection of
James Donnell Tilghman

BEVERLY: DETAIL OF
IRON GRILLWORK

BEVERLY

being broken by a single landing. A similar stairway leads from the second floor to the attic with its remarkable door.

Two rooms, a livingroom and library, are directly back of the hall, each possessing a hand-carved fireplace, heavy base boards and fluted chair moulding. The livingroom mantel is the more elaborate, with fluted panels, applied moulding in the form of a square and dentils under the mantel shelf. The window frames have ears at the top and panels of wood alternate with panels of plaster to form a dado. At the ceiling the walls are finished with a heavy cornice. A diningroom with two large windows on each side is directly behind the livingroom and study and is furnished with excellent examples of early American walnut and mahogany, its most interesting "piece" being a curious box-like bit of mahogany, mounted on fluted legs. In outward seeming it is much like a sewing table, but inwardly it is contrived far more like a Chinese puzzle and comes apart in a curious way. It may have been an ingenious cabinetmaker's idea of a cheese-box—or it may have been something else. No one ever has identified it. The diningroom mantel once stood in the ball room which occupied the entire back of the house and now is used as a kitchen. Five feet high and with a shelf which is little more than a wide moulding, it is carved ingeniously with rococo designs, its architrave at the fireplace edge having a tesselated line.

The back hall parallels the front hall and also has its stairway. Square fluted spindles form the balustrade and the rail and newel post are of walnut. The wall beside the stair is panelled and the ends of the steprisers are carved with scroll work.

Naturally the most pretentious room of the house, the ball-room, is forty feet square and the finest woodwork was used in its trim. A wainscot decorates the walls below the chair rail, with fluted panels underneath the windows. The windows, two on each side, have elaborate ears, and the mantel in this room, though not as elaborate as the one which originally stood there, is authentic and of good design.

The old colonnade and kitchen which departed at right angles from the "little house" are gone, but traces remain in the stucco to show where they stood. A tremendous cellar runs under the entire house, one end of it being walled off into rooms which were lathed and plastered for use of the slaves.

The second floor has been considerably altered by some time owners of Chanceford to make room for closets and bathrooms. Over the front hall, however, a tiny bedroom retains its original size and a superb chamber occupies the space over the ballroom. One of the bedrooms is designated the Washington room and is filled with mahogany period furniture. Old prints representing Washington at all phases of his life, from early manhood to his death, hang on the walls and patchwork quilts bordered with glazed chintz cover the poster beds.

In the master bedroom the most interesting piece of furniture is a wig table, with a faded silken receptacle for the preposterous fol-de-rol hanging below a vanity box.

A few bushes are all that remain of the box maze which once stood in front of the house, the rest of it having been sold. A modern garden of old fashioned flowers stands where the old one bloomed, their brilliant petals making a strong contrast with the green and white of the house.

* * *

Completely isolated from the world—and the world well lost in the process—is Cellar House Farm, on the Pocomoke. Down at the tip end of Maryland on the Eastern Shore, this old place is a survival of the days when the rivers of the State formed its highways, but even then Cellar House Farm was remote enough for a smugglers' retreat.

For a century and more this estate has been associated with the names of some of the oldest families on the Eastern Shore. The Duers, who bought it in 1798, have lived in the house. It has been owned by the Dennises and by the Covingtons and now belongs to a Miss Howerton, who bought it from the Covington estate a number of years ago. Everything about the house, however, seems to justify the belief held by those who know the country that it is much older than its recorded history.

Because of a latter-day envelopment of shingles the house does not, even from a short distance, appear especially ancient, but a closer inspection which fails to disclose any two windows on a line with each other, arouses instant conviction that here is a structure which must have been built during the very early days of Lord Baltimore's colony.

The house is small and faces the river. Until it received its coat of shingles it presented to the world a construction of brick ends and weatherboarded front and rear walls, a type excellently suited to building when bricks were hard to get and timber was plentiful. All of the outer doors are stout affairs of two thicknesses, the inner layer being applied diagonally. The front door has the original massive lock, with a key so heavy that the householder who sought to take it with him when he left home must have developed a noticeable list on the side of the pocket where he carried it.

In plan Cellar House is simplicity itself. The front door opens into a small, square hall around which the other rooms are ranged on three sides. But in spite of this apparent geometric regularity which is generated in this fashion this old domicile could take prizes easily as the original crooked house. No two of the windows are the same size. The wide floor boards are

[379]

just as they came from the tree. The doors sag and the walls are uneven. Everything is eloquent of primitive workmanship which has acquired an appeal accentuated in the "greate room" by the really splendid panelling at the fireplace end and in the room above it.

The "greate room" has become a modern livingroom. Its two windows face the river and its deep fireplace is marked by a flat arch in the Elizabethan manner. The overmantel is panelled horizontally to the ceiling and fluted pilasters tie up—as the architects say—fireplace and overmantel into one composition. Painted an ivory white, with deep inset wine cupboards between the fireplace and the sidewalls, this panelling combines with the dado and moulded chair rail to form the trim of as livable a room as any Colonial house can produce.

The stairway is panelled too, and painted ivory white with a black handrail. Each step is painted black and a broad panel around the inside of the well string repeats the same color with anything but dismal results. This stairway is entirely of black walnut, a discovery which was made when repairs were in progress a number of years ago, but successive layers of red, green, black and brown paint made the idea of removing the accumulated coverings out of the question and the present color scheme is the result.

On the second floor the room over the livingroom reproduces the proportions and the decorative panelling of the room below, with powder cupboards replacing the ones designed for wine. Throughout the house the small windows have broad muntins between the panes and much of the original glass is in place. In the attic, close beside the chimney, is a window so tiny that it is scarcely more than a peep-hole and this, according to a legend of the neighborhood, was used for observation in Indian days.

H-and-L hinges appear on nearly all of the doors and every nail in the house was made by hand, some of the heads being so small as to be almost invisible and others almost as large as a dime. When the house was built a brick archway is said to have formed a secret passage which connected the cellar with the river and through it, local lore insists, were carried vast quantities of contraband captured by pirates, which was taken to Cellar House and then disposed of in the best way possible. Persistent digging has brought to light a few arch bricks, but the entrance in the cellar to a secret passage way is nowhere evident.

Another story connected with the house is even more gruesome and declares that a Frenchman who once owned the place and was so misguided as to cast his lot with the smugglers paid for his evil doings with the loss of his wife's affections. Such a career as his kept him necessarily much from home and during his absences his wife is said to have become deeply infatuated with the captain of a boat which more and more frequently pushed its nose between the narrow wooded banks of the Pocomoke. Their liaison inevitably was discovered and the infuriated Frenchman avenged his honor by murdering his wife whose ghost is said to patrol the banks of the river, wailing for her sailor lover.

During the Revolution the house is reported to have been the headquarters of a company of Continental soldiers, but no marks of this occupancy remains to verify the tale. Who owned the place before it came into the hands of James Duer is uncertain. Old records in the Covington family indicate that a "William Allen formerly lived on the plantation," but of him nothing is known. Captain Benjamin Dennis who bought the property in March, 1803, paid for it, "three thousand dollars, current money of Maryland." This Captain Dennis was a large landowner, planter, lawyer, officer of militia and Captain of the Wicomico battalion of Worcester county in 1776. He had nine children, six daughters and three sons, but the sons left no male descendants, and the property descended through the feminine line into the hands of Mrs. George M. Covington, whose heirs sold it to the present owner.

*   *   *

A house contemplative and gay by turns, its walls grown wise and careless of the racing years is Beverly, in Worcester County. For more than two centuries Beverly was the rooftree of the Dennises who came to Maryland before 1700 by way of Virginia and who have been conspicuous ever since in law, in politics, and on the land, furnishing Maryland and the nation with jurists and congressmen, planters and "rebels." The place now belongs to Mr. and Mrs. Conklin Mann, recently of New York.

Facing the Pocomoke river, (named for an Indian tribe) Beverly is one of the few important pre-Revolutionary houses left on the extreme end of the Eastern Shore peninsula and is equally interesting as the home of a notable family and as a monument of Colonial architecture. Its proportions are generous and well disposed, its construction as solid as a skyscraper. Here, in short, is a genuine blend of the formality of the Georgian era with the hospitable inclinations of an Eastern Shore Marylander.

No other house in Maryland has an entrance like that at Beverly. Up from the lawn which slopes gradually from the house to the river, a flight of deeply worn stone steps, built fan-fashion, leads to the front door. On each side the steps are guarded by an ornamental railing of wrought iron which turns on the lowest in a spiral about a rod which rears high above the railing and is capped by the head of a duck, a heartfelt tribute to this toothsome bird once to be found in enormous flocks on the rivers of the Eastern Shore and still very abundant. Over the front door the wrought iron grillwork continues in the form of an arch, with a fixture at the top for a lantern which formerly hung there and was lighted at night to serve as a beacon for the boats on the river.

Double latticed doors open before the entrance door, a modern substitute of small-paned glass set in a white-painted framework. Above the door a broad white lintel serves as a base for the small semicircular transom of the type which antedates by at least half a century the elliptical pattern fondly supposed by many to be the *sine qua non* of the genuine "Colonial" house and which did not, as a matter of fact, come into being until the Nineteenth century.

Above the front door a window in the Palladian manner is both decorative and a study in folkways, for it constitutes another interesting illustration of the efforts made by Colonial builders to capture fashionable effects of the day without the necessary resources and skill, but achieving an artistic result despite such handicaps. At the roof line a wide cornice, supplied with dentils and modillions forms a band across the facade.

To persons interested in the mechanism of Colonial building the vigorous brick walls of Beverly are deserving of more than a passing glance, even under their coat of yellow paint. The slightly projecting base is inset with small windows, heavily latticed, through which air is admitted to the cellars. The water-shed is formed of pulvinated brick, and the line of demarkation between the first story and the second is formed by a projecting course laid in English bond, contrasting with the Flemish bond of the rest of the walls.

All of the windows, though no two are the same size, are in perfect alignment. Two are set on each side of the doorway, with those of the second story directly above them. Apparently, the lack of skill as shown in the Palladian-like window did not extend to the matter of symmetry on the part of the artisans who built the walls. All of the windows have ornamental sills and broad lintels and those of the first story are set under flat brick arches, which impart a decorative quality. The panes are tiny, with four to each row, and are separated by broad muntins which make a house look so exceedingly venerable. Unlike many early Maryland houses, Beverly has outside latticed shutters, provided with ornamental holdbacks of wrought iron.

From the land side of the house the prospect is entirely different from that on the river front. Originally the road to Beverly passed from the main highway through an avenue laid out on a grand scale and outlined by cedars, black against the sky. Some of the old trees still stand to mark the course of the quondam avenue, but the present lane approaches much nearer to the gardens and leads to a pair of ornamental wooden gates which are formed of narrow palings in a design suggestive of the Chinese influence which swept over the Colonies as well as over Europe in the days when America was young. Beyond the gates a tree-shaded driveway curves to a two-story pillared portico which, though added long after the house was built, still is very old and seems quite to belong.

To the left of the entrance is a wing which formed the original house, with colonnade and kitchen, at Beverly. This wing is so much lower than the big house that the entire flight of worn steps, which preceded the portico on the land side before the portico was built, has been set up in the kitchen before the door leading into the diningroom.

Within, Beverly lives up to expectations aroused by the exterior. The square entrance hall narrows under an ornamental arch to a corridor which divides library and diningroom. At the right of the square hall rises an elaborate stairway, broken by a single landing and provided with a scroll step and a mahogany handrail.

To the left of the entrance from the river front, through a deeply set door, is the panelled drawingroom, its fireplace opposite the door presenting a welcome in cold weather before the threshold actually has been crossed. The fireplace is faced with marble, but no mantel shelf is there to draw attention away from the blazing logs and attract it to itself. Beverly was built before the craze for mantels arrived, its rectangular panelling of bevelled edges and raised fields having no need of such an addition.

The rear drawingroom, now used as a library, is panelled across the fireplace and wainscoted. This room has been supplied with the mantel which was not there in the beginning and shows an early type carved in the center of the frieze with a panel in sunburst design.

Opposite the library is the diningroom, the most inviting place in the house. This room, too, is panelled across the fireplace end, and quaint china cupboards are built into the panelling which deviates from the straight and narrow course at one side of the fireplace to turn a corner to the door leading into the old wing.

The kitchen at Beverly is a room for pewter plates and blunderbusses reared against the wall. Its worn, uneven floor is flagged with dull red brick, mellowed by the application of soap and water and in the fireplace the old crane and Dutch oven still beg to be put to use. Windows like the one before which Jess sat in Barrie's "Thrums," watching for the son who never came, let in the light. It is the traditional Sabbath day's journey across the kitchen and above it are five bedrooms divided between the second floor and the attic. A winding stair, exactly eighteen inches wide and ladderlike in its pitch, leads from the second floor to the rooms above.

In the main house each of the bedrooms has its own fireplace, that in the front bedroom being considerably more elaborate than the others, with an ornamental fireback of wrought iron.

The upper hall is divided, like the one below, by an arch ornamented with strapwork, and is lighted at each end by a Palladian-like window. The old H-and-L hinges appear on the doors, hinges that are real works of art, and the attic shows in heavy beams and rafters, numbered at the ends, so that each fits exactly into the position designed for it, in the brickwork of the huge chimneys, placed two at each end of the house, and in various other ways the capacities of the Colonials who "hewed the beam and laid the architrave."

The Dennises of Beverly came to America in 1638, the first of the name in this country being John Dennis who sailed on the Merchants' Hope after examination by the minister at Gravesend, England, "touching his conformite" to the Church Discipline of England and after taking the "oath of allegiance and supremacy," he settled in Accomack County, Virginia. His son, Donnoch Dennis, came to Maryland, taking up large tracts of land near Dividing Creek in what is now Somerset county and in Worcester county. Donnoch Dennis's holdings included a portion of the lands of Beverly which he acquired in 1669. By subsequent additions he increased the size of the Beverly tract until it included nearly two thousand acres.

In the various patents granted him, Donnoch Dennis is described as "gent." Governor Copley in 1685 appointed him high sheriff of the county which then embraced the territory since become Worcester, Somerset and Wicomico counties. His cattle mark which, in those days of commons was required by law to be registered, was "Clpt in ye left year, and a hole in ye same year: a fleur de luce in ye ryght. Recorded June 20, 1669."

Donnoch Dennis was admitted to the bar of Somerset county, but it does not appear that he ever engaged actively in the practice of his profession. He fathered an enormous progeny, many of whom, nine generations removed, still live in Maryland and the vicinity and some, holding positions of responsibility in the State and nation, maintain the family leaning for the land, law and politics established almost three centuries ago.

Littleton Dennis, the great grandson of Donnoch Dennis, who was born February 3, 1728, and died May 6, 1774, built the present Beverly house which is said to be the third or fourth on the present site. The others, in all probability, were used solely by tenants as Littleton was the first of the name to adopt Beverly as his residence. The house was in process of construction for many years and was built of the best and most durable materials. All of the lumber was of the best quality heart pine and oak, either hewed out of the whole tree or sawed by hand in a "saw pit," a primitive and laborious procedure. By this process logs were rolled on a frame platform and a large saw manipulated with one man standing on the top of the log to pull it upward and another man below to pull it downward. The site of this operation is still known as the "Saw Pit field." The bricks used in the building of the house were burned on the place and the wrought iron grillwork for the railing on the river front was imported from England.

Littleton Dennis died before his home was finished but the work went on and was completed by his widow, who had been Susanna Upshur, daughter of Rachel Revell Upshur of North-ampton county, Virginia, who died from the effects of a bite inflicted on her heel by a mad fox. A few months after the death of Littleton Dennis in 1714 his widow and their children moved into the house where their descendants lived for nearly a hundred and fifty years. Susanna survived her husband about a decade. Both are buried under the box-like marble tombs in the family burying ground near the house.

A tradition exists that on windy nights old Susanna still walks the vaulty halls of the house her husband begun and she finished. Many a one of her trembling descendants has had to cover his head with the bed clothes in the old tester beds to shut out the image of his grandmother's ghost parading the dark rooms.

Littleton Dennis was an excellent lawyer and a very successful one in the financial sense of the word, for he laid the foundation of a large fortune which he invested in many farms and numerous slaves. His elder son, Henry, when a young man, sailed from Beverly for the West Indies on a day in February, 1785, and never was heard from. None knew where or how his vessel was lost. The second son, Littleton, followed his father's footsteps in the law and from 1800 to 1806 was one of the judges of the newly created Court of Appeals of Maryland. He was an ardent Whig, too, and his specialty seemed to be serving as Presidential elector, qualifying in 1801, 1813, 1817, 1825, and 1829 for this position.

John Dennis, who was but five years old when the Revolution began, was elected at the age of twenty-five to Congress, taking his seat in 1797. He served in that body for ten years, until his death, taking a high position as speaker and lawyer. He was one of the five Federalists who transferred their votes to Jefferson, thereby breaking the deadlock between Jefferson and Aaron Burr.

In the seventh generation from the original immigrant, Littleton Purnell Dennis also was a member of Congress, his death occurring in Washington in 1834. This brilliant member of the Dennis family was educated at Yale and served several sessions as a member of the General Assembly of Maryland from Somerset county. He was a bachelor, extremely popular, and noted for his wit which was so keen that his *bon mots* were long remembered and quoted by the late Governor Wise of Virginia and other contemporaries who cherished a warm admiration for his character and conspicuous talents.

The seventh generation was one of the most significant in this entire line, as well as one of the most picturesque. Littleton Dennis Teackle, nephew of Littleton Purnell Dennis and son of Elizabeth Dennis and her husband, John Teackle, built the Teackle mansion which stands at the head of Main Street in Princess Anne, a massive structure now occupied by three separate families.

In that same generation John Upshur Dennis, who was born April 10, 1793 (the year of the French Revolution) and who died in 1851, combined the typical existence of a Southern Maryland planter with a genius for business. From the Pocomoke river he exported cypress staves in his own vessels to the West Indies, bringing back cargoes of molasses. He was born at Beverly and died there, and there he is buried, together with his three wives, the first of whom he espoused at the age of nineteen. His third wife had been the beautiful Louisa Jane Holland, a girl of less than half his age, who survived him for forty-nine years.

This John Upshur Dennis had twenty-one children, of whom more than half reached maturity and some were older than his third wife. In this connection, two traditions rise up to disturb the calm of the Dennis family. The first holds that John U. Dennis and his brilliant and gallant eldest son, Littleton, were both suitors at the same time for the hand of Louisa Jane and that the widower father by virtue of craft begot by experience, got the lead over his unsophisticated son.

The second of the two traditions maintains that old John Upshur Dennis, handicapped by the poor transportation facilities at Beverly which consisted only in sailing craft, accepted delivery at the plantation wharf of the tombstone for his second wife together with the handsome coach he had ordered in anticipation of the successful wooing of the third. The beautiful child installed at the head of a household with stepchildren older than herself had a stormy time of it, and not unnaturally. The storms broke with unabated fury after the loss of the restraining hand of old John Upshur in Christmas week, 1851, leaving Louisa Jane a widow at thirty-one, the head of a turbulent tribe. Her will and her courage were only exceeded, apparently, by her wisdom and faith in the Presbyterian religion, and she lived to see the day when old-time enmities and jealousies were at rest.

Littleton Dennis, the son of John Upshur Dennis, who lost his sweetheart to his father, was brilliantly educated before he was graduated in medicine at the University of Virginia. In addition to his interest in his profession the family predilection for politics cropped out early in life. He served in the Maryland State Senate and then in the House of Representatives and in 1870 was elected to the United States Senate. He also was president of the old Eastern Shore Railroad Company. His home was at Kingston Hall in Somerset county, and one of his sons, John Upshur Dennis, became judge of the Supreme Bench of Baltimore City.

Beverly, in the eighth generation descended to Samuel King Dennis who married Sallie Crisfield, daughter of John W. Crisfield, of Princess Anne, and half-sister of Judge Henry Page, of the Court of Appeals of Maryland. He was educated at Princeton and served several times as a member of the State legislature, relinquishing his seat in the State Senate to the late United States Senator John Walter Smith. Two of his sons now occupy positions of distinction, one of them, Alfred Teackle Dennis, Ph. D., being vice-chairman of the United States Tariff

Commission, and the other, Samuel K. Dennis, being chief judge of the Supreme Bench of Baltimore City.

Both of the latter were born at Beverly and both, from boyhood, have been interested in public affairs. Alfred Pearce Dennis went to Princeton and was editor of the Princetonian. For the two years following his graduation he held a fellowship at Princeton and then taught history at Wesleyan University and at Smith College, finally abandoning pedagogy to go into business. He has served as commercial attache at the United States embassies in Rome, Paris and London, and has written much on historical and economic subjects.

Judge Samuel K. Dennis entered politics as private secretary to Gov. John Walter Smith before he had been graduated in law from the University of Maryland with the class of 1903. The following year he was elected to the General Assembly from Worcester county. When the Maryland Tuberculosis Sanatorium was organized in 1906, he was a member of its board of managers, serving in that capacity for more than twenty-three years and as president of the board after the death of the then Senator John Walter Smith in 1925.

For many years he has been chairman of the publications committee of the Maryland Historical Society. He was a member of the St. Louis exposition commission and served for more than twenty years as an attorney to the Democratic State Central Committee. During the years 1915-1920 he was United States District Attorney for Maryland.

John M. Dennis, also a representative of the tenth generation of this extensive family, is a great-grandson as well, of Maryland's first elected governor, Thomas Johnson. He was born at Frederick, and is treasurer of the State in addition to being president of the Union Trust Company of Baltimore.

None of them now lives on the land their forefathers held but one of the beams in the cellar at Beverly shows a scar, scarcely healed since it was made several years ago. From the beam a generous piece of wood was cut away, not with wanton intent, but to be made into the gavel used constantly by Judge Samuel K. Dennis to maintain "order in the court."